THE ASTROLOGER'S MANUAL

MODERN INSIGHTS INTO AN ANCIENT ART

LANDIS KNIGHT GREEN

CRCS PUBLICATIONS

Post Office Box 1460
Sebastopol, California 95472
U.S.A.

Library of Congress Cataloging-in-Publication Data

Green, Landis Knight.
  The astrologer's manual.

  Bibliography: p.
  Includes index.
  1. Astrology. I. Title.
BF1708.1.G73 1988   133.5   88-16755
ISBN 0-916360-42-3

Published by permission of Simon & Schuster, Inc.

Library of Congress Catalog Card Number 74-16082

INTERNATIONAL STANDARD BOOK NUMBER 0-916360-42-3

First CRCS Publications Edition Published in 1988.
Distributed Worldwide by CRCS Publications.

Cover Design: Image and Lettering by Tony White.

CONTENTS

Preface

The best way to approach astrology is first of all to understand the meaning of the essentials: signs, houses, planets; and then to learn to interpret the planetary aspects, or geometric relationships, between the planets in the horoscope. Newcomers should not try to take on too much at once. Read about the signs—then think about each one and how it corresponds to a particular horoscopic house and a planetary "ruler." In time the symbols of astrology will become the components of a second language which has many dimensions, levels, and facets. Each reader will get out of this information what he puts into it, as in any other system of symbolic knowledge. Such an approach will bring rewards which are profound and which generate an ever greater sense of individuality. The more a person meditates upon astrology, the more he is put in touch with the wisdom of the past; at the same time, he develops a fuller understanding of man's future intellectual growth. But what is most emphasized is a realistic appraisal of his own position in the present, in the particular life that he is living (according to the distinct solar system patterns seen in his horoscope).

It is here that I wish to acknowledge—if that's possible—the enduring assistance given to me by my Virgo friend, Iride Ravaioli, during the long years while the MANUAL was being written. Also, I would like to thank the friends, colleagues, and family who helped in various ways in preparing the manuscript, especially my sister-in-law, Susan Goodenough Green. For those who might be interested, my own birth took place at 2:10 P.M. on June 15, 1940, in Blackfoot, Idaho.

CHAPTER I

ASTROLOGY'S PLACE IN THE MODERN WORLD

The twentieth century may be remembered by future historians as, among other things, the great renaissance of astrology. This rebirth has not been easy as a result of the confusion surrounding this ancient discipline. It is the aim of all serious astrologers to help clear up some of this misunderstanding by showing how and why astrology is relevant for modern man. Properly understood, astrology is an important key to psychological and spiritual insights which may be less obtainable in other systems of knowledge. Its immediacy lies in the fact that it deals with time and space as described by the cyclic motions of the Sun, Moon, and planets of this solar system. Astrology is the study of these cycles and patterns as they affect man.

Today the better astrologers hold firmly, though not rigidly, to the truths and standards of the earlier practitioners of the art, while they reinforce these ancient maxims with modern astrological and scientific thought. A new time and a new age require the reorientation of earlier concepts. As we enter the age of Aquarius, which is ostensibly the time of *Homo sapiens*, we must make new tools for understanding our place in the universe. Old truths and observations will have to be translated into the language of the new time. Astrology holds a great wealth of information that few modern scientists or scholars know exists. The main intention or goal of those who teach astrology is not to prove or defend the practice as a science, but to show how its scope is broader than the strictly empirical horizons of modern science. Any open-minded skeptic (I was once a skeptic myself) could hardly fail to see the spiritual or trans-scientific cohesiveness of astrology in the course of an objective and extensive study of its principles. These principles and the techniques of astrology are discussed in later chapters. Many of its zealous opponents—these are almost always those who have failed to thoroughly study the subject—ignore astrology's true depth and historical significance. They dismiss it as mere superstition, a pseudo-science, or as a popular form of wishful thinking. It will not always meet the laws of statistics or the tests of the laboratory, so it is considered to be "unscientific" pap for unhappy housewives and those who are gullible.

At the other extremes are some of the more superficial or under-educated enthusiasts of astrology who make extravagant claims about its position and worth in the development of human culture. Without any proof, some maintain that in ancient Atlantis the astrologer-priests had knowledge which far exceeds anything known today. Perhaps this is true. However, the development of astrology is somewhat obscure and such claims should be accepted carefully, if at all. The beginning student has to weed out what is speculative from what is well-established in astrological practice.

Astrology's Legacy

For the present, it might be helpful to note that the oldest known records of astrological lore date from about 3000 B.C. in Babylonia; that astrology reached its first peak in Hellenistic Greece, decreased in importance when the Roman Empire fell, and was later re-introduced in the West via Islamic scholars. At the same time it had spread from Mesopotamia to Egypt and India, and eventually to China, where the stars and planets were already being observed. The Mayans, and to a lesser extent the Aztecs, developed a system of astronomy and astrology. In the New World, as in Mesopotamia, the emphasis was confined mainly to the prediction of such events as war, natural disaster, weather, and affairs of the kingdom. The Spanish conquests brought to an end any further development of stellar science in the Western Hemisphere. In the ancient world, it was mainly in Greece that astrology took on the more humanistic, individual qualities that again make it so popular. It was originally the possession or domain of the priesthood and royalty which it served: those were times when man was essentially bound by his local horizons and the fields he tilled; and in those times science and art reflected local needs. Appendix I gives further information on the historical development of astrology.

In the modern world, man's needs are broader and more complex, there being greater horizons in every sense as his knowledge of his place in the solar system and universe becomes more sophisticated and precise. The abstract and concrete become ever more interwoven as science and religion begin, hesitantly, to touch hands. Yet we are only a very small step, in terms of bio-geologic time, from our star-worshipping, pyramid-building ancestors. The movement toward self-understanding may have only just begun. This is why I believe man should consider every aspect of knowledge: spiritual, geological, biological, psychological, astrological, etc. We should not be so hasty to embrace or divorce insights simply because we are prejudiced in favor of our own field or background. No person could begin to assimilate the vast amount of data and knowledge that is now available. In fact, only an intellectual megalomaniac would even try. More than ever, what is needed is an open-minded kind of intelligence.

The early Greeks were not frustrated and burdened with this vast amount of information and technology. They had time for love, art, and music as well as the pursuit of knowledge. Pythagoras equated music and solar system rhythms in what he called the "harmony of the spheres." He, along with other ancient soothsayers and healers, including Hippocrates, seemed to link astrology to art, science, and religion. Certainly, astrology has affected the development of much of man's formal knowledge, including ceremonial magic (religion), philosophy, mythology, law, medicine, literature, psychology, commerce, navigation, and agriculture. This collective knowledge is based on man's ageless and unavoidable observations of the four seasons, the lunar phases, and the revolutions of the planets, or "wanderers," through the zodiacal constellations.

As life on this planet evolves it is affected by the revolutions of other celestial bodies, just as all of the components of a molecule or atom are linked in a mutually dynamic process of energy and matter acting on the field of time and space. Evolution (ineffable development of life force) and revolution (observable time/planet sequences) go hand in hand. The unconscious or archetypal symbols of the planets, the Sun, and the Moon, and their geocentric relation to the Earth, reveal ever deeper truths about mankind as we evolve toward greater complexity and understanding. At this point in our development it is not always easy to see how astrology, with its awareness of the effect of the cycles of time and change, fits into this process of intellectual differentiation and growth. After all, the development of complex bodies of knowledge, in fact of civilization itself, from simple observations to comprehensible definitions, is a long evolutionary process and an event that transcends our individual sense of time and change. The gap between observation of the four phases of the Moon by our ancestors and the discovery of Pluto in 1930 is great; yet one thing ties the modern scientific star-gazer to the old astrologer–astronomer: both have relied upon intuition to some degree. One who no doubt understood the endless cycles of nature in this manner was Pao Hsi, the ancient Chinese astrologer-cum-naturalist who created the basic trigrams of the *I Ching* (Book of Changes). Modern astrologers, perhaps lacking this ability, have compensated with new scientific knowledge, including direct observations of "new" planetary bodies and other solar system phenomena. The old masters accounted for these bodies (namely Uranus, Neptune, Pluto) and the planetoids (minor planets) intuitively and symbolically through their myths and oracles. In reading the wisdom of the *I Ching*, one begins to feel that there really is very little that is "new under the Sun." The eternal mosaic is there; only our perception of it changes.

Several of the sixty-four hexagrams of the *I Ching* refer to the value of observing the planets, Sun and Moon. Hexagram sixteen, "Yü," teaches that

> Natural laws . . . are not forces external to things but represent the harmony of movement immanent in them. That is why the celestial bodies do not deviate from their orbits and why all events in nature occur with fixed regularity.[1]

Observation of regular solar system events and patterns is one of the main concerns of astrologers. Natal astrology is the study of the synchronous effects of the bodies of the solar system on individuals, particularly as these bodies appear to transit the constellations of the Zodiac. The Zodiac is viewed as a belt of stars extending for about eight degrees on either side of the ecliptical path of the Sun and planets in relation to the Earth. This almost circular belt is divided into twelve *signs* or categories of experience, each containing thirty degrees of zodiacal longitude.

The Horoscope

A *horoscope* is a graphic picture of the positions of the planetary bodies in the Zodiac relative to the birth of an individual at a specific time and place. As a "blueprint for living" it gives clues to understanding an individual's character and destiny, potential relationships, events,

---

[1] Richard Wilhelm, *The I Ching or Book of Changes,* trans. Cary F. Baynes (3rd ed. Princeton: Princeton University Press, 1967), p. 68.

inborn tendencies, and capacities, as well as the nature of the governing will in achieving goals. The celestial sphere surrounding the globe is symbolically divided into twelve departments, or *houses*, which make up the familiar pie-shaped wheel of the horoscope. The planets (Sun and Moon so-called for convenience) and symbols for the signs they occupy are placed into this wheel.

There is a natural correspondence between the houses and the twelve signs. For instance, Aries, the first sign of the Zodiac, has to do with matters similar to those of the first house. Because the Earth rotates on its axis every twenty-four hours Aries corresponds to only about two hours of first house influence out of twenty-four, and thus each succeeding sign lines up with the first house *cusp* (beginning) for approximately two hours daily. The cusp of the first house in an individual horoscope is traditionally called the *rising* or *ascending sign*, and to know which sign rises at any moment on the first house, or "eastern horizon," one must know the exact time and place of birth. The various essentials of the horoscope are discussed more in detail in later chapters.

For the present, it might help to keep in mind the fact that the houses represent actual spatial settings or terrestrial circumstances of experience, while the signs of the Zodiac lend a certain basic or archetypal coloring to the planetary energies. The house divisions are based on the Earth's daily rotation on its axis, whereas the Zodiac is an expression of the Sun's apparent geocentric annual movement; that is, the houses reflect the hours of day and night while the signs are an expression of the four solar seasons.

The rising sign describes the personality or mask of the outer self, the basic attitudes of the individual. In contrast, the Sun's position by sign and house denotes his deeper or inner self, sense of individuality, and purpose. The Moon symbolizes feelings and the subconscious aspects of personality; Mars is related to conscious drives and immediately observable levels of energy; Mercury to native mentality and to communication; Venus to affections and face-to-face alliances; Jupiter to ideals and travel; Saturn to duties and responsibilities; Uranus to objective hopes and friendship; Neptune to sacrifices and solitude; and Pluto to the collective unconscious and a person's relation, generally speaking, to his own generation.

Planetary *aspects*, the critical distances in terms of zodiacal longitude between the planets in relation to the Earth, are the most important factor in astrological analysis and they deserve special study. The number of possible geometric combinations of the seven basic aspects is very great, and it is for this reason, among others, that the general statements one sees in most popular astrological literature for one's Sun sign, especially some of the predictive travesties appearing in daily newspapers, must be tempered by a thorough evaluation of the individual horoscope as a whole. Mars in Aries is somewhat different than Sun or Moon in that sign. Several planets in a particular sign will modify in some way the generalizations that can be made about that sign. Altogether, there are a great number of factors that have to be synthesized when interpreting a horoscope. Each birthchart is unique, requiring special attention.

Correctly delineated, the horoscope is a precise tool based on real forces, events, and relationships occurring in nature. It is also a symbolic diagram of one's purpose in life. The horoscopic view is one that places each individual at the center of his own universe. Cosmic or solar system powers are not then regarded as separate agencies, but as expressions of a unity of action that help to make up the character and motives of the individual. This can be perceived in the Stoic concept of the Macrocosm being expressed simultaneously in the Microcosm. Everything in the solar system (every atom) goes more or less in a circle or shares in that going. Astrology is the study of the circle of experience; the Buddhists and Hindus refer to this as the great wheel of life, death, and rebirth.

An Intuitive Discipline

Technically speaking, astrology is not an exact science. Some knowledge of basic mathematics is required, and some skill, patience, and time are needed to set up a chart, but the average astrologer does not, like his predecessors, also have to be a mathematician and an astronomer since ephemerides are published annually for the positions of the planets. He can even use an electronic computer to set up the horoscope. Astrological analysis might better be classified as an intuitive art or science which requires the development of a receptive state of mind that can correlate those elements in the chart in terms which are meaningful spiritually and psychologically. Such an ability requires a meditative patience for details, a serenely open mind, and the capacity to reason.

Modern astrology, then, is partly a science and partly an intuitive discipline, and a good horoscopic reading is a synthesis of both. The conscientious astrologer will not overemphasize prediction, but he might describe the general effect of current or future solar system cycles (transits) in the individual's horoscope. The reading reflects the particular abilities and personality of the astrologer, his intellect, values, and outlook on life, much in the same way as the psychologist imbues his interpretations with his own views. What the better astrologers have in common is a broad education (not necessarily one that is formal), the ability to use tools and concepts from related fields, and a flexible method of analysis which helps promote individual growth and responsibility. However, one should not expect an astrologer to tell everything there is to know about oneself. Each is, after all, limited by his own Sun sign and horoscopic patterns, among other things. In certain cases it might even be wise to consult more than one astrologer in order to get a rounder view of one's chart, although doing this may confuse some individuals more than help them.

Astrology's less intelligent adherents display an inner weakness in their ambitious attempts to predict the future in terms which are too explicit or precise. Such individuals may overlook the effect of several strong variables that are often, if not usually, impossible to perceive in a first glance at a chart: some of these are race, sex, geography, myths, taboos, language, class, educational background, and other sociocultural factors that can modify the basic meaning of horoscopic patterns. Careless predictions can even do harm to those with a weak will; they may end up waiting impotently for the events of the future with the view that time is their adversary rather than something to be used to realize their best potential. To know some of the possibilities of the future without becoming unduly entangled in a state of doubt and apprehension—that is the art of astrology, at least as far as prediction is concerned. This is not an easy thing to master, for even the most experienced astrologers can fail to make smooth transitions daily, monthly, or yearly, due to excessive concern for the outcome of some planetary pattern to be formed in the future. Free will works within a greater Will, just as in a clock small wheels and gears effectively operate (cooperate) in unison with larger gears and the mainspring. The Sun has its planets and the planets have their Moons. To know to what degree we are dependent and to what degree we can independently assert ourselves without going against the dictates of nature and time is a prerequisite for living intelligently. True freedom lies in recognizing the boundaries and limits of life as well as its opportunities, and this is true both physically and psychically. In India they speak of realizing one's *dharma*, that is, one's essential duty or law for living. The horoscope shows this quite clearly.

The Appeal of Astrology

In the great philosophies of the Orient, with their ideas about *karma* (the sum and the consequences of an individual's actions during successive phases of his existence) it is believed that human existence is transitional, recurring, and always an expression of one's earlier lives. Supposedly, each moment of time begets the next moment, each incarnation creates the karmic conditions, the sow-as-you-reap patterns for future lives. Karma is thought to be an endless chain of births, deaths, and rebirths from which it is apparently no easy task to escape into what is conceived as being a blissful state of non-existence (if one can imagine that) called *nirvana*. Many astrologically oriented people accept this idea to some degree, and the real believers among them attempt to simplify their lives by becoming more and more attuned with the cycles of change denoted by the planets and the solar seasons. This may require a large amount of inner discipline, patience, adaptability, and not least, a sense of humor about one's self as a passenger on "spaceship Earth." A partial or superficial awareness of astrology may cause the weaker soul to worry excessively about his position in time. Falling short of a correct understanding of its principles, its potential strengths, and its current weaknesses, and being unable to synthesize the factors meaningfully in his own chart, he may turn to oblique occult or magical practices. Such lack of correct information, sparse study, and suspension of reason is what characterizes those interested in "black magic" or in the more fantastic forms of astrology. It is little wonder that some of the critics of astrology see in it the fodder of the superstitious and absurd. Serious-minded astrologers everywhere must bear this stigma with courage. Astrology *is* to some extent an occult discipline, as are physics, psychology, parapsychology, and hypnosis, but it is not just the starry ceiling of Merlin's house as some would like to believe. It is more transcendental and at the same time more natural than any form of magic or witchcraft.

Astrology does, unfortunately, too often attract those who are mentally, emotionally, and sexually troubled and who are desperately but superficially seeking simple solutions or answers for their complex problems. But they really do not believe in the astrological genie; therefore, how could it really hurt (help) them? Many of these people avoid the solutions to their problems at any cost. They will not turn to psychology because they feel (at least subconsciously) that it *will* help them, and that they may have to face rather painful revelations. Such people are easy prey for would-be astrologers who unscrupulously take their money and give them false notions about themselves to lean on. A good astrologer is less likely to have such a clientele.

The people who come to see him are usually above average intelligence and they are keenly interested in understanding themselves. The individual may have turned to astrology after the insights of religion and the social sciences fell short of his needs for enlightenment. If he is strong and searching he will not become dependent upon his astrologer. In many places, the outstanding problem is that of finding a good astrologer. There are thousands of unbalanced and unstudied charlatans, not to mention amateurs, who would read your fortune, describe your character, and predict your life's course in the most haphazard or dishonest manner imaginable, either in person or via the mail. Some simply enjoy the power they feel in directing the lives of others. Even some of the astrologers who belong to "professional" or "astro-spiritual" organizations may not necessarily be qualified to interpret your horoscope properly. There is not yet a way in which the public can be insured against astrological quacks in the same way that we license doctors. Even if there were legal standards, they might reflect only the views of the astrologers who set the standards. Astrology is still on ground that is too unstable for there to be any chance of effective legalization in the near future. The best insurance is to learn from friends and acquaintances who the dependable and thoughtful astrologers in your area are.

There is another important point, but one that should not discourage a person from having his chart read: partly because it is an intuitive art working with concrete facts (planetary positions), there is probably no single approach or school of interpretative astrology that has all of the answers. So let the beginner be eclectic and wary in his approach to this subject, which is just now awkwardly coming out of many centuries of cultural hibernation and intellectual suppression. Astrology, which has been called the "queen of the sciences," has not yet learned how to properly wear all of her wonderful clothes. I believe she will in time.

As history repeats itself, astrology can be seen to have its greatest rebirths at times when spiritual revolutions occur. At such times the concepts of astrology can help to perpetuate eternal truths by revealing how we can attune ourselves with current natural cycles. This science of individuality is especially relevant today. In our complex civilization impersonal modes often dominate the individual and he loses or never even realizes individual freedom and self-respect. Astrology reveals genuine human differences and it celebrates the idea that each person is a unique traveler through time. Few disciplines are so humanistic.

Astrological Literature

The demand for arcane knowledge about one's individuality and purpose has caused a burst of books on astrology and related subjects in the Western world. Some of the best books may be solo efforts, constituting years of frugal observation, research, and study. These may not be readily available in the average book store. Other writers have produced many books, some good and some quite poor in quality. Still others have written patronizing books of incredible superficiality. Some books are too erudite or stiffly written for the general reading public, while others are so poorly written that a learned reader would be put to a test to read them from cover to cover. Many of the popular works are merely copies of earlier works and they may repeat the same old errors, generalizations, and outdated thoughts that plague astrology. Older texts are not necessarily more or less informative than those written by later astrologers with a "fresh view." Much of the material written about astrology is riddled with half-truths, superficialities, archaic or irrelevant concepts, unnecessary repetitions, or unfounded speculations. This should not discourage one from studying the subject. The best approach is to read as widely as possible with an open but cautious mind, weeding out the errors and non-essential material as one progresses. Many people have devoted their lives to improving the standards of education in astrology, and all sincere practitioner-writers have something valuable to add to the field, both old and new.

View Toward the Future

The practical astrologers of the next few centuries should, whenever possible, consider making astrological knowledge more consistent, both in literature and in practice, reinstating it as the spiritual science and art that it is, or could be. In the meantime, astrology will have to do its best to join as much as possible in the development and synthesis of metaphysics and modern science. It will have to firmly decry the charlatans in its ranks and beware of dogmatism as it seeks stability. Man is now *on* the Moon, in addition to being influenced by it in his everyday life. Aquarian age astrologers will have some entirely new things to do. It is quite possible that new planets or forces will be discovered, corresponding to the further development of the collective psyche of mankind just as the discovery of Uranus, Neptune, and Pluto synchronized with the emergence of the mass man, depth psychology, aviation, atomic energy, and other "marvels" of the age of science and electronics, the age of Aquarius. New tools for investigation and new areas to be investigated can be expected to develop. The discovery of new planets could help further astrology by helping it clear up certain

Fig. 1. "Aquarian Disk."

ambiguities regarding the rulership (a planet rules the sign with which it has the greatest functional similarity) of Virgo and Gemini, which presently share rulership by Mercury, and Taurus and Libra, which are both presently ruled by Venus. Even Leo could find a new ruler, it being somewhat doubtful that the Sun could rule any particular sign. An intramercurial planet might be discovered or the minor planets (the planetoids) might be found to have some effect in terms of rulership.

Astrologers and astronomers alike should not be hasty in thinking that they have mastered their arts and deciphered all of the puzzles of the solar system. We should make the best of the knowledge and symbols at hand, just as the Greeks, Chinese, and other ancients were able to perceive truths using the tools and concepts of their own time. True seers and scientists perceive the limits of their knowledge, and they know that their knowledge is eternally limited by time. The master astrologer, if one exists today, would probably have a keen sense of history; he would travel the roads of life with love, reason, courage, and caution. Where he would see weakness in himself he would also perceive the opportunity for self-enlightenment as he rises above his problems. His complete sense of being human would be an overwhelmingly positive asset in his being an able counselor. This would be true for a great psychologist as well, for nothing teaches the necessity for the proper blend of compassion and detachment better than one's personal experiences. The enlightened astrologers and other spiritual-psychologists of the future will be little different at heart than Socrates, Shakespeare, the author of Ecclesiastes 3, Gotama Buddha, and other teachers of the past whose hearts have been touched by both joy and sorrow in great measure. The time is coming when people will no doubt enjoy a more enlightening form of astrology. The new teachers will have all of the wisdom of the past, from every land, with which to augment their own observations.

The Great Zodiacal Ages

Because it deals with the orderly and predictable unfolding of time or change, astrology helps to show us which rules of life are valid at any given moment and which are not, which truths endure through the ages, and which are more or less transitory in their application. It reminds us to ask whether or not an idea is important for a particular individual, situation, or time, and ultimately it brings us to realize that we must act in harmony with nature's schedules and programs if we are to succeed. It also helps us to become aware of cycles of time greater than our own life span, cycles which are important in understanding the progress of mankind as a whole.

The most significant of these cycles are the twelve great zodiacal ages, each lasting about 2160 years and forming part of a long cycle known as the "precession of the equinoxes." This is a slow displacement of the star sphere in relation to where the Sun crosses the equator at each equinox. The entire cycle lasts 25,920 years and then repeats itself. The sequence of the ages is the opposite of that of the signs which share the same names, the latter forming a counterclockwise sequence, whereas the ages move clockwise. Thus, the age after Aries would be Pisces rather than Taurus, and so forth. The last age, the one we are just ending, is that of Pisces. The new age is that of Aquarius. The Piscean age might have been best symbolized by the Neptunian octopus which extends its arms in several directions at once. This is the gradual extension of the ideas born of the previous age, that of Aries. The Arian age was that of iron, city states (individuality), and conquest, among other things. The ideas born of that period will probably continue to affect man for many centuries to come. Pisces was a time of great sacrifice, woe, and suffering, attributes associated with that sign. The sign of mankind, Aquarius, implies a large number of people in the world, and it shows the role of science in creating and solving complex problems of relationship and global association.

If, putting aside the idea that each sign, age, or constellation is strictly confined to thirty degrees, one accepts the idea that a sign's cusp overlaps the adjacent sign by a few degrees, somewhat like the colors of the spectrum, then the first discernible seeds of the Aquarian age might be seen in Franklin's kite, the discovery of Uranus (ruler of Aquarius), Marx's first writings, Edison's light bulb, the first airplane flight, or some other typically Aquarian event or discovery. No doubt the effects of the last age will continue to be felt quite strongly for some time to come, but it would appear that Piscean isolation, solitude, and sacrifice (and bondage) are being transformed into more objective associative experiences and institutions. There is now communication on a global level and an explosive development of science and technology.

Some (and perhaps the majority of) astrologers believe that the Aquarian period has already begun, while others set the beginning date as much as several centuries in the future. Nobody knows for certain, but it is highly likely that the harnessing of atomic energy, electronics, aviation (Aquarius is an air sign), and other cultural and scientific dynamics, such as population explosion and political-economic revolution, are indicators of a new path for man for several centuries into the future. Those who believe in repeated lives might say that we will have many opportunities in this age to gain knowledge of ourselves as social animals as well as spiritual entities. Supposedly, people incarnate less in other ages than in the age of man. Perhaps so, but one thing seems certain as put by a friend: "History is in us and we are in history." We are never outside the inherently predictable patterns of change as they emerge from the great vortex of the universe. As man emphasizes new or additional spiritual values (as he does at the beginning of every new zodiacal age) the weaker standards of the past must yield the right of way to the future. That is why the present is always so difficult for man. He knows that he must look forward to the future, yet the "sins" of his past actions slow or thwart his very progress. It is amazing how few people grasp this simple point; indeed, it seems to be an affliction of our species to avoid responsibility for our actions, both collectively and individually. In this new age we are traveling constantly and rapidly away from our old customs and communities toward new ones. Will we be able to find new values and levels of reason as we pull the rug out from under ourselves with the hands of war, poverty, greed, pollution, rape of resources, and population explosion? One hardly dares to speculate on what the future will be like.

The more realistic astrologers, understanding human nature and observing the planetary cycles and the passing of the ages, do not believe that universal love and lasting peace will soon come to this planet. Some might wonder if they will arrive at all. Much of the current talk among the general public about realizing the humanitarian glories of the Aquarian age seem to stem to a large extent from wishful thinking at a time when the future actually looks rather grim. One who accepts the idea of karma would not see too much hope for the nearer future (2000 years is really a very short period of time). There have already been a great number of ages of Aquarius. Why has man not already reached some angelic state of cooperation? The answer lies in the fact that he is still evolving: the ages have more to do with revolution and less with evolution. But man is growing—it would appear—so the idea of a true *Homo sapiens* or man (person) of knowledge should not be discarded. I believe that such a possibility on a collective level lies much further in the future than in the next few centuries or ages. Meanwhile, as individuals, we might emulate the great heroes and sages of the past or present who have already achieved such high levels of development and universal relatedness. In the Aquarian age we will most likely become aware of the *need* for universal harmony and cooperation among men, and not necessarily achieve the actual or complete realization of a utopian world community.

Astrological Guidelines

A penetrating knowledge of astrology enables a person to better understand his involvement with his family, friends, acquaintances, and co-workers in the light of zodiacal responses to current cycles of change. Roles, duties, and responsibilities cannot be more exactly defined than through astrology. Through an objective astrological appraisal of our fellows we might learn how to wisely raise our children and reach for mutually correct and flexible goals of a humane and constructive nature.

Astrology can help a person to determine whether his life is a metaphysical descent, to teach or share knowledge; whether it is an ascent, to learn and acquire knowledge; or some combination of the two. It cautions him to avoid wasting time in seeking out things that have been thoroughly experienced or developed in past lives or at earlier stages in the present life, while at the same time it indicates what he presently needs to develop in his character. Even if he does not accept the idea of repeated lives and the laws of destiny and karma, astrology can still help the individual find wise guidelines for directing his will at all levels of experience.

In either case, whatever is most important or urgent is pointed out by the patterns of the planets in his horoscope. Each person becomes a true individual at the moment when he begins to pursue his deeper aim or purpose in life, rather than blindly following some course prescribed by others, whether they be family, friends, or teachers. This course may not be easy, but it is usually the best one for him to pursue. Man, being a self-seeking social animal, must find the balance between his own needs and desires and those of others around him. This is what his life is all about—a life in many ways more confusing and tragic than the lives of other creatures of this world, who for the most part, act with instinctive certainty in the course of their daily existence. Man alone has responsibility for the conditions of the Earth as a whole. He can, on a grand scale, modify the land, the sea, and the atmosphere; yet he has trouble both collectively and as an individual in seeing the nature, much less the ends, of this great burden. In many ways, modern man seems less able to understand this dilemma than did his ancestors who lived more closely in tune with the rhythms of nature. Some people believe that astrology can help us to return to an awareness of the role of time in these cycles of nature, that it can help give us the proper geocentric orientation to the soil from which we spring. Astrology does not take us out into space; it brings the cosmic down to Earth, making us realize that we are an integral part of the solar system, which is in turn a mote in the vastness of the universe. The Sun, Moon, and planets are a direct and dynamic manifestation of the Tao, the Great Spirit, Brahma, God, or whatever one wishes to call the Creative force. In the *I Ching*, hexagram thirty-two, "*Hêng*," says that

> Heavenly bodies exemplify duration. They move in their fixed orbits, and because of this their light-giving power endures. The seasons of the year follow a fixed law of change and transformation, hence can produce effects that endure . . . In that which gives things their duration, we can come to understand the nature of all beings . . . the superior man . . . always keeps abreast of the time and changes with it.[2]

Here, as elsewhere in the *I Ching*, the idea of the eternal permanence of revolutionary cycles (planetary motion) and evolutionary cohesiveness is put forth in terms which are understandable to the student of astrology. By observing the current motions or transits of the planets one "keeps abreast of the time." The inner will or self is thus increasingly able to act with spontaneous certainty. This truth was expressed many centuries ago in China. With our new knowledge of the solar system and the universe beyond, we should be able to understand and utilize these patterns of change more precisely, but we may never know why or how the ancient sages of China knew so much so long ago. In awe of those masters, Confucius himself much later added extensive commentaries to the Book of Changes. And still, like astrology, it endures. "By contemplating the forms existing in the heavens we come to understand time and its changing demands."[3]

For the thoughtful and disciplined person, astrology is an impartial and dynamic self-examination that sees no end in the search for inner truth and wisdom. To repeat an important point: the horoscopic wheel shows one's main purpose in life, one's duties, limitations, shortcomings, talents, and the nature of one's various bonds with others. The intricacies of the individual's experience can be seen in the cyclic and synchronous patterns of astrological change occurring from the first to the last breath of his life. At no point in this life (as long as the heart continues to beat) is one ever outside the influence of the forces of the solar system.

Astrology is not a sometime thing. It is, instead, like a great eternal clock, the ticking of which cannot be prevented although it is ignored by many. Neither is it a static concept, because new knowledge of the solar system gives the practice greater breadth and new vitality. The

[2] Richard Wilhelm, *The I Ching or Book of Changes,* trans. Cary F. Baynes (3rd ed. Princeton: Princeton University Press, 1967), p. 127.

[3] *Ibid.,* p. 91.

astrology of Mesopotamia (in fact all of the astrology that was practiced prior to Uranus' discovery in 1781) was limited to the visible boundaries imposed by Saturn. The discovery of Uranus, Neptune, and Pluto shows a major transformation in the collective psyche of mankind and in its collective karma and experience. Three thousand years ago knowledge of the trans-Saturnian planets would have been largely superfluous since man had not yet evolved to a level where his ideas or experiences corresponded to the qualities and changes denoted by Uranus, Neptune, and Pluto. This implies a cultural shift in priorities, goals, authority, and values; a transition from the rural horizon-bound man to the man communicating via satellite with another person in a city on the opposite side of the world.

Through astrology, modern man can learn to be truer to himself and to develop his own will to act impartially and thoughtfully without copying unnecessarily the habits, values, and goals of others. Unrealistic ego projections, comparisons, and judgments can thus be avoided, while communication and tolerance for others are enhanced. Involvements can be better understood. When a person knows his own horoscope, in addition to those of others with whom he is in close contact, he does not have to guess of what stuff their character is made or how he should treat them. In time he can come to appreciate the subtle differences of each zodiacal and planetary manifestation, even those which may cause him to react with emotional or mental discomfort. These are often the signs with which he is supposed to be incompatible, but no sign is really incompatible with another, such as Leo with Scorpio, or Capricorn with Cancer or Aries.

Signs actually complement one another, each forming a part of an organic, psychological or spiritual wholeness—the Zodiac. The real problem of compatibility lies in our difficulty in acknowledging and aligning ourselves with zodiacal parts different from our own due to some weakness of will or the influence of our own egos. Aries may often need to develop some of the practicality and reserve of Capricorn; Capricorn may, in turn, need to learn from Aries the value of warmth and directness. Gemini is the opposite of Sagittarius, but these two signs need not be opposed if they can both accept the reciprocal values of communication and truth, qualities these signs are apt to reveal in more enlightened examples. Very often, too, we react negatively to a particular sign because our natal Moon—denoting subconscious feelings—happens to be located in that sign. Or some other strongly placed planet may be in frictional geometric relationship with the other bodies in the chart, causing a certain amount of frustration to be concentrated in one area of the Zodiac. It is natural for a person to see his own shortcomings in others, even while ignoring them in himself, but learning more about the signs and planets may help him to obtain more objectivity in his relationships. At the same time he must become watchful lest he judge people by their Sun sign or rising sign alone. This point could hardly be overemphasized. A horoscope, like the person it symbolizes, is vastly more complicated than the simple (though admittedly often correct) generalizations made about the signs.

If any part of a person's life dominates the remainder excessively, or if any planetary position denotes disbalance, there is apt to be a personal struggle or loss of vital energy and rhythm in a person's life. Horoscopic analysis teaches the difficult-to-realize truth that the Golden Mean or the Middle Path is the only real basis for peace and self-contentment. Each planetary vibration must be utilized at the right time and in a manner which is in accordance with the individual's actual abilities and place in life. Freedom of choice really operates within this fact; that is, free will works within the harmonious Will of a more universal Self as it is revealed or projected in our biopsychic experience. We can see the workings of the planets and the changing seasons of the Earth as the expression of this one great Intelligence.

Why and how astrology works, why its symbolism is really valid; this nobody can explain; but neither can we explain dreams, life and death, or love and hate. What does appear obvious is that all creatures and planets are an inseparable part of a revolving and evolving God-ness, a portion of a great pantheistic mosaic, that at the same time—through man at least—seeks to understand itself. It is in trying to understand or be in harmony with this divine pattern and experience that one finds peace. Not to try to understand may be to live at the mercy of doubts and fears aroused by what appears to be a world of random events and chaos. Those who study astrology in depth perceive that it is truly a science of hope based on insights about one's actual place in time. It is a spiritually oriented science of the Earth (not the stars so much) which makes each person the center of his own experience. Its symbols relate to nothing other than life on this planet as it is being influenced by the other members of this solar system. A heliocentric or Sun centered form of astrology would have little meaning, even though we know that the planets all revolve around the Sun, not vice versa, since we do not live on the Sun and the Sun lives in us. The symbolic relationships of astrology are valid, perhaps even more so than they were in the period preceding the Copernican concept of the solar system. We can now pull the energies of Uranus, Neptune, Pluto, and the asteroids (that is, the things these planets represent) into focus while still using the third planet from the Sun as the main point of reference, our main observa-

Fig. 2. The Dodecanarian Zodiac.

tory as it were, even though this is a symbolic or synchronous relatedness.

The new astronomical orientation did not actually change the validity of astrology, although its unreflecting critics may wish to use the great Copernican breakthrough as "scientific" proof that astrology is nonsense because it adheres to a geocentric or Ptolemaic orientation to the celestial bodies. Astrology is and always has been for the most part something measured largely by the changing seasons, the phases of the Moon, and the aspects or geometric relationships between the planets in relation to Earth. Pure and occult scientists alike should see both the geocentric and the heliocentric viewpoints of the solar system as being meaningful; the former viewpoint is a symbolic and apparently reflective reality from which we can translate cosmic energies. The heliocentric view is a breakthrough because it reminds us that behind all symbolic truths and relativistic views lies a deeper truth, a more ineffable and blinding reality, the very force that is the cause of life and death on our planet—the Sun.

In astrology, the Sun corresponds to our deepest self. Astrology should never be considered to be more than a stairway leading to this deeper self. This is perhaps why the ancient stargazers built pyramids and related structures which had their apex in the heavenly vault where the Sun reaches its zenith. They longed for wholeness and communion with the life force just as we do today as we reach out into infinite space in our obelisk space ships.

A profound vision of human nature that enables man to easily pass through the obvious zodiacal aspects of personality characterizes the master astrologer. He can perceive the inner self spoken of by depth psychologists, Zen Buddhists, psychedelists, and others of a mystical bent. This may seem to be contrary to what one would think, but it is his very understanding of the basic laws governing human nature that allows the conscientious astrologer to avoid putting people into strictly astrological categories at the expense of their deeper being. Like the effective psychologist, he comes to know what really motivates others, and he is not easily fooled by appearances to the contrary. By looking at a chart, for instance, he can distinguish the outer personality, as denoted by the ascending sign, and the deeper will, as described by the Sun sign. He will also know the difference between the effects of Moon or Mars in a particular sign or horoscopic house, and so forth with each astrological factor.

Astrology is always more meaningful when it is reinforced by ideas from other fields, and this includes the social sciences, occult science, and to some extent natural sciences. The modern astrologer is not lacking in available material with which to enrich his perceptions. Never in history has there been so much information of such a great variety. Each person can bring to this wealth of information his own insights, at the same time taking what he needs for his own development and enlightenment, but he must first know what he needs and then what he can contribute to his fellow man. Astrological analysis can provide important clues.

In times past, it was mainly the astrologer-priests who had access to astrological knowledge. Since the Hellenistic period others in the community have become interested in acquiring this knowledge. It is true that in the age of Pisces it was partially hidden, perhaps even tainted to some extent by superstition, dogmatic religion, and science alike. In the age of Aquarius—the Waterbearer of Hope—we will probably make considerable progress in understanding this ancient scientific art, but one might say that we have just begun to understand ourselves as living and dying beings on a tiny planet encircling a below-average-sized star in one galaxy (one type of galaxy) in the inconceivable number of galaxies in the Universe. We must *continue* to learn that man is *of* the Sun, and it is presently from its third planet, Earth, that we have to make our astrological observations. When (should it ever happen) the last man has left this planet, we will no longer need a terrestrial astrology based on the four seasons, the Zodiac, and a geocentric relatedness to the rest of the solar system. If we go to Mars or some other planet or solar system—perhaps to escape a ruined Earth—we will then formulate an astrology based on that planet, its star, its Moons, and the neighboring planets.

As creatures with an emerging reason and higher intelligence we should try to realize that our being is the transitory occurrence and re-occurrence of matter/energy, and spirit, on a field of time and space within Eternity—an endless wheel of life, death, and rebirth, in which each horoscope is a meaningful, but fleeting shadow of a deeper Self. To know these patterns of selfhood, as expressed in the horoscope, is to comprehend one's place in time. Astrology defines our limits as well as our limitations, but it does this in such a way that the responsibility of what we do with this self-understanding rests mainly on our own ability to act in a manner appropriate for the time. Only the perfectly innocent can afford to ignore the dictates of time as revealed through astrology: young children, true sages, and saints. For the rest of humanity, every moment is a turning point, every circle leads to another.

CHAPTER II

The Main Considerations of Astrology

There seem to be at least four general themes or areas of emphasis in modern astrology. The first finds support in those astrologers who are practical by nature and who take a fairly scientific interest in the subject. They may have an emphasis of earth signs (Taurus, Virgo, or Capricorn) in their own horoscopes. These astrologers look for patterns which may prove or reveal certain points, perhaps borrowing or adapting tools and concepts from the analytical sciences. This group makes planetary tables and other useful tools for other astrologers; observation is more important here than speculation or experimentation. The second group corresponds symbolically to the air signs (Gemini, Libra, and Aquarius). These astrologers are concerned mainly with psychological aspects, counseling, education, and information about astrology, and they are interested in human relationships. The third group, which is most closely related to the fire signs (Aries, Leo, and Sagittarius), is interested in the more speculative, ethical, philosophical, or religious aspects of astrology. The last group, corresponding to the water signs (Cancer, Scorpio, and Pisces), is inclined toward the more occult side of astrology. This might include an interest in predictions, extrasensory perception, and other psychic phenomena. These fields overlap, and each astrologer is a combination of two or more of these types because his horoscope has planets within the various elements or houses with which they naturally correspond.

Certain shortcomings in each group must be guarded against. The earth sign type may overemphasize practical or material considerations. The air sign practitioner can become too sophistic or intellectually ab-

stract. The fire sign astrologer may be too idealistic, romantic, speculative, or fanatical in some religious sense. The water sign type may be
emotionally subject to negative unconscious forces and a view of life
that is too ethereal. A well-balanced astrological view should include
considerations for the practical, the social, the spiritual, and the emotional sides of human nature. It is the task of the astrologer to interpret
each planetary relationship in the chart in as many meaningful ways
as possible. Jupiter in a horoscope can indicate law, religion, adventure,
athletics, travel, and many other things. The Moon in Leo can relate
to emotional matters that have to do with children, creative self-
expression, private enterprise, or other things described by that sign.
Each case shows several potentials, and the astrologer has to learn
which are the strongest so that he can properly counsel his client.

Natal Astrology Defined

The study of the synchronous effects of the planets upon individuals
born at a specific time and place is referred to as *natal* or *genethliacal*
astrology. The natal astrologer is generally more interested in analyzing character and life purpose than in simply revealing the future. In
some ways he may resemble a vocational counselor, priest, psychologist,
or sexologist more than a soothsayer or a medium who tells one's fortune by some psychic or divinatory means. There are some, however,
who are both good counselors and seers. Most astrologers practice some
form of natal astrology. The greater part of this book is devoted to this
facet of the science.

Horary Astrology

There is a kind of divinatory astrology called *horary* astrology. This
deals with specific matters "of the hour," a horoscope being erected
for the moment when a critical need becomes manifest as a question
to be answered, especially regarding the future. There is an attempt
made to secure or foreshadow a view of the future from looking at the
present chart in a particular oracular manner, according to specific
rules and symbolic interpretations. The natal horoscope shows the basic
patterns and events likely to occur in a person's life. In contrast, a
horary chart is a view of the universal present or future, of one moment
of time as it might relate to that person. Comparison of the natal and
horary charts can often yield additional insights into the problem or

question at hand. Obviously, one cannot attempt to do horary astrology until the basic essentials of natal astrology have been thoroughly mastered and intuitive faculties developed. This usually takes a number of years. Horary astrology is sometimes used in conjunction with the *I Ching*, the Tarot system, or some other divinatory method.

Mundane Astrology

A third branch of astrology known as *mundane* astrology attempts to understand world events and political trends in nations and countries. It should eventually include the study of sunspots, magnetic storms, eclipses, comets, great conjunctions between planets, and other cosmic solar system phenomena. Many mundane astrologers (for example, Nostradamus, Tycho Brahe, and William Lilly) attempt to predict future events such as wars, earthquakes, famine, political upheaval, and other significant matters affecting the masses. Many of these predictions have failed because the astrologer was given to excessively visionary soothsaying rather than objective reasoning. The lack of accurate planetary tables, or ephemerides, for periods prior to 1800 and an absence of information on the trans-Saturnian planets may have also contributed to the remarkable lack of success in many cases. In addition, astrologers are not certain exactly when each great zodiacal age begins, so it is not easy to obtain a clear historical zodiacal view, a perspective which is essential for accuracy in the prediction of cultural changes on a large scale. This does not mean that all of the observations of the mundane astrologers are inaccurate; it merely cautions one to avoid believing every prediction, especially those which are obviously sensational. There are many forces in the universe of which we may not yet be aware, including geologic, biological, and psychic forces that could account for certain trends and events on a collective scale. Unlike the natal astrologer, the mundane astrologer often does not have a natal horoscope with which to relate current positions or transits of the planets, unless it is the horoscope of the founding of a nation or some similar event.

Nonetheless, mundane astrology is the oldest form of the science. Natal astrology became popular only after the Greeks introduced their humanistic and individualistic ideas into Chaldean star lore. Perhaps in the future we can look forward to a time when mundane astrology will become more of a true predictive science, especially as it is combined with other sciences, such as computer technology. Until such a time it is best to be wary of any wild astrological speculations about where we are heading, culturally and socially.

A Major Turning Point

The practice of astrology has been undergoing a tremendous revolution in the Western world, attracting people from diverse areas of concern with its symbolic language. This renewed interest has been largely spearheaded by the younger generation, whose views have been affected by the kaleidoscope of psychedelic substances, mystical religion, and various occult practices and traditions. The twelve signs of the Zodiac have practically become household words in America, although admittedly not at a very deep level of meaning or interpretation. For the most part this interest has all of the appearances of a fad. Matchbook covers, clothing, jewelry, and even coffee cups advertise one's Sun sign, catering to the ego. Astrology is still—in the late twentieth century—treated with levity by most people, and it is seldom taught in our public schools.

Nevertheless, the turning point for astrology seems to have arrived. New works by young astrologers are appearing, and the better works of the older astrologers are being read by well-educated and critical students. Almost everybody knows their Sun sign (denoting individual sense of purpose), and many can tell you what sign they have rising (outer personality), and where their Moon and Mars are located. A new means of communication has developed. The ideas and language of astrology will no doubt in time be assimilated much in the same way that Freudian terms have become everyday speech. There will probably be an increase in "schools" of astrology. Some will emphasize practical or scientific matters. Still others will use astrology to reinforce or describe esoteric concepts or practices from other fields. There are already books out on "esoteric" astrology, the psychology of astrology, and other facets. Various theosophical societies have written considerably on the subject. Their works appeal strongly to those who are mystically inclined or who relate to complex metaphysical explanations of human existence. However, the esoteric or occult approach, strictly speaking, belongs more to the age of Pisces, the age of mystery religion and initiation into hidden rites and lore, than to the age of open communication and friendship, the age of Aquarius. In the coming age the astrologer is apt to be more like a psychologist than a temple priest. In the Piscean age there were times when a person of knowledge had to hide from a hostile public; in certain cases he had to join a secret society in order to preserve and protect the truth. Aquarius does not favor such secrecy and seclusion. Instead, it looks forward to the future with the hope that much of this ancient knowledge will be translated into forms which will improve the condition of man as a whole. There is little hope

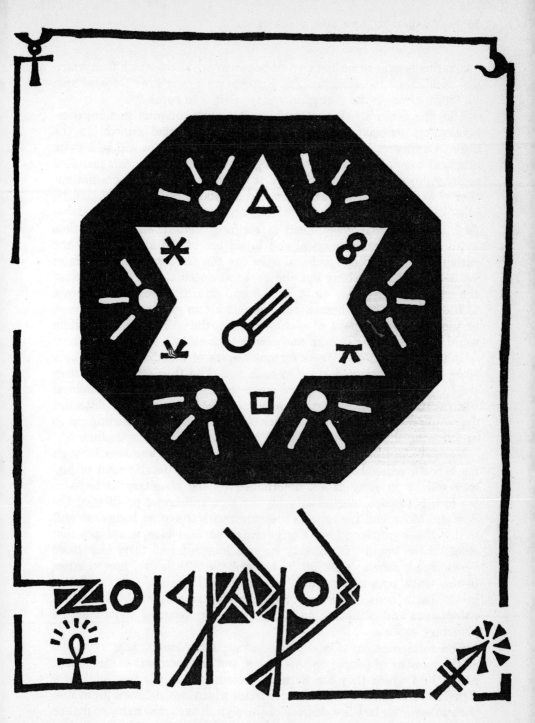

Fig. 3. "Zoidiakos."

(Aquarius is said to be the sign of hope) in anything which is mysterious, hidden, or too esoteric. The Piscean era was a time for wise men to "keep silence"; the Aquarian age is "a time to speak."

Like the other air signs, Gemini and Libra, Aquarius signifies communication, associative relationships, and intellectual growth. In the age of Capricorn, which follows the Aquarian age, there will be a more practical orientation if the earth sign qualities of that sign manifest as they normally do. Some believe it will be a time of impersonal authority and order, at the worst a world of robots. Still others optimistically hypothesize that the age of Capricorn will be a relatively stable period when global government is realized, that it would be a time when man can make practical and broad use of the ideas born in the earlier ages. The other zodiacal ages are too far away—thousands of years—to allow anything but the broadest speculations. Also, because the constellational ages move in the opposite or retrograde sequence of the zodiacal signs themselves, it is difficult to gain an accurate view of the true development of events; that is, the shift in the prevailing world view or *Zeitgeist* from one period to another.

It takes seventy-two years for one degree of a zodiacal age to pass since there are thirty degrees in each age. The thirtieth (rather than the first) degree of a sign corresponds to the beginning of a zodiacal age because of the retrograde movement of the ages. The fifteenth degree represents the zenith of each age; the two halves leading up to or following the midpoint represent the flowering and the decline.

Each student of astrology can think this matter of the ages through for himself, remembering that his view about the development of history will be to some extent determined by the planetary patterns in his own horoscope, particularly by the sign and house position of the Sun and Moon and the aspects they form with the other bodies, as well as by the sign ascending. Considering the Sun sign/house position alone, there would immediately be one hundred and forty-four basic views. For instance: the Sun in Aries in the fifth house, Sun in Aries in the tenth house; Sun in Cancer in the fifth house, Sun in Cancer in the tenth house. This is not even taking into account the various rising signs and planetary positions which can occur in a chart or the planetary aspects.

The total number of possible astrological combinations is as varied as the number of people on this planet and the moments of time (and place) into which they are born. A person born at the beginning of a sign is apt to have some characteristics which are different from one born toward the last few degrees of the sign. Even a few minutes makes a difference between two horoscopes. A different degree of the Zodiac "rises" on the eastern horizon every four minutes. Every second of time is astrologically different from every other second. The Moon moves from one sign to another about every two days. Uranus goes into a new sign in the zodiacal sequence every seven years. Someone born twenty-two months (about two years) after you or before you will have Mars in the same sign that it occupies in your chart. The conjunction of a planet in your chart with a planet in another person's horoscope is often something that cannot be easily ignored, especially if either of the two luminaries are involved. These and many other details and patterns are the concern of the astrologer.

A person who has never studied astrology may have no idea how complicated it actually is. This includes most of the self-styled critics of the art. Such study takes years of patient and penetrating meditation on the basic astrological factors. One can never learn in one life and probably not in a hundred lives of full time study, all there is to know about astrology. There is always something new to add; a new planet, an exciting new concept from some related field, or a cycle that has not been observed before. There will always be some disagreement as to what these new terms or discoveries (for example, Pluto) signify in astrological symbolism. Is Pluto the ruler of Aries, or, as most believe, of Scorpio? Can Mars still be regarded as ruler of Scorpio? These are typical problems that modern astrologers have to solve. There are quite a few areas of disagreement, including the division of the minor houses of the chart, the value and meaning of the Moon's nodes, the validity of progressions, and other touchy problems. There are even two different zodiacs used in setting up charts.

Tropical Versus Sidereal Zodiac

Traditionally, the Zodiac is defined as a belt of fixed stars in the celestial sphere extending for about eight degrees on either side of the apparent ecliptical path of the Sun, Moon, and planets in their relation to Earth. Containing three hundred and sixty-five degrees, the Zodiac is divided into twelve equal parts of thirty degrees each which make up the familiar signs of the Zodiac. These are discussed in detail in the next chapter. The division of this circle is perhaps somewhat arbitrary since one could also divide it into eight, nine, or ten signs, each consisting, respectively, of forty-five, forty, or thirty-six degrees. Various eight-sign zodiacs were used in India and China, but the symbols for the signs varied and some of these were lunar zodiacs. The twelve-sign, or dodecanarian, Zodiac is well-suited to the needs of modern man. As he has evolved, man has modified, through his creative myth-making faculties, the symbolism of the Zodiac. The signs seem to be the very expression of the collective unconscious Carl G. Jung has spoken of in his various works, and these archetypes correspond to actual realities in human life.

Some confusion surrounds the fact that there are two Zodiacs: the *tropical*, or moving Zodiac; and the fixed, or *sidereal*, Zodiac. The former is based on the seasons and is widely used in the modern Western world. The sidereal Zodiac, which is confined mainly to India, is based on the constellations of "signs" bearing the same names as the signs of the tropical Zodiac. Where this confusion began, and where the concept of the Zodiac itself originated, is not certain. In the second century B.C. the Greek Hipparchus discovered that there was a slow westward movement of the equinoctial points along the plane of the ecliptic. This movement is now called the *precession of the equinoxes*. It was found that the signs no longer corresponded to the constellations which bore the same name, and that every 2160 years—a whole zodiacal age—the equinox withdrew by one constellation. Thus, it would be 25,920 years before the constellations would again be lined up with the signs having the same names. The tropical Zodiac is based on the vernal equinox, on the four seasons which mark the Sun's annual path as viewed geo-centrically. One must remember that the signs of the tropical Zodiac are not the same as the twelve constellations of the fixed Zodiac which bore their names almost twenty centuries ago. The constellations no longer correspond to the seasonal signs; in fact, the constellation of Aries is displaced almost thirty degrees from the vernal equinox which marks the beginning of the sign Aries annually.

The constellations may be seen to relate to the twelve zodiacal ages, and they move backward in relation to the vernal equinox over a very long period of time. The signs are an annual matter and relate to the season-oriented, individual aspects of human experience. The "person-centered" astrology in this book is based entirely on the tropical, or moving, Zodiac. One should keep in mind that the tropical signs are a constant and observable reality about which there is no doubt or variation; the zodiacal assignations to the fixed stars, the constellations, are somewhat arbitrary because the exact beginnings and endings of ages or constellations are not precisely defined, at least not to the satis-faction of most tropical astrologers.

These boundaries could be off a number of degrees. The zodiacal con-stellations are, after all, a product of human consciousness, and it is possible that the original boundaries, even the original zodiacal symbols and images could have in some way been lost or modified to meet local needs and beliefs. The astrology of the Mediterranean and Near East could have been a carryover, perhaps altered, from some other culture which has long been extinct. Few of the constellations bear any definite resemblance to the signs with which they are supposed to correspond. Why should we think of the twelfth constellation as a pair of fish; why not a dolphin or an octopus, or even a hermit? The eighth constellation could possibly be imagined as being symbolized by an eagle or a dragon as well as by a scorpion. The fourth constellation might be imagined to be a tortoise instead of a crab. The whole matter of the origin of the symbols, boundaries, and correspondences between the constellations of stars and the signs of the Zodiac is not altogether clear. Man may have to add or drop certain symbols in the present or future ages, being careful to distinguish between the twelve signs and the twelve constellations. The two are not identical, as most people believe, although they are related.

The fact remains that the discovery of the precession of the equinoxes by Hipparchus did not strike a blow to astrology as some of its critics believe; rather, it was the point at which Western man was first able to discriminate between the collective development of his own kind, as denoted by the great ages or constellations, and the dynamics of individuality as denoted by the twelve signs. Citizens of the Grecian city states were among the first in recorded history to celebrate individuals other than royalty, warriors, or holy personages. Their heroes and gods were in many ways like themselves. Their culture was one of the finest intellectual expressions of the age of Aries.

Planetary Rulership

To return to natal astrology, the remaining chapters give basic information on the planets, signs, and houses. Learning astrology is very much like learning a new language. First, the grammar or basic factors should be understood, and only later, with practice, will one become fluent. This takes patience and hard work.

One of the first things to be understood and memorized should be the rulership of the signs. That planet whose characteristics and functions have the most affinity with a particular sign is said to be its *ruler*. As new planets have been discovered, new rulers have been assigned to certain signs, clearing up troublesome ambiguities in previous classifications. The ruler of a horoscopic house is that planet which rules the sign appearing on the cusp or beginning of that house. The term *Sun sign ruler* refers to the planet which rules one's birthday sign, such

as Mars for a person born when the Sun is transiting Aries; or Saturn
for one born when the Sun is in Capricorn. The Sun sign ruler can
greatly modify the position of the Sun in those cases where it is emphasized in a horoscope. The *ruler of the horoscope* as a whole is generally considered to be that planet ruling the sign which appears on
the beginning of the first house, the so-called ascending or rising sign.
This planet can often depict, by its position and aspects, a special
means by which one initiates some particular new phase of experience.
Because of its affinity with the first house of the chart it is a point of
consciously directed revolution of attitudes, personal ideals, and values.
Planets within houses are said to be co-rulers, or sub-rulers, of those
houses. There is some disagreement concerning certain rulerships. Both
the currently accepted and the traditional rulers of the signs are shown
in Table I. The larger asteroids, or minor planets, might be investigated
as being the possible rulers (taken together) of Taurus or Virgo; or
Virgo might actually be ruled by an intramercurial planet (Vulcan),
a small body so close to the Sun that it cannot be seen from Earth.
Thus the dual rulership of Mercury and Venus would be relieved. Even
Leo might find a ruler other than the Sun (how could the source of
all life be associated with only one sign?), perhaps a planet very close
to the Sun which is hidden from our view. There seems to be no substantial reason to continue associating Saturn with Aquarius or Jupiter
with Pisces, and Pluto seems to be a much better candidate for Scorpio
than Mars, which is the ruler of Aries.

TABLE I

PLANETARY RULERSHIP OF THE ZODIACAL SIGNS

ZODIACAL SIGN	CONTEMPORARY RULER	TRADITIONAL RULER
Aries	Mars	Mars
Taurus	Venus	Venus
Gemini	Mercury	Mercury
Cancer	Moon	Moon
Leo	Sun	Sun
Virgo	Mercury	Mercury
Libra	Venus	Venus
Scorpio	Pluto	Mars
Sagittarius	Jupiter	Jupiter
Capricorn	Saturn	Saturn
Aquarius	Uranus	Saturn
Pisces	Neptune	Jupiter

The Rising Sign

Another factor that the beginner must understand is the *ascending* or *rising* sign. The ascendant, as it is often called, is that degree of the Zodiac which appears on the eastern horizon at the exact time and place of one's birth, and which is usually placed on the beginning or cusp of the first house of the horoscope. It is not a planet or a house itself; it is one point of the Zodiac appearing on or near the threshold of the first house of the chart. A new degree appears there approximately every four minutes; hence a new sign rises about every two hours as the Earth spins on its axis. The cusps of the other houses are also important, as will be shown later on, particularly the cusps of the other "angular" houses, the fourth, seventh, and tenth. The first house is important because it refers specifically to the individual more than the remaining houses. In fact, the houses become increasingly impersonal as they proceed from the first to the twelfth. The nature of the rising sign is modified by the patterns in the horoscope as a whole, especially the positions and aspects received by the planet ruling the rising sign, the Sun, Moon, any planets actually located within the first house close to the ascendant, and very often Mars because it, more than any other planet, has a natural affinity with the first house through the correspondence of Aries with the first house. This will become more obvious as one learns the basic correspondences between the various astrological factors.

There is some difference of opinion about what the rising sign means and how important it and the other four angles (cusps of houses 4, 7, and 10) are in the overall chart. Most astrologers would probably agree that the ascendant denotes one's outer personality, appearance (especially the head), mannerisms, basic likes and dislikes, and what might generally be called temperament, although all these things would also be described to some extent by the planets themselves. Some see the rising sign as a fairly static mask that changes only with age, a sort of shell that serves and protects the inner self denoted by the Sun, and the feelings and subconscious, symbolized by the Moon. Others believe the rising sign is more important or as important as the Sun or Moon positions, although somewhat less tangible or more abstract. As such, it is conceived to be that point where the spirit enters the body at the moment of the first breath. My own view is that the rising sign probably varies in importance from one chart to another, that both the outer and the more individual sides of human nature can be expressed there. When you meet someone, it is often his rising sign (and Mars too) to which you react rather than his Sun sign. Later you may discover that his heart (Sun) lies elsewhere and that your initial reaction is less important than it seemed at first.

The rising sign can act as a sort of personal funnel or filter system for all of the planetary energies in the chart. If the idea of repeated lives is true, it seems that the ascendant might be the essence or quintessence of one's past efforts and purpose. The Sun would then demonstrate what one is working out karmically in the present incarnation; it would describe, by its sign and house position, as well as aspects, the main setting and purpose in the present. Viewed in this way, the Moon represents the vital energy or fuel one uses from day to day (of varying quality and quantity from one chart to another) to obtain the ends determined by one's karma or "destiny." The Sun sign *dictates* what the main karma or purpose will be in each horoscope and the Moon *reflects* this through our daily routine and general emotional posture. The remaining planets act as significant modifiers of these solar/lunar energies, aims, or functions. Mercury, Venus, and Mars are significant mainly at the personal level; Jupiter and Saturn primarily at the broader level of social responsibility; and Uranus, Neptune, and Pluto at the more universally oriented, collective phases of experience. This picture is to some extent speculative—all of the bodies work at all three levels of experience as they form unique geometric patterns in a chart. In any case, the rising sign always remains a primary and persistent point of self-awareness, identity, self-interest, and personality.

The most salient personal point in the chart is that point of reality to which we most instinctively adhere for our own protection or gain, and from which we take our initial intuitive glance at the things in our immediate environment. We tend to hold to the things denoted by the ascending sign, whether we like it or not, because it is like the unclouded mind of the infant and young child within us, the most pure and intimate non-planetary factor in our horoscope. Yet, it would seem that the rising sign varies in importance according to the individual's position in life and the actual role of personality in obtaining what he needs. Certainly the strength of the deeper character described by the Sun is reinforced by an effective outer expression of that will. Personality is an outer attribute of the inner self, but in human relationships its effect can be very great. Many textbooks list basic interpretations for the rising sign, aside from the general interpretations for the Sun signs. This text includes the rising signs in the general discussion of the twelve signs in the next chapter.

Archaic Concepts

The last thing to be mentioned before going on is the problem of terminology. In astrological practice one will encounter such terms as "dignity and debility," "malefic and benefic," "fortunate and unfortunate," "positive and negative planets," "exaltation and detriment," and other similar old-fashioned terms. Modern astrologers are dropping these dreary and often confusing terms; they recognize that every planetary position is important and natural, and that the simple good/bad interpretations are too subjective for intelligent understanding of a horoscope.

Each planet and each sign has many sides and potential ways of being expressed. One will find a "changeable and superficial" Gemini person, a "cranky and sullen" Capricorn, or a "sloppy and clinging" Cancer native, but one will also find positive expressions of these signs. A planet receiving many frictional aspects—so called "afflictions"—such as oppositions of one hundred and eighty degrees or squares of ninety degrees, may actually reveal a deep or heroic individuality and more inherent strength than a chart containing mainly non-frictional aspects. As times change new terms must be added and old terms and concepts dropped or modified accordingly. For every astronomical discovery made some adjustment has to be made in the language of astrology. There is no room for over-simplification, nor should we hang on to elaborate ideas, terms, and methods that in the past may have served well to compensate for lack of knowledge (empirical data, actually). Every new planet announces a new dimension or level of intellectual perception. Astrologers should let those terms and symbols from the past which still have meaning endure, let archaic terms go their own way, and look forward to a time when astrology will be better equipped to present itself to the modern world.

CHAPTER III

SOLAR ARCHETYPES: THE ZODIACAL SIGNS

 The Zodiac itself was discussed in the last chapter. Much of what is said in this chapter about the individual signs holds true for the corresponding horoscopic houses, but the houses are treated separately in Chapter IV because they represent something different in effect than the signs. The definitions for the signs given here are valid mainly for those occasions when they are occupied by the Sun, Moon, and rising sign; to a lesser extent by Mercury, Venus, and Mars; and to an increasingly less personal degree by Jupiter, Saturn, Uranus, Neptune, and Pluto. For instance, the Sun in Gemini or Gemini rising, or even the Moon or Mars therein, will reproduce more observable individual qualities of that sign than the slower moving bodies such as Saturn and Neptune. Later you will learn to synthesize the various astrological factors, knowing how much emphasis to give to each position or planetary pattern in the chart. Meanwhile, it is best to get a general idea of what each of these factors represents.

Born on the Cusp and Double Sign

Certain people born at the beginning of one sign and the end of another are said to be born *on the cusp*. When this happens they should check with an astrologer to be certain as to exactly where their Sun is located. The term "cusp" has two applications. First, it refers to the boundary between two sequential signs; and second, it refers to the beginning of a horoscopic house. Whether or not two adjacent signs

45

overlap each other in effect, combining qualities of both, is a matter of debate among astrologers. If so, this would make the fifteenth degree the strongest of any given sign (each has thirty degrees), the point that would most effectively epitomize the outstanding characteristics denoted by that sign. One born with Sun at the first degree of Leo might be influenced by adjacent Cancer; a person born when the Sun is at thirty degrees Leo would apt to be influenced to some extent by Virgo, the sign that follows Leo. The idea of being born on the cusp would probably not be effective for more than three to five degrees on either side of a sign, at least in some way that would be obvious. But this concept is not something to overemphasize. Sun in Libra is still Sun in Libra. Sun in Pisces is Sun in Pisces. What varies most is the remainder of the chart, and the house of the horoscope that the Sun occupies is also an important modifier of what that Sun sign signifies.

Another term which may be familiar, if not a little confusing, is *double sign*. What this usually refers to is the situation when the Sun and ascendant are of the same sign. It might also be extended to include the Sun and Moon occupying the same sign, or when the Sun is in a house which corresponds to the sign it occupies, such as Virgo and the sixth house, or Capricorn and the tenth house. Naturally, such a situation places an emphasis on the sign in question.

Planetary Stellium

When it happens that three or four planets, including either the Sun or Moon, occupy one sign, the grouping is called a *stellium*. Venus and Mercury are so close to the Sun, never more than forty-eight and twenty-eight degrees, respectively, that they can normally be omitted or given less emphasis in determining whether a group of planets constitutes a true stellium. Any of the following situations where planets are in the same sign will also emphasize that sign, although they would not be classified as stelliums: Sun and Moon, Sun and Mars, ascendant and Mars, Mars and any two other planets, Jupiter or Saturn with the Sun or Moon and one other planet, and quite often Jupiter and Mars when they are in close conjunction. Generally speaking, Neptune and Pluto are too slow moving and too universal in effect to be by themselves significant in terms of a sign's emphasis at the individual level. In almost all horoscopes the two most important factors are the Sun and the Moon. Experience will show where the emphasis lies in each horoscope. In addition to any of the signs containing a preponderance of planets, any of the twelve houses may contain a majority or be emphasized in some other way. This must be considered when analyzing the positions of planets. House and sign position of planets are factors which can vary in effect. A person born at any time of the year—under any Sun sign—at 11:00 A.M. will have the Sun in the tenth house of their chart. One born at 5:00 P.M. will have the Sun in the seventh house of their horoscope. This applies to each hour of the day, every day of the year.

Mutual Reception

Planets may occupy the sign or natural house ruled by one another, swapping positions or visiting each other's place, so to speak. This is called *mutual reception*. For example, the Moon, which rules Cancer (and the corresponding fourth house), may be in the twelfth house or Pisces, while Neptune, ruler of Pisces and the twelfth house, may be in the fourth house or in Cancer. When this happens there is a special emphasis in matters described by the appropriate planets, houses, and signs. Another example: Saturn, ruler of Capricorn, in Aries; and Mars, ruler of Aries, in Capricorn. Mutual reception is all the more important if the two bodies in question are also closely aspecting each other. It is one of the many subtle things to look for in the course of analyzing a horoscope.

Signs as Archetypes

It would probably not be wrong to say that the signs are a transcendental expression of the inventiveness of human consciousness, that they are cosmic or solar archetypes arising from a deep need to order and understand this consciousness. But this would not explain how or why the Zodiac exists, why the signs actually do reveal realities of experience, albeit often symbolic and at an intuitive level. One can say that Sagittarius, often symbolized by the Archer, relates to religion, law, long trips, foreigners, gambling, and many other matters. By observation one can see that this is so. Whenever Sagittarius occurs in strength in a chart, one or more of these characteristic concerns will be emphasized; for instance, dealings in some matter related to foreigners, long trips, or things from other lands. These matters might also be emphasized if Jupiter—ruler of Sagittarius—is prominent, or if the ninth house (corresponding to Sagittarius, the ninth sign) holds significant planets. These same rules apply to the other signs and their corresponding rulers and houses.

What is actually known about the Zodiac is that it is a sensible way of dividing the four solar seasons into equal parts, each representing a unique function or phase of experience. At some point in the past its symbols were probably transferred to the stars themselves, to the constellations which constitute the Sun's apparent path around the Earth. In almost every land this circle was divided into eight or twelve parts. Zodiac means "wheel of life" (Greek *zoe:* life, and *diakos:* wheel). Who invented this idea of a wheel of life? Totemistic ancestors? Sages like those who created the *I Ching*? Are the signs a carryover from a vanished culture? The Zodiac persists, yet it is not clear just when and where it had its origin.

As a contemplative tool, as a means of viewing the past and future, the Zodiac has no rival. The signs, which represent distinct *phases of experience*, also reveal different *kinds of experience:* cardinal, fixed, and mutable; fire, earth, air, and water; yin and yang. It is mainly in meditating upon their various relationships with each other—always viewing them as parts of an organic and psychic whole—that one comes to understand the deeper metaphysical and psychological implications of the twelve signs. The Zodiac is an intricate and lucid language all to itself, a way of thinking and ordering reality that covers every facet of terrestrial human experience. This includes every potential human relationship, goal, propensity, and hope. The Zodiac is the wheel of life as it is symbolically conceived and projected through the human intellect. The more pristine and intuitive this intellect is, the broader one's view of the laws of change affecting man will be. In the course of studying the Zodiac one can come to realize the truth expressed in *Ecclesiastes 3:* "To every thing there is a season, and a time to every purpose under the heaven. . . ."

Zodiacal Elements

Since at least the time of the Greek Empedocles and the emergence of the dodecanerian Zodiac, astrologers have classified the signs according to four primordial *elements* and three functional *qualities*. More recently, psychologically oriented astrologers, adopting the ideas of psychologist Carl G. Jung, have adapted these elements to four psychological types or functional categories. The elements of the Zodiac—fire, earth, air, and water—each contain three signs which form a harmonious triad. The zodiacal qualities—cardinal, fixed, and mutable—each contain four signs which form a cosmic cross.

CARDINAL SIGNS	FIXED SIGNS	MUTABLE SIGNS
Fire: Aries	Fire: Leo	Fire: Sagittarius
Water: Cancer	Water: Scorpio	Water: Pisces
Air: Libra	Air: Aquarius	Air: Gemini
Earth: Capricorn	Earth: Taurus	Earth: Virgo

Fire and air signs are said to be masculine or *yang;* water and earth signs are classified as feminine or *yin*. It might be more accurate to classify fire signs as pure yang, water signs as pure yin, air signs as yin yang, and earth signs as yang yin, since the last two elemental groups tend to have somewhat androgynous qualities.

Generally speaking, the Jungian concept of psychological functionality relates to the signs as follows: fire signs, intuition;[1] earth signs, sensation (a "spade-is-a-spade" reasoning and a form of observation which is basically empirical); air signs, thinking; and water signs, feeling. These four functions (see Fig. 4) are broken down further into intermediate functions that are a combination of two adjacent main functions; for instance, thinking plus intuition results in "intuitive speculative thought." Aries, the primary fire sign, represents pure intuition, the urge to explore, while the fire sign Sagittarius is intellectually inclined toward the air sign mode, and is thus classified as an intuitive speculative type. Libra is the sign of pure thinking, and next to it, inclined toward the fire signs, toward intuition, is Aquarius, the air sign of theoretical thought. Like Sagittarius, it is classified as an intuitive speculative sign, but it is related more to the function of thinking than to intuition. A third cardinal sign, Capricorn, represents pure empirical sensation (the general earth sign mode). Adjacent to it, toward the air signs, is Virgo, and adjacent to the cardinal air sign Libra is Gemini. Both Gemini and Virgo are mutable signs that are classified together as empirical thinking types. Virgo leans toward the practical earth mode, toward facts of a concrete nature; Gemini is more in communication with Libra, which represents pure thinking (that is, reflective reasoning). The cardinal water sign Cancer, symbolizing pure feeling and the most yin of all zodiacal signs, is in the last quarter of the diagram. Next to Cancer, situated toward the element of fire, is Pisces, and next to Pisces, near the sign Aries, is Leo. Pisces and Leo relate to

[1] Throughout this book the term "intuition" is generally used to describe a super-cognitive process, a will-directed activity that enables the individual to synthesize various psychic insights, observations, feelings, and external perceptions. The term is also used to describe one of the Jungian psychological types, here identified with the fire signs. This is a simpler inner perception or natural awareness, the effects of which are directed outward. The more complex intuition spoken of above transcends any such psychological/astrological classifications.

"intuitive feeling," the former more to feeling and the latter more to intuition because it is a fire sign. In the last intermediate section, between pure sensation and pure feeling, are Taurus and Scorpio. These two signs are both classified as "sensory feeling" types, the first oriented toward the earth mode and the second toward the water mode.[2]

This classification creates psychological opposites which differ dramatically from the zodiacal opposites based on the sequential or seasonal relationship of the signs. Intuitive signs are opposed here to the empirical/sensation signs; the signs identified with feeling are psychologically the opposite of those considered to be thinking types.

One thought that might be added to this is the idea of extroversion and introversion, what Jung calls "attitude types." Extroversion implies an orientation to things or matters outside oneself. Introversion means that energies and relationships are directed primarily back to oneself. Fire signs might be seen as being subjectively extroverted and purely yang; water signs would then be classified as subjectively introverted and purely yin in nature. Earth signs would be objectively extroverted yin (or yang-yin); and air signs would be objectively introverted yang (or yin-yang). Combining these ideas with the concept of the three qualities—cardinal, fixed, and mutable—yields a deeper understanding of the signs. This psychologically cohesive view is a perfectly woven fabric of knowledge that has taken centuries to complete. To imbue the symbols of astrology with the observations of modern psychology is to bring it forward to meet the needs of the time. Not being a psychologist myself, I can only hope that those who are appropriately trained will find other important connections which must surely exist between the social sciences and astrology.

Certainly it seems that a preponderance of planets in any position or pattern will provide important clues about the psychological and social posture of that particular person in whose chart the pattern occurs. In this way one might be able to see what he needs to develop in his effort to "individuate" himself; that is, what is needed to obtain a harmonious sense of self in action. The houses which correspond to the signs, as well as the rulers of the signs, will provide important insights about which zodiacal element or zodiacal quality predominates. For example, a person with Aries rising and several planets in Leo or Sagittarius will undoubtedly be of the intuitive type: he will have to follow his "hunches" to obtain what he desires. Also, several planets in the first, fifth, or ninth houses, particularly the Sun or Moon, may indicate a

[2] A good summary of Carl G. Jung's work can be found in Jolande Jacobi's *The Psychology of C. G. Jung* (5th ed. New Haven: Yale University Press, 1962).

Fig. 4. Correspondence between the four zodiacal elements and the four psychological functions as defined by Carl G. Jung: intuition (fire signs), feeling (water signs), sensation (earth signs), and thinking (air signs).

nature that expresses itself—positively or negatively—along mainly intuitive lines.

Determining the actual psychological function is usually not so simple. Everything in the chart must be studied and carefully weighed, one point against another. The Sun sign might point to the main function, with Mercury (since it is so close to the Sun) acting as an important modifier. Or the ascendant might represent the main function, with something else in the chart signifying the "auxiliary function." The Moon sign might be the auxiliary function or it might be found to be the least developed mode, even signifying a point of inner weakness in less developed individuals. Mars seems to be a good candidate for representing an auxiliary function because it has so much to do with conscious drives and the way a person "comes on." Because it is expansive by nature, Jupiter might emphasize a particular function when in combination with another key planet, especially the fire sign or intuitive mode. Saturn would put certain limits on the psychological makeup of a person as it would refine the earth sign or sensation mode. Uranus probably relates naturally to intuitive thinking wherever it is emphasized, and it seems that Neptune would be involved where intuitive feeling is evident. Pluto probably affects the deeper strata of the sensory feeling mode, perhaps even lending it a compulsive quality. Pluto would not be prominent where intuitive thinking is concerned because this latter mode requires an open set of circumstances that is quite the opposite of what Pluto symbolizes. The Moon's role in feeling would be most obvious where it is placed in a water sign or in a house corresponding to that zodiacal element. Venus would be prominent where pure thinking is apparent. However, pure types of any psychological or astrological type are very rare, if indeed, they occur at all.

Fire Signs: Aries, Leo, and Sagittarius

The fire signs symbolize the activity of the self or ego in those phases of experience related to self-expression or to a creative and dynamic externalization of inner impulses that can be identified as being intuitive in nature. Here there may be charisma and a capacity to inspire, lead, direct, and encourage others. There is always something to conquer through sheer will, the following of speculative urges or hunches, or an application of personal energy in a manner that is direct, even at times impulsive or reckless. Aries seeks to impress others and it needs to be admired for its singularity of purpose or its resolve; Leo dramatically expresses itself and seeks an audience which will respond to its various qualities of character; and Sagittarius is driven to expand its horizons in some manner where the keynote is self-realization through an active participation with others, that is, through gregariousness.

Where there is a lack of spontaneity, will, self-enterprise, and power of personality, the fire signs will be thwarted by aspects from planets in earth or water signs. Fire signs are most expressive, bold, intense, and adventurous where the element is reinforced by strong placements of Mars and Jupiter, in addition to the rising and Sun signs. A strongly placed Saturn may curb their amplifying power to some extent. The weakness of the fire signs lies in a tendency to dominate others, bombast, rashness, and an ill-regulated directness with others. If Saturn can force order on the spontaneity of the fire signs, Neptune may drain some of the energy from their will. In exceptional cases Neptune can enhance the creativity of the fire signs or denote a warm compassion. Uranus here, and in a strong position, may increase the speculative side of the fire signs; it will also indicate dramatic changes in one's friendships and social ideals. Venus in a fire sign may incline one to choose a mate who has some of the qualities associated with this element. Mercury here may suggest an intuitive mentality. When the Moon is in Aries, Leo, or Sagittarius it can reveal a warm nature, but many times it indicates a willful subjectivity and an excessively emotional expression of the qualities of the fire signs. Indeed, the Moon may bring out a fire sign's worst qualities if the Sun is in a yin sign and not well aspected. Mars and Jupiter reveal the nature of the fire signs better than the other planets; in addition, the rising sign has a natural affinity with the fire mode or, to be more precise, the cusps of the first, fifth, and ninth houses.

Here, as everywhere in astrological analysis, one must also consider the house position of each planet. The Sun, Mercury, and Venus might, for example, be in Sagittarius, but in the twelfth house. Such a position would reduce or confine the fire sign qualities somewhat because the twelfth house—through its affinity with Pisces and Neptune—is related more to the water element than to fire. On the other hand, these same Sagittarian planets would be emphasized if they happened to be in either the first, fifth, or ninth houses because these houses correspond to the fire triad.

Water Signs: Cancer, Scorpio, and Pisces

The water signs are associated with the subconscious realm, with feelings and psychic forces which are intrinsically subjective or hidden from view. Like the water signs, the fire signs are also subjective, but their energy is being directed outward and upward rather than inward and downward as with the water signs. Keywords associated with the water signs are receptivity, penetration, permeation, protection, and pathos. They can shelter others, relieve suffering, and contain and collect the necessities of life. Cancer is the mother and the home. Scorpio indicates the mutual nourishment and exchange of resources that occurs in close partnerships with others. Pisces best symbolizes care and concern for the victims of misfortune; it is the idea of nourishment applied on the broadest scale. Water signs are sensitive emotionally. The weaker qualities of these signs are excessive emotionality, insularity, secretiveness, possessiveness, lack of order, and the seduction of others through feelings, sentiments, or guile.

The Moon is especially strong when in this mode. So, too, are the Sun and rising sign as they would be in any of the four elements. Neptune and Pluto therein have a strong, although subtle and difficult-to-determine influence. Mars seems to overtly manifest the qualities of these basically hidden signs, as does Jupiter to a lesser degree. Mercury in a water sign suggests that thoughts and communication are much influenced by feelings and subconscious impressions. Venus therein may indicate an attraction to a more yin, emotional partner, or to one whose main concerns are with security and shelter. Saturn in a water sign could indicate repression of feelings, or it may positively manifest itself as controlled feelings and common sense in meeting responsibilities. Uranus here may mean that there will be emotional changes—some quite unexpected—surrounding the home and friends. The Sun or Moon in a water sign is best reinforced by stable positions in the other water or earth signs. Fire and air placements may increase the necessity for personal and socially significant emotional adjustments. Air may cause the water to vacillate emotionally or to be on the defensive in relationships. Fire with water can create emotional outbursts, or steam, as it were.

Air Signs: Gemini, Libra, and Aquarius

The air signs represent the various phases of social and personal interrelationships. Gemini is the sign of informal relationships such as those having to do with acquaintances, neighbors, siblings, playmates, fellow students, and peers. These are essentially non-amorous relationships other than friendships which could be classified as "accidental," "chance," or "side-by-side" relationships. Any close companions found here would likely be fellow travelers in some sense of the word.

The next air sign, Libra, represents close comrades, formal partnerships, marriage, or other "face-to-face" relationships where there is a definite bond or alliance between two parties; it can also signify competitors and open enemies.

Aquarius is the sign of friendship, of those broader special interest associations outside of one's family and marriage. Aquarius also represents one's colleagues in some associative experience such as in a club or some other organization which one might freely join.

Together these three signs relate to social adaptions, communication, abstract intellectual activity, and various social agreements, customs, and manners. Faults attributed to the air signs are indecision, pedantry, lack of sympathy (or empathy), and undue detachment or aloofness. The Sun, Mercury, and Venus are usually well placed in an air sign, particularly if there is also a yang sign rising. Uranus here may bring out special intellectual characteristics, often in friendships. The Moon or rising sign in the air mode may tend toward indecision unless the Sun or Mars are strongly aspected or in a fire sign. Saturn here can indicate some degree of seriousness in one's relationships as well as in one's ideas; it also can describe various kinds of social inhibition. The effect of Pluto is difficult to determine, although it may suggest some kind of regeneration in one's relationships where there is an exchange or mingling of ideas and resources. Neptune can signify confusion in relationships, or it might be the signature of some form of deception or inability to communicate some important idea. In more spiritually enlightened people it might indicate a subtle intellectual creativity and ability in communicating with others. Jupiter well-placed in an air sign enlivens the mental side of personality and broadens one's ability to communicate or exchange ideas. Mars here also sharpens the mental faculties, but it can suggest strife and argument if it is severely aspected. Of course, what is being said in this section about the effects of planets in the four zodiacal elements is very general and necessarily brief. Each of these positions can imply a great deal more than what has been mentioned. A planet in any sign anywhere in the horoscope is there for a special reason, and it is an oversimplification to say its effect is inherently good or bad. This is true regardless of the zodiacal sign or the planet involved.

Earth Signs: Taurus, Virgo, and Capricorn

The earth signs, which correspond to the sensing or empirical psychological mode, are the most practical of the four types, generally speaking. Their world is one requiring regulation, management, utility, and a sense of duty. To air and fire signs they may seem too "down-to-earth" or too concerned with material matters. The constructive nature of the earth signs is reflected in a pragmatic view which concerns itself with what is tangible, observable, and solid. They are interested in whether or not something "works." Defining and placing limits is one of their basic tasks. The earth signs perceive abundance and success in terms of understanding and sticking to these limits, duties, or responsibilities. Where they may show weakness is in a too materialistic orientation to life, petty concern for detail or order, and a lack of receptivity to new or untested ideas. They can be (and should be) devoted to their work because these three signs have to do with matters related to employment and material gain. In general, Taurus works for itself, calling on its own resources and talents; Virgo works for others to support a family (Cancer and Leo) and it is apt to adopt the skills and techniques of others to augment its own talents; and Capricorn, ideally speaking, works for mankind or society in some professional capacity where responsibility is shouldered and capital is increased through others outside the realm of the family. Naturally, these are the ideal situations; not all Virgo people serve, not all Capricorn individuals are skillful managers of great projects, and not all Taurus natives are adept at making money or building things.

The Sun and Saturn in earth signs, as well as the ascendant and Moon to a lesser degree, best express the more obvious earth sign qualities. Earth combines most effectively with water, less readily with the signs equated to air and fire. Uranus, Jupiter, and Mars have some of their outgoing power reduced, or rather, contained for practical ends, when they occupy earth signs. Neptune can lend a deeper purpose to the sometimes routine tasks associated with these signs. Mercury and Venus take on the qualities of the earth element as readily as they do the others, suggesting a rather practical orientation in dealings with others. Pluto in one of these pragmatic signs may be a warning to be thorough and correct in determining the practical ends of one's actions in dealings with others in order to avoid serious losses (should it receive frictional aspects from other planets).

The fire signs envision, inspire, and prophesy or speculate about the future; they are the stimulators. The earth signs are effective at planning and making up viable programs and schedules. Air signs have ideas and use logic to obtain socially significant ends; they can compare and combine various concepts and things. The water signs are the nourishers; they also collect and store things. Most people are a combination (with varying degrees of success or failure) of all four elemental types. It does happen from time to time that one element will contain a striking majority of the planets, or a complete lack of planets. In such cases the astrologer has to determine whether this is a blessing or a burden and how the individual compensates for this emphasis or dearth.

Zodiacal Qualities

The four zodiacal elements each contain three signs basically harmonious with one another, and which share similar characteristics in terms of life purpose, personality, and intellect. The next matter of concern is that of the three zodiacal *qualities:* cardinal, or initiating; fixed, or synthesizing; and mutable, or modifying. The four signs of each quality have a dissimilar elemental or psychological basis, but they share in a *complementary life purpose* much in the same way that the four solar seasons are part of one process, yet distinct from one another. The four signs of each quality form a mandala or cosmic cross. These signs are said to be "incompatible" with one another; however, this is somewhat misleading. What they actually represent are three basic areas of experience and adjustment: the crosses that each of us has to bear in the process of becoming more individual.

Corresponding to the equinoxes and the solstices is the cardinal cross consisting of Aries, Cancer, Libra, and Capricorn. It begins with individual fire and ends with universal earth. The second cross, the fixed mandala, includes Taurus, Leo, Scorpio, and Aquarius, and it begins with an earth sign and ends with an air sign. The third cross is the mutable pattern outlined by Gemini, Virgo, Sagittarius, and Pisces; it begins with air and finds completion in water. These waters, symbolized by Pisces, contain the seeds of life which are brought forth in Aries, the sign immediately following Pisces. We associate Aries with spring, but is it really the first sign? Where did the seed come from in the first place? What is shown here is that there is no absolute first and last on the zodiacal wheel of life. The eternal serpent (Ouroboros) is found to be biting its own tail: no zodiacal quality begins with a water sign or ends with a fire sign. One might ponder the mysteries of the zodiacal qualities further. The same is true regarding the four elements. Could it be that we naturally associate the earth signs with the more corporeal and overtly conscious aspects of human experience (the body) and identify divinity with air signs (Heaven, the gods, the Word)? That would leave us to equate water signs with Soul (the collective uncon-

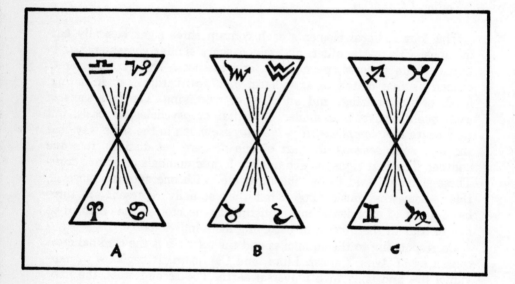

Fig. 5. The three zodiacal qualities: A. cardinal, B. fixed, and C. mutable.

scious?) and fire signs with Spirit (the superconscious). Somewhere in this we might observe the essence of the myth-making faculties of man and his need for religion.

Cardinal Signs: Aries, Cancer, Libra, and Capricorn

The cardinal signs denote initiation, creation, challenge, trial, action, causality, ambition, responsibility, fortification, burdens, support, and influence. Aries symbolizes selfhood and the desire for immediate extension; Cancer, security and depth; Libra, relationships and breadth; and Capricorn, conscious goals and height. Cardinal signs lead, carry others, arbitrate, and present themselves openly. Their real power is exoteric or overt rather than esoteric or covert. These four signs find that their duties, boundaries, and goals change from time to time, and that problems arise when they fail to realize their inherent capacity for adaption and change in the light of these new challenges or crises. Cardinal signs represent the immediate role of the individual in various public affairs and in the conflicts of the time. They describe the primary impulses for individual security, liberty, and freedom, and the basic responsibilities upon which they are attendant in the family, marriage, and community as a whole. Rules and standards have to be followed to obtain the most favorable results, though this may prove to be very difficult when the signs are weakly placed in a horoscope.

Busy and insistent, the cardinal signs are easily enthused by the various things to which they hold. Their strength lies in an ability to assess reality on an immediate and often urgent basis. Their conclusions are general, quick, and decisive, even premature at times. Hence, a creative and satisfying balance should be sought in the light of constant change between such poles as firmness and gentleness, action and reserve, and independence and dependence. Aries and Libra are signs having to do with individuality and its attempt to find a complement in the mate or partner: self goes to meet not-self. Aries seeks, explores, intuits, ventures, and projects itself against the horizon. Libra, the opposite sign, waits for Aries to arrive; it weighs, reflects (in every sense of the word), reasons, and enhances Aries through the spirit of its own individuality. Aries is the sharpest of all the signs. Libra has the greatest breadth.

Cancer and Capricorn represent the vertical axis of experience. What has the deepest roots is opposite to that which obtains the greatest height. Together, these two cardinal signs represent the experience of paternity. Cancer is associated with the home and mother, with all those things of a feminine or insular nature that ensure survival. Capricorn is the father, his means of livelihood, and the rules of society that make it possible to live successfully. In this case the emphasis is on the role of one's heritage and relation to the authority of the family, clan, tribe, or nation.

Taken together, Cancer and Aries constitute those things which might be termed individual-familial. Libra and Capricorn are motivated by things that are more public or less personal, those things and standards which could be identified as being social-universal. Each cardinal sign begins a new phase of experience, a new season, as it were. The next chapter shows how the cardinal signs are related to the angular houses and their respective cusps, the ascendant, nadir, descendant, and midheaven.

Fixed Signs: Taurus, Leo, Scorpio, and Aquarius

The fixed signs which immediately follow the cardinal signs correspond naturally to the succeeding houses of the horoscope: the second, fifth, eighth, and eleventh. Keywords for these four signs are empowerment, evaluation, consolidation, execution, direction, order, experience, insemination, magnetism, accumulation, and endurance. Taurus obtains and utilizes personal energies and materials close at hand. Leo expresses itself intuitively, often dramatically, in some enterprising manner. Scorpio shows how we use the resources of others, particularly those of the mate or partner, or how these resources are combined in some way with those of our own. Aquarius is the repository for one's various social urges, the currency of communication and complementary intellectual activity available through friendship and special interest associations. It is the task of fixed signs to concentrate, evaluate, stimulate, endure, and find agreement in values and materials. Their purposeful ventures may seem to be too slow or plodding to the cardinal signs who are often faced with immediate decisions that cannot be put off. Fixed signs tend to stick to the same frame of reference in dealing with the problems they encounter. They are less given to sharp changes than the cardinal signs. Their real power is sometimes exoteric or overt and sometimes esoteric or covert. For them, boundaries, duties, and goals are fairly easy to determine, but troubles arise when they make the fixing of these boundaries a more difficult task than is necessary. Fixed signs relate to the processes of evaluation of the various phases of experience, especially those concerned with shared experiences and rewards (or losses). They signify those ideas, things, values, and people which the individual considers of most concrete value in affirming his self-actualization. The idea is to *form something* so as to make it of tangible value at the moment.

Taurus and Scorpio, its complementary sign, have to do with the accumulation and disposal of one's resources. Each reminds the other that life and material things are only transitory. Leo and Aquarius have to do with the problems of self-expression, both singularly (Leo: creativity) and in manifold relationships (Aquarius: friendship). Any effective association along the lines of special mutual interest (Aquarius) is quite naturally dependent upon an intelligent exchange of ideas between strong-willed individuals (Leo) with good powers of evaluation (Taurus) who are able to share and transmute (Scorpio) their various personal resources for the benefit of the whole. The cosmic cross formed by the Ox, Lion, Eagle, and Man—the ancient tetramorph—symbolizes the necessity for sharing the wealth of the world. There can be no universal love, as symbolized by Aquarius, unless things are intelligently shared at the other three stages. On a less ideal scale, one can say that this sharing and willingness to give and take to the right degree is what marks the best kind of friendship, marriage, and relationship to one's children. What could be more important than this sharing of wealth, whether it is creative, psychic, intellectual, or material? The way in which this wealth is distributed is one of the chief concerns of the mutable signs, the third of the zodiacal qualities.

Mutable Signs: Gemini, Virgo, Sagittarius, and Pisces

The mutable signs may be the latest in the development of the Zodiac from eight signs to twelve signs. They represent things not formerly the concern of the common man or the masses: distribution of wealth, education, intellectual activities, religious knowledge, and administration of the kingdom or realm. Keywords for the mutable signs are demonstration, dissemination, modification, accentuation, adjustment, refinement, review, aid, repair, and utilization. The mutable mentality is interested in pursuing or refining ideas already set into motion by the cardinal signs and further evaluated by the fixed signs. It develops rather than creates anew, but in the mutable mode lie the seeds for new steps to be taken by the cardinal signs which follow the mutable signs. These new ideas or information, data, fresh ideas, revelations, and images find their release through the cardinal mode. Mutable signs use reason, serve, make judgments, and determine what sacrifices and final adjustments have to be made. Their real power is esoteric or covert; and for them, duties, boundaries, and goals are often difficult to determine or define because they are by necessity mutable in nature. Problems are most likely to occur when inappropriate goals and boundaries are forced upon these signs. In general, these duties should be determined by how they can best employ their manifold energies and talents for the moment, for the mutable signs lack the single-mindedness and crisis-meeting ability of the cardinal signs and the determination and consistent strength of the fixed signs in pursuing a goal.

As signs of review, the mutable signs represent the main modifications, the final steps in the development of basic drives and values at all levels of experience: mental, physical, spiritual, and emotional. There is an expansion here of the concrete boundaries and values, denoted by the fixed signs, into more abstract or ethereal realms, the emphasis often being directed toward the future. Gemini and Sagittarius, representing man's greatest degree of mobility, have to do with the intellect, learning, and travel. The quiver of the Archer is filled with the arrows of information compiled by versatile Gemini. Gemini obtains abstract facts, and Sagittarius takes these and expands them on a broad scale, often infusing these ideas with its own enlightening insights. Gemini is the vagabond with all of his belongings on his back; he travels lightly. Sagittarius is the explorer who must travel on a broader basis. His vehicle and luggage are apt to be more complicated than those of Gemini. Virgo and Pisces also travel; the former is the eternal traveling merchant, the Marco Polo of the Zodiac; the latter is the pilgrim who must bear the burdens of a solitary trek. Virgo and Pisces "serve" others and stay in the background (if they are wise) as much as possible in order to avoid the dangers of being in the limelight (which is experienced most pointedly by the cardinal signs). The function of these two yin mutable signs is to heal, mend, or give support to others in some practical (mainly Virgo) or emotional sense (Pisces).

Karmically speaking, the mutable signs must give more than they take. A weak and selfish person will perceive this as some form of bondage rather than as an important service. Doctors, teachers, priests, psychologists, plumbers, lawyers, reporters—all those who inform, aid, or repair—will have strong planets or rising sign in the mutable mode. The mandala formed by these four signs is the mandala of self-understanding, the final performance of the ideal human intellect. It could be that man will understand this intellect somewhat better by the time the age of Sagittarius (denoting truth and understanding) arrives four thousand years from now; and if not then, perhaps by the age of Virgo or the age of Gemini which come much later on. In the age of Pisces, we began to become aware (painfully, it would seem) of the vastness of the human mind as it is projected on the mutable mandala.

The crucifixion of Christ on the cardinal cross (established authority) for his belief in the ideals symbolized by the fixed signs (sharing, love, and freedom of spirit) symbolizes this new collective awareness as it is expressed through the mutable signs. Some may call it empathetic understanding or compassion, the courageous revelation of a broad love and truth at the very peak of man's inhumanity to man. From this concept of Piscean self-sacrifice (remember the death of Socrates and the suffering and solitude of Buddha as well) and voluntary simplicity arose the new religions which have helped to shape man's ethical ideals, destiny, and history for more than two thousand years.

This is not to say that man suddenly stopped treating himself savagely. What the awareness of the mutable cross represented in the last great age is only a beginning in a long process of growth which optimists hope will end in some expression of universal love. In the age of Aquarius man must pay attention to what the fixed signs represent. As long as people are repressed because of their age, race, class, or sex, there can be no true freedom. In the age of Capricorn, which follows this age (the ages defined by the constellations move in the opposite direction of the signs), mankind will again, as in the age of Aries, be confronted with the problems or solutions which relate to authority as symbolized by the cardinal cross. Each age corresponding to a cardinal sign marks a new season in the development of man. The Greek states, Pharaoh, and the Roman Empire lie behind us; the atomic age, as some wish to call the present period, will also become our heritage. To grasp the meaning of the signs in one's own horoscope in the light of these great ages is to know which way the "wheel of fortune" turns. The three crosses made by the zodiacal qualities provide the best insights into this larger view. People whose charts contain strong planets in the fixed signs are apt to be instigators—like it or not—during the Aquarian age. Cardinal signs will be somewhat less prominent than they would be during ages with which they correspond. The mutable signs will be more engaged in using their energies to redefine wealth of all types than they would be in the four ages corresponding to their own mandala.

Zodiacal Hemicycles

There are four zodiacal *hemicycles*, each containing six signs and beginning with a cardinal sign. The first, beginning with Aries and ending with Virgo, has to do with the essentials of survival facing the individual in the business of everyday living. Here his roles and experiences in the family, neighborhood, and at his job can be seen. What is sought is sustenance and shelter and their attendant pleasures and rewards.

Opposite this hemicycle is the one which begins with Libra and ends with Pisces, the sign one hundred and eighty degrees removed from Virgo. This half of the zodiacal wheel symbolizes the modifications made by others on the individual's basic ideas about wealth, family, shelter, children, pleasure, and work. Both his personal properties and his sense of selfhood are modified by the ideas and goods of others such as partners, foreigners, authorities, colleagues, and even secret enemies.

The attitudes acquired in childhood and early adulthood from one's family, playmates, co-workers, education, and recreation are modified by the last six signs. Sagittarius is a further expansion of the basic ideas and educational habits acquired in early childhood. Capricorn is the advancement in the community in reputation and career (Virgo denotes apprenticeship) which has some social significance beyond the strictly familial concerns symbolized by Cancer, the opposite sign. Aquarius, the sign of friendship and special non-familial associations, shows how we gradually replace or add to our involvement with our children and our personal pleasures and avocations, as described by Leo. In doing this we align ourselves with some objective cause or special activity in association with others. In contrast, the rearing of children requires a personal involvement and commitment of feelings. Pisces, the last sign of the second hemicycle, shows how we seek or take retirement from the toil (Virgo) of our daily lives, how in solitude we find the peace and time to review our actions. Thus, the first half of the Zodiac might be seen as the *source* of all the primary impulses for living, and the last six signs might be considered to be an objective *reflection* or expansion of these subjective impulses in the community or world as a whole.

A third hemicycle begins with Cancer and ends with Sagittarius. There is in this hemicycle an intensive involvement with courtship and love (Leo); family and heritage (Cancer); marriage and face-to-face relationships (Libra); definition of roles and duties (Virgo); exchange and combination of resources (Scorpio); and advancement for mutual satisfaction (Sagittarius). Here, the person has to align himself with others in terms of close cooperation toward what ideally should be some mutually satisfying goal or goals. The last sign in this hemicycle, Sagittarius, represents the final stage before the transition from the familial and social to the more universal or world-wide aspects of experience. There is usually a need in this instance for a proper balance (Libra) between private family concerns and those of a more public nature. Cancer, the first sign in the hemicycle, shows our roots in the family, tribe, or nation, our heritage as it is perceived emotionally.

Virgo and Leo, respectively, suggest the themes of work and play. Virgo is constructive work which has a practical aim. With Leo the activity is more for recreation or it seeks to fulfill some basic creative urge. Libra and Scorpio reveal the nature of the marriage and other partnerships and the condition of the family's wealth or basic resources as they affect one's partner, and vice versa.

The last hemicycle begins with Capricorn and ends with Gemini. The signs contained in this hemisphere together represent the greatest achievement in those objective phases of experience where the individual himself plays a decisive role in affecting the welfare of the world as a whole. Those things which relate to his family or marriage are not as much a part of this picture as are the rewards (and pains) of a sharper, yet broader social relatedness. Aquarius, the second sign in the hemicycle, shows how we are embraced by others of like mind, particularly those who approach us after we have proven ourselves to be productive citizens (Capricorn) of our community or nation. Pisces shows the necessary lessons of humility the individual encounters in the course of his success, honor, or even fame, all these things being associated with Capricorn and the tenth house. Aries follows all of this as the reassertion of one's pride and sense of individuality; it is the return to that state of innocence which can be equated to that of the infant (spring). Once he has arrived at this point the individual can begin a whole new phase of experience or he can pursue new, socially significant goals which are at the same time personally advantageous. Taurus symbolizes the personal rewards or tangible satisfaction obtained from one's recognized achievements (Capricorn). Gemini, the perennial vagabond, shows how the individual impartially makes his departure from the public eye (Capricorn), leaving behind material success (Taurus), and continuing with only the necessities for survival over his shoulder. This last step is important because for every ascent in life there must be a carefully regulated descent. One returns to his roots, as symbolized by the sign which follows Gemini, Cancer; it is mainly in this sense that Cancer is often regarded as representing the closing part of one's life.

A majority of planets, including the Sun or Moon, in one of the zodiacal hemicycles is sure to provide important clues about the main direction toward which an individual's will is inclined. The road each must travel is unique, with different sojourns along the way. Seldom, if ever, will the actual sequence of events outlined by a hemicycle evolve in an individual's life. Their discussion here merely provides an ideal model of the various phases of human existence.

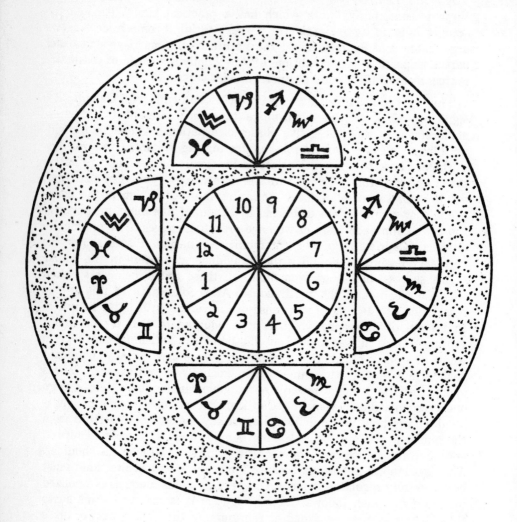

Fig. 6.   The four zodiacal hemispheres.

Zodiacal Quarters

Before the individual signs are discussed some mention should be made of the zodiacal *quarters* and their corresponding quadrants in the twelve horoscopic houses. The first quarter, which includes Aries, Taurus, and Gemini, represents stimulation, basic resources, ideation, and individual matters. It is the spring quarter and corresponds to the first, second, and third houses of the natural horoscope. The second quarter, consisting of the summer signs of Cancer, Leo, and Virgo, corresponds to the fourth, fifth, and sixth houses. In this second group of signs individual resources are built up, developed, and refined. Growth and expansion take place inside the environment of everyday responsibilities and interaction with family, children, and fellow workers.

The autumnal quarter, which includes Libra, Scorpio, and Sagittarius, can be defined by such terms as consolidation, combination, supplementation, and readjustment. It is here that individuality finds itself flowering in areas which are essentially extrapersonal. In the opposite quadrant, the first, the individual has to call upon his own talents and resources; in the third quadrant the ideas and possessions of others play an important part in his existence. Capricorn, Aquarius, and Pisces make up the last zodiacal quarter. Keywords here are synthesis, fruition, realization, and actualization; the result of all previous actions and associations finds its expression in this quarter. Yet, in the last quarter of the Zodiac are found the seeds for a new cycle because the seasons and the signs which mark the seasons continue to follow one after the other. Further keywords for the zodiacal quarters are provided in Fig. 7.

The Individual Signs

The descriptions given below for each of the twelve signs are suited mainly for the Sun sign, denoting will and purpose, and the rising sign, denoting personality and attitudes. They are also useful in studying the reflective effect of the Moon in a particular sign, and to a lesser extent, the other planets, especially Mars, which is often a signature of one's individuality as it is expressed in apparent drives and levels of energy. Mercury's sign position does not describe the individual so much as it does the means by which he adapts and communicates with others in daily life. Venus' position usually tells more about one's partner or ideal mate than it does about one's own personality. The posi-

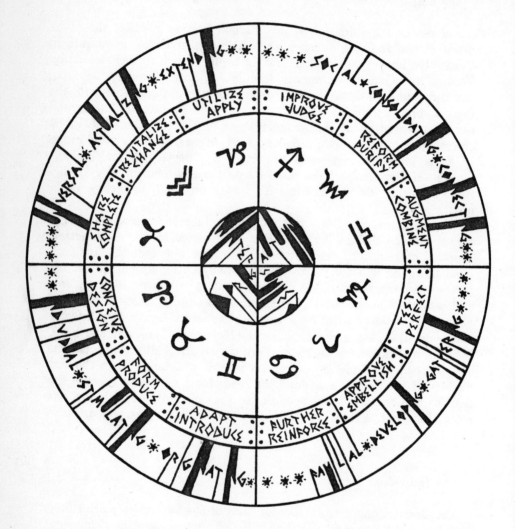

Fig. 7. Zodiacal quarters. The first quarter is individual-stimulating-originating; the second quarter is familial-developing-gathering; the third quarter is social-consolidating-connecting; and the fourth quarter is universal-actualizing-extending. These four quarters correspond to the four solar seasons.

tion of Mars reveals more about one's own sexual drives than does Venus. One looks to the sign occupied by Jupiter to understand ideals, and to Saturn to see where specific responsibilities are apt to be felt most strongly. Friends will to some extent be described by the sign Uranus occupies in a birth chart. The sign Neptune is in tells something about where seclusion might be sought, where sacrifices must be made, or it can be an area of potential "self-undoing." The sign Pluto occupies shows how one is tied to his generation through the values they might hold. However, the following brief interpretations apply mainly to the Sun signs.

Aries ♈ March 21 to April 20

First sign of the Zodiac
Corresponds naturally to the first horoscopic house

Ruled by Mars

Zodiacal quality: cardinal
Zodiacal element: fire
Complementary sign: Libra
Jungian type: pure extroverted intuitive
Psychological opposite: Capricorn
Gender: subjective yang

Relates to: initiation, exploration, impression, inspiration, individuality, self-reliance, incentive, action, leadership, sharpness, courage, discovery.

Other keywords: intuition, perception, curiosity, conquest, fortitude, energy, particularization, radiance, warmth, promotion, personalization, enforcement.

Lower expressions: impulsiveness, lack of restraint, narrowness of view, lack of foresight, overbearing nature, brutality, combativeness, narcissism, vainly seeks admiration.

Positive Aries types are initiators with a spirit of self-reliance and a degree of energy which is effective in exploring new horizons. Where there is no vacillation or excessive subordination to others there is apt to be some planet strongly placed in Aries. Here obstacles are met and overcome, the idea being that there is something to be conquered, or some challenge to be met. The quality and nature of Arian courage and virtuosity are, of course, modified by the position of Mars, ruler of Aries. The level-headed and intuitive versions of this sign are also much influenced by the sign appearing on or near the first house cusp, that is, the rising, or ascending sign. Otherwise, the ascending sign or the position of Mars may distort the personality.

Although Arians (and those with the sign rising) tend to have the power of a persuasive personality, they have to learn to develop thoroughness, reserve, tact, and receptivity in their rather pointed dealings with others. Excessive self-confidence or use of force works against the Mars type of person when he desires to ascend too rapidly or when he goes too far out of his way to gain the admiration of others. On the other hand, the sign becomes bogged down when it becomes unduly reflective or indecisive. More than the other signs, Aries must know how to take immediate action in dealing with the personal crises it is bound to encounter. Jupiter, as ruler of Sagittarius, another fire sign, is quite pronounced when in Aries. So too, are the Moon, Venus, and Saturn, all rulers of cardinal signs. Mars or Sun in Aries brings out the characteristics of the sign most effectively.

Taurus    April 21 to May 21

Second sign of the Zodiac
Corresponds naturally to the second horoscopic house

Ruled by Venus

Zodiacal quality: fixed
Zodiacal element: earth
Complementary sign: Scorpio
Jungian type: extroverted empirical (sensation)
Psychological opposite: Sagittarius
Gender: objective yang-yin

Relates to: construction, production, investment, evaluation, practicality, wealth, profit, resources, transactions, order, common sense, contentment, constructive talents.

Other keywords: accumulation, substantiation, appraisal, domestication, foundation, patience, firmness, calmness, stamina, attachment, valuation.

Lower expressions: materialism, stinginess, excessive conservatism, procrastination, stubbornness, impatience, awkwardness, dullness.

Positive Taureans are characterized by genuinely valuable efforts in the utilization of the various personal resources they have at hand. A steady and constructive pace brings the greatest rewards. Consistency and thoroughness in cultivating one's crops and in making sure there are seeds for future crops are essential for this earth sign. By conserving energy and paying attention to small but important things, the Taurus person is able to build things that last and which bring personal contentment and security. What some of these people may need to develop is self-humor, emotional sensitivity, and a more universal outlook. A view of life which is too inflexible can cause one to overlook valuable rewards in realms of experience other than the material or practical. A narrow selfishness is apparent in less developed Taureans, who at the same time may feel they can run the (business) affairs of others.

This sign is the builder, and as such, should concern itself with the quality of the tools it uses and the materials that go into whatever it makes. In serious transactions it should not feel reluctant to ask others for their specifications, credentials, or whatever. But it, like the other two earth signs, should be careful not to overlook intangible factors which can ruin its good works. Any planets in the second house of the horoscope will modify a Taurean Sun or Moon. Venus has traditionally been associated with Taurus.

Saturn in Taurus is usually thought to be well placed, somewhat less so, Uranus and Jupiter. But there is no cut and dry rule: any planet in any sign can produce either positive or negative results, depending upon the individual's response to the aspects the planet receives. A person with any planet in Taurus must take the time for careful and methodical evaluation of the things denoted by that planet (and house it occupies); he has to "bring down to earth" some important thing which will be of personal value to himself. This fixed sign also has to be careful that it does not at any point exhaust its personal resources or it may find itself in some grave danger. To know the true value of what one possesses and what one is able to build is the main purpose in life for Taurus.

Gemini   **May 22 to June 21**

Third sign of the Zodiac
Corresponds naturally to the third horoscopic house

Ruled by Mercury

Zodiacal quality: mutable
Zodiacal element: air
Complementary sign: Sagittarius
Jungian type: introverted empirical thinking (abstract facts)
Psychological opposite: Pisces
Gender: objective yin-yang
Relates to: communication, translation, correlation, illustration,
information, education, study habits, intellect, logical induction, short
or speedy trips, side-by-side relationships such as siblings, neighbors,
acquaintances, peers, nonamorous companions.
Other keywords: bipolarity, versatility, adaptability, informality,
charm, definition, polarization, enigma, chameleon changes.
Lower expressions: changeableness, superficiality, ambivalence, un-
certainty, inconsistency, plagiarism, verbosity.

Positive Gemini individuals are talented translators in various phases
of experience; their bipolar intellect gives them the capacity to consider
two or more points of view simultaneously. The position of Mercury
is important because it is never more than twenty-eight degrees away
from the Sun; and therefore there can only be three types of Gemini
mentality: Geminian, Taurean, and Cancerian. The position of Mercury
in the horoscope of the Gemini person shows his outlet for intellectual
energies; along with the position (by house) of the Sun, it shows how
the Gemini seeks to correlate information in some informative or communicative form. Any planets in the third house will also strongly influence people who have the Sun, Moon, Mercury, Mars, or ascendant in
Gemini. The nature of the intellect and faculties of communication
will be colored by whatever planets are involved in Gemini.

Saturn in this sign enhances a serious mentality, while Jupiter in
Gemini may increase any jovial or easygoing tendencies in the chart.
What the Gemini native may need to develop is a sense of pragmatism,
outward confidence, and a capacity to review (and preview) words and
ideas. A too-changeable nature can work against the Gemini, who may
also tend to spread himself too thin. Many Geminis think they have
a message or information for others—if they do, they should be careful
to be as thorough as possible, without being too expansive or spread
out at the same time. Concise, logical, and true statements made in
the present have lasting value, and they can always be elaborated upon
(by Sagittarius, ideally) at some point in the future. Gemini is at its

best when it remains light, adaptable, objective, and teaches (if it is so inclined) in an informal manner. Intellectual detachment that leaves room for compassion might be the higher goal of the third sign of the Zodiac.

Cancer    **June 22 to July 23**

Fourth sign of the Zodiac
Corresponds naturally to the fourth horoscopic house

Ruled by the Moon

Zodiacal quality: cardinal
Zodiacal element: water
Complementary sign: Capricorn
Jungian type: introverted pure feeling
Psychological opposite: Libra
Gender: subjective yin
Relates to: nourishment, security, protection, support, the home, the mother, the tribe, heritage, feelings, memory, psychic power, sentiment.
Other keywords: impressionability, empathy, receptivity, collection, storage, shelter, tenacity, sensitivity.
Lower expressions: insularity, defensiveness, clannishness, clingingness, sentimentality, emotionality, moodiness, peevishness, sloth, chauvinism.

Positive Cancerians manifest a need and capacity to nourish and protect others in some manner. Their powers of empathy often make them tenacious champions of the underdog or the common man. To understand a person with Cancer rising or Sun in Cancer one must know the house and sign position of the Moon, ruler of the sign. Decisions are often made by these people on the basis of their personal feelings or impressions about something or someone; they can take this to an extreme, revealing a too-narrow and subjective view lacking realistic boundaries. Too much insularity can make them miss new opportunities. Any lack of poise or dignity will work against them in the public eye.

Cancer people are skilled in collecting the essentials of life, but some of them confuse useful objects with those which have only sentimental value; hence their homes or places of storage may look as though they are inhabited by a "pack rat." This exaggerated need for security and shelter arises from some distortion of the feminine instincts, Cancer being the most maternal of all the signs. Even men born under Cancer may show strong feminine characteristics—positive and negative—although a rough exterior may hide this from the casual observer. Cancer is the sign associated with the personal unconscious, especially as it is affected by the environment of one's early childhood. It readily absorbs the impressions which arise from the deeper levels of the unconscious, and in this respect it may enhance a creative imagination.

The highest activities that Cancer people can relate to are those where they are able to care for or nourish others in some capacity. In a tribe, it is this sign which is apt to be the chief. Wise Cancereans know that there are times when they have to move sideways or backwards in order to achieve success; they have less success when they seek recognition or honors (a Capricorn matter). Moving with the tides of life, they should never carelessly give up their home or shelter for some superficial purpose. In this respect the patient turtle seems to be as effective a symbol for the sign as the clinging crab. In studying this sign (and its opposite sign, Capricorn), it is helpful to note that it may be quite different inside than it appears to be on the outside.

Leo ♌   July 24 to August 23

Fifth sign of the Zodiac
Corresponds naturally to the fifth horoscopic house

Ruled by the Sun

Zodiacal quality: fixed
Zodiacal element: fire
Complementary sign: Aquarius
Jungian type: extroverted intuitive feeling
Psychological opposite: Virgo
Gender: subjective yang

Relates to: creative self-expression, enterprise, recreation, avocations, romance, affection, courtship, children (procreation), humor, fashion, enjoyment.

Other keywords: aggrandizement, strength, self-confidence, earnestness, warmth, benevolence.

Lower expressions: egotistical pride, ostentation, insatiability, mirth, childishness, infatuation, indolence, tension, anger.

Positive Leo individuals, or those with the sign rising or several planets therein, are magnetic and warmly outgoing in their dealings with others. They are the epitome of a firm gentleness. The goal they seek is one allowing self-expression, joy, and some demonstration of ethical concern for others, especially in regard to any children they might have to rear. Aries points the way for others, whereas Leo, also a fire sign, sets an example and directs them in some manner. The terms *creation, recreation,* and *procreation* describe the various ways in which the Leo person will express himself. What he may need to develop is a broader view of life and of the objective needs of the future. Living at any impractical or overindulgent level in the present tends to create problems later on. Insincerity and a domineering or manipulative tendency is sometimes seen in Leo natives. This may be accompanied by bombastic or excessively dramatic behavior, or a lack of restraint in expressing ideas and fiats. Yet, some Leo people, if their fire is squelched, may find themselves too much in accord with the ideas and desires of others, too frustratingly conforming. This causes a lack of rhythm in their compulsive expressions of boldness and exuberance; however much they roar like lions they seldom go out to catch the game. To compensate for this weakness and inability to be individually expressive they may become pseudo-extroverts, or they may be unduly concerned with showing off their adornments but not their hearts.

Where there is a childlike spontaneity and a well-regulated sense of humor and play, there will be a positive expression of Leo. Such people often have a rainbow-like talent for fantasy which enables them to cheer or entertain others, or to inspire them to creative action. In that case they become leading or directing forces in the community or family. The more this power (some might call it love) is centered benevolently on one's own heart, the greater the influence of the Leo character on those around it will be. Where this power is not heartfelt and freely demonstrated there may be a gruff, grim, and even cruel expression of the Lion.

Jupiter and Mars are emphasized in Leo, in addition to the Sun, Moon, or rising sign. Neptune here can be a signature of creativity if it is well aspected. Saturn incurs responsibilities along the line of matters related to Leo, and Uranus may show some conflict or shocks between one's offspring (enterprises, creations) and one's associative urges (friends, objective associations) if it is frictionally placed in the horoscope. Mercury and Venus readily take on the characteristics of Leo in terms of communication and social dealings with others, indicating an attraction to out-going, warm-spirited people. These two planets, in the chart of a Leo native, may also be found in Virgo or Cancer, accounting for qualities which are quite unleolike. (This is true for any Sun sign, as already mentioned, because these two modifying bodies are seldom more than one sign removed from the Sun sign.) Any planets in the fifth house of the chart will also modify what can be said in any particular instance. The Moon in Leo tends to bring out the weaker or less desirable side of the sign when it is poorly aspected or responded to by the individual.

Virgo ♍   August 24 to September 23

Sixth sign of the Zodiac
Corresponds naturally to the sixth house

Ruled by Mercury

Zodiacal quality: mutable
Zodiacal element: earth
Complementary sign: Pisces
Jungian type: extroverted empirical thinking (concrete facts)
Psychological opposite: Leo
Gender: objective yang-yin

Relates to: analysis, observation, repair, service, work, efficiency, discrimination, craftsmanship, instruction (how to do it), assistants, coworkers, health, hygiene.

Other keywords: digestion, examination, precision, criticism, succinctness, simplicity, purity, pragmatism, inventory, dependability, indoctrination.

Lower expressions: vain criticism, false sense of modesty, undue scepticism, pettiness, fussiness, selfishness, self-prostitution, enslaves self to "serve" others.

Positive examples of this sign are practical and well ordered. They are adaptable and somewhat more mobile than Taurus, the first of the earth signs. Introspection and the power of observation are associated with Virgo. There is also a capacity to adjust, improve, modify, perfect, and repair things. Virgo seeks to prevent disorder and fix what is not operating properly; it also has to account for the various working parts of any organic whole. Virgo may be the mentor or the minister in the kingdom—the power near the throne (Leo). In warfare and peace alike it is the quartermaster and supplier of necessary goods. Virgo's analytical ability makes it well suited for any job requiring attention to detail and speedy conclusions along practical lines. "Will it work?" is the question concerning this pragmatic sign.

Negative manifestations of Virgo take the form of excessive attention to non-essential details in the light of more significant issues or matters. What may need to be developed in some cases is a more expansive outlook, warmth, sympathy for the weaker individuals it may be forced to work with, and a less critical and analytical sense of itself in social relationships. Virgo's self-undoing might lie in any uncalled for attempt it makes to seek prominence for its efforts or work. According to astrological tradition, it should serve in such a way that it avoids crisis and controversy. It should always be cautious, methodical, and aware of the value of its own skills and fine craftsmanship in whatever it does. This discriminating and orderly sign (sloppy Virgo people are poor examples of the sign) is also influenced by any planets which are in the sixth house of the chart. Through Virgo, we ensure that our crops will be bountiful and usable.

Libra   **September 24 to October 23**

Seventh sign of the Zodiac
Corresponds naturally to the seventh horoscopic house

Ruled by Venus

Zodiacal quality: cardinal
Zodiacal element: air
Complementary sign: Aries
Jungian type: introverted pure thinking
Psychological opposite: Cancer
Gender: objective yin-yang

Relates to: face-to-face relationships, marriage, partnerships, union, cooperation, arbitration, justice, mediation, equality, contests, open enemies, aesthetics.

Other keywords: attraction, agreement, harmony, peace, poise, grace, balance, detachment, comparison, reason, choice, enhancement, contract, arrangement, endorsement.

Lower expressions: rationalization, vacillation, contradiction, competitiveness, allurement, aloofness, insipidity, undue dependence upon others.

Positive Librans form sound unions with others in order to find the right complement of qualities necessary for their success. Cooperation, especially with a close comrade or mate, is usually demanded of Libra, and the influence of the partner on the individual's attitudes and sense of purpose can be very strong. Libra may also give the ability to counsel other people; it is an effective arbiter in situations where there is conflict. Its inherent detachment and ability to weigh or reason matters is, perhaps, the sign's most positive characteristic. It is also the sign associated with art and beauty, especially the appreciation of design and form. When this characteristic is not fully developed Libran tastes are likely to be colorless, unoriginal, and neat to the point of being rather sterile. A compulsive need to balance everything or to divide things up evenly may reinforce this tendency.

What Libra people—this can include those with the sign rising or Moon therein—may need to develop are more practical goals, self-confidence in asserting themselves, and an appreciation of simple, less symmetrical things and experiences (things, for instance, related to Cancer). The negative example of this sign can never make up its mind because it endlessly weighs things, hoping somehow to be able to imbue them with its own standards of perfection and harmony. This can be very frustrating to the individual and to those around him; therefore, in defense, he may compensate for this weakness by putting on a harsh (pseudo-Arian) demeanor. However, inside he is constantly watching for approval from others. Where he can be direct and *decisive after weighing things properly* (at the right time and to the right degree) he becomes a potential leader or counselor capable of resolving the disputes and problems of those around him. The strong Libran is also an excellent tactician. The type and quality of alliances he forms define the nature of the rewards he will obtain throughout life.

Venus is powerful when in Libra, epitomizing many of the sign's more noticeable qualities. Moon, Saturn, Mars, and Uranus are also quite important when placed in Libra, often denoting delicate situations or conflicts which require tact and reflective reasoning to resolve. Jupiter in Libra tips the scales toward a great sense of social justice if it is well aspected. Neptune here might incline one toward the arts if the horoscope otherwise indicates this. Mercury in Libra is logical if it is reinforced by similar placements; otherwise it can contribute to moments of painful indecision or vacillation. The position of Venus and any planets in the seventh house will also reveal something about the Libran character.

What most distinguishes Libra from Gemini, the first air sign, is that the "twins" represent accidental or side-by-side relationships of an informal nature, while Libran relationships are more formal or contractual (therefore more critical) in nature. With Libra, certain roles, commitments, and duties are outlined. This is true in a marriage as well as in a chess match, and in purely Libran situations there may be little physical contact between the two parties. Indeed, any union that is required will become possible only after both parties have understood and voluntarily agreed to the terms of that union. Conflict arises when the scales are not balanced.

Scorpio ♏︎   **October 24 to November 22**

Eighth sign of the Zodiac
Corresponds naturally to the eighth horoscopic house

Ruled by Pluto

Zodiacal quality: fixed
Zodiacal element: water
Complementary sign: Taurus
Jungian type: introverted sensory feeling
Psychological opposite: Aquarius
Gender: subjective yin

Relates to: investigation, penetration, regeneration, demolition, research, extrasensory perception, sexual release, death, wills, legacies, taxes, partnerships assets, shared or combined resources.

Other keywords: catharsis, purgation, baptism, hidden power, magnetism, discipline, clarification, elimination, intensification, determination.

Lower expressions: secretiveness, willfulness, obsession, alienation, divorcement, destructiveness, possessiveness, jealousy, wrath, a caustic manner.

Positive Scorpio individuals (the eagle and serpent are also symbols for this sign) or those with a strong planetary emphasis in Scorpio are concerned with matters related to the sharing of various types of wealth or resources. Inferior qualities and things can be cast out and replaced by enduring things which can be shared or transformed into something (socially) useful. Regenerating personal traits requires a resoluteness and intense sensitivity that can be sure of passing through the dangers associated with any kind of self-renewal or reorientation of personal values and goods. Life as such may be viewed by the Scorpio person as being like a glacier across which he must travel (fixed water), one which is filled with many emotional and sensual crevasses, or many temptations to use his magnetic personality and keen insight to gain personal advantage. The last thing the Scorpio person should be concerned about is personal advantage; as the eighth sign, the one immediately after Libra, its motives are best directed to proper alignment with the talents and resources of others. Theoretically, Scorpio is the sign which can enrich others. In contrast, Taurus, the opposite sign, has to be careful to keep its own possessions intact because it normally has to rely more on itself than on others. When Scorpio shares what it has with its partner it is itself enriched, but this sharing is purely an act of will.

The highest Scorpio type—the eagle—uses his penetrating intelligence to regenerate defective things. In relationships he may be able to help his companions reform or eliminate emotional and sexual problems which cause them pain or discomfort. Scorpio is also associated with the surgeon, the devoted and painstaking scientist, the biologist, the depth psychologist, and others who study the forces of life and death. Like Cancer and Pisces, the other water signs, Scorpio is covert and oriented toward the feeling mode; it may also demonstrate some psychic powers of which the individual himself may not be aware. Some of these powers can be dangerous or destructive if they are not well directed. In attempting to rid an organism—himself perhaps—of some negative or undesirable quality the less developed Scorpio is apt to injure the surrounding tissues, defeating his attempt at revitalization. He lacks the inner concentration which is found in the more developed examples of the sign.

If it is inclined to be shy and oversensitive, Scorpio may have to learn to be more socially adept and outgoing—attributes ideally suited to Aquarius and Leo, which are also fixed signs. There is a secretive version of Scorpio which conceals its intentions and weapons, and in an almost sinister way, seeks to manipulate others or undermine their security. Sexual excesses or obsessive conflicts may also be present when a planet is found in Scorpio. A struggle with passions is often a prelude to some deeper transformation or release. The ego is transformed and one catches a glimpse into the enigmas surrounding sex and death, or into what Jung called the collective unconscious. This release and the inner clarity which follows is called *satori* by Zen students. Psychic power and the ability to heal others may also be present in certain individuals born under Scorpio (this is true for the other water signs as well).

Any planet in Scorpio will denote, through its house position and aspects, situations where one will have to experience some personal catharsis or metamorphosis of feelings. Also significant are any planets in the eighth house of the chart or a strongly placed Pluto. This sign clears the way for better things, but this act of will-directed change or self-transformation in the light of a new relatedness (denoted by Libra) can prove to be terrifying for weaker examples of the sign. In serious cases—and Scorpio is deadly serious—it is nothing less than mustering the courage and energy to look death in the eye, or to yield completely one's ego and desire to control in the act of sexual union. It is no wonder that this sign is seen as evil by those filled with fear of the unknown. Those same people might do well to meditate on the awesome beauty in the web of the spider, the effectiveness of the agile serpent, the strength of the ever-vigilant and devoted eagle, or the means of defense of the timid scorpion. Scorpio teaches that we may often find ourselves in those things we fear. From those things which prove to be truly dangerous, we learn to be cautious. The greatest danger in an iceberg lies below the surface of the sea. The careless grasshopper—at whatever stage of metamorphosis he might be—becomes the spider's dinner. Many of the secrets of life (sex) and death (spiritual reawakening) lie in Scorpio.

Sagittarius   November 23 to December 21

Ninth sign of the Zodiac
Corresponds naturally to the ninth horoscopic house

Ruled by Jupiter

Zodiacal quality: mutable
Zodiacal element: fire
Complementary sign: Gemini
Jungian type: extroverted intuitive speculative thinking
Psychological-opposite: Taurus
Gender: subjective yang

Relates to: encouragement, speculation, expansion, adventure, intuitive judgment, hunches, idealization, formal education, philosophy, religious quest, foreigners, journeys, athletics.

Other keywords: guidance, sincerity, frankness, joviality, generosity, self-understanding, improvement, declaration.

Lower expressions: recklessness, juvenile behavior, romantic excesses, evangelism, exaggeration, unreliability, gambling, quixotism.

Positive Sagittarians or those who have strong planets therein, especially Jupiter or Mars, show a high-mindedness which seeks to infuse practical matters with a spirit of idealism. They encourage others, teach them new or alien concepts, and they do this largely through the power of personality, much like Aries and Leo. Frankness, boldness, and an expansive manner, combined with swift judgment, make some Sagittarians good leaders in those broad undertakings which require energy, strength, and mobility. The more knowledge and understanding they acquire, the more they can accomplish. What Sagittarians may need to develop is a sense of logic to go along with their broad enthusiasm, patience with practical details, and more concern about the end results of their often impulsive actions and grandiose plans. Too much zeal can work against the person governed by Jupiter, causing him to take unnecessary chances or make snap judgments; and feeling frustrated, he may become arrogant, overbearing, and falsely self-confident. He may, in this event, attempt to teach you something you learned before him, or try to persuade you to gamble on some romantic or speculative venture.

In taking on large jobs the positive Sagittarian will maintain his warmth of personality in order to find helpers to take care of small but important details to which he may not have time to give personal attention. His helpers (or students) will admire his spirit of natural gregariousness. If the individual imagines himself to be a knight worthy of emulation he will have to act like one in every respect. The more intellectual Sagittarians need a vehicle for their thoughts; thus, they will be students on the road of understanding before they become teachers, usually expanding on the ideas of some other individual who started down the road somewhat earlier. To Gemini, Sagittarius adds its own ideals and intuitive thoughts; Gemini seldom has the time to expand or travel far with the "message." Gentleness, warmth, and modesty are qualities which an influential Sagittarian will seek to develop in order to temper his basically extroverted energies. The Sagittarian who boasts, shows off, or shoots for the target with defective equipment becomes dangerously lost in life's jungles.

Any planet passing through the sign of the Archer entreats the individual to speak the truth, for the truth is the basic concern—or should be—of those born under this sign. Any planets in the ninth house will also reflect Jupiterian qualities. To develop good judgment is to some degree being able to hit that at which one is aiming. The courtroom judge, the airplane pilot, the stockbroker, the car salesman, the wrangler, the backwoods hunter, the football quarterback, the mountaineer, the explorer, and other Jupiterian types of people have to be good judges in order to be able to make swift and just decisions. They will, as expressions of a mutable sign, always have to adapt to new and ever broader changes they are bound to encounter on one of life's many roads: Sagittarius must travel.

Capricorn ♑ December 22 to January 20

Tenth sign of the Zodiac
Corresponds naturally to the tenth horoscopic house

Ruled by Saturn

Zodiacal quality: cardinal
Zodiacal element: earth
Complementary sign: Cancer
Jungian type: pure extroverted empirical (sensation)
Psychological opposite: Aries
Gender: objective yang-yin

Relates to: responsibility, management, organization, capitalization, authority, the father, superiors, ambition, achievement, career, honors, blessings, prestige, administration.

Other keywords: establishment, control, obedience, elevation, salience, acknowledgment, integrity, constancy, concern, confirmation, actualization, wit.

Lower expressions: undue cynicism, misanthropy, insensitivity, coldness, false sense of martyrdom, manipulation, pretension.

Positive Capricorn people are able to capitalize on things of worth and quality. Time is taken to achieve excellence and recognition in matters which some other signs might consider to be too mundane. This can be responsibility in managing some enterprise of a practical nature, or in acting as the organizer in some objective group endeavor. Capricorn is well suited to carry responsibilities for others in the community or nation, but because it is the most visible or salient sign (cardinal earth) it must learn to be cautious and thorough in discharging these duties. Due to this naturally exposed position, Capricorn individuals (and those with the sign prominent) may have to take on a rather cool, businesslike, and reserved personality, even though they may be quite gentle and yielding inside. In contrast to Cancer, the most maternal sign, Capricorn best symbolizes the paternal side of human nature. In a good parent the difference between the two functions may be difficult to discern, especially in the Aquarian age (equality on a broad basis) when roles are becoming less distinct.

The position of Saturn and of any planets in the tenth house will affect the Capricorn native very strongly. Saturn warns the individual to be as sure-footed as a goat when it is wandering through perilous heights. Carelessness, lack of order, and ill-defined duties can all contribute to a fall from one of the peaks of Saturnian ambition. In a serious place there is little room for impulse, brusqueness, or emotion that might weaken the power of command. By the time something or someone has arrived at Capricorn *everything* should have found its proper place.

Really high-minded Capricornians can handle any controversy, criticism, competition, or responsibility they might encounter. They are "on top of things." The sign looks to the future—Aquarius follows Capricorn—through the eyes of the past, and it sees much of the vanity in man's present ambitions, acts, and desires. Although a Capricorn person (I am speaking here of a mature goat, not a young kid) finds himself in a position of authority and influence he knows that there is always a higher authority to which he himself must answer, a superior (actual or symbolic) to whom he must bend. He is, after all, only a manager, president of the company, spiritual guru, or "son of

God." The weaker examples of Capricorn may need to develop more directness, warmth, sensitivity to the feelings and sentiments of others, and a more diplomatic manner in face-to-face relationships.

The failing of this sign might often lie in an overly serious or taciturn nature. This posture can cause mistrust, as others believe that Capricorn is scheming to control them in some way—and perhaps it is. Any coldness, gruffness, conceit, or brooding also depreciates the sign in the eyes of the other signs. Most people need some degree of intimacy, and few like to be depressed by a gloomy person. Planets in Capricorn represent situations in which some barrier or sense of duty has to be defined, or some rules created or followed, usually to the letter. At its zenith, Capricorn is, in effect, more public or universal than it is personal, and is furthered by maintaining integrity in all things and striving for clarity.

Aquarius  **January 21 to February 19**

Eleventh sign of the Zodiac
Corresponds naturally to the eleventh horoscopic house

Ruled by Uranus

Zodiacal quality: fixed
Zodiacal element: air
Complementary sign: Leo
Jungian type: introverted speculative thinking
Psychological opposite: Scorpio
Gender: Objective yin-yang

Relates to: friendship, experimentation, altruism, special interest associations of a manifold nature, colleagues, cosmopolitan ideals, communal urges, interaction, future hopes, invention.

Other keywords: progress, trust, freedom, synthesis, unification, diversification.

Lower expressions: diffusion, disorder, anarchy, disrespect, carelessness, excessive bizarreness, prolixity, indiscriminate associations, pride of intellect.

Positive Aquarians are often diversified in both their thinking and their relationships. A note of altruism can motivate the individual to seek alliances with like-minded colleagues, or he might use his strong mental energies to organize, improve, or invent (the combining of previous concepts) something of value. His strength lies in the softly magnetic and mild quality of his personality, in the tactful and graceful manner in which he aids others in their creative or constructive endeavors. Reason, rather than emotion, is his forte, and he uses this intuitive reason to tie or fix different elements together in whatever he happens to be involved. Most important is the fact that he is only as successful as the quality of friendships and objective associations he is able to establish: Aquarians seldom get anything done solely through their own actions. The exercise of their intellect and will depends upon those around them.

Weaker Aquarians may find that they have to develop a better relatedness to practical things; they have to learn how to assert themselves more decisively while retaining their individuality when in association with others. The scatter-brained (this sign has a radial quality about it) Uranian/Aquarian individuals try to befriend everyone with whom they come in contact, and this may lead to certain unexpected shocks in relationships. These same individuals generally display disorder in other facets of their life as well, diffusion being the dominant trait in their character.

When it is being objective and well ordered, Aquarius finds freedom of choice and the will power to act with speed and breadth. Originality reinforced by positive relationships and by an eye that looks toward the future mark the truly rare and brilliant Aquarian. Being bizarre for its own sake is a certain indication that the individual is operating at a lower level of the "sign of man." The majority of Aquarians are neither non-conformists nor great altruists; they conform pretty much to the values and ideas of their friends and they seek an easy-going pace.

Any planets in the eleventh house of the horoscope will modify the Aquarian nature, as will the position and aspects of Uranus. Planets placed in this sign reveal some need for the individual to align himself with friends, colleagues, or associates in order to obtain some mutually satisfying end. In its most refined or ideal meaning Aquarius symbolizes the angelic person, the spiritually androgynous individual who transcends the traps of sexual roles, ethnocentric views, greed, and man's own inhumanity. This *Homo sapiens* does not simply talk about improving our lot: with his friends, he does something about it. His inventions are truly useful, his ideas bring men closer together, and his associates circulate and add to his ideas for man's future. His intellectual detachment is freedom itself, for it is completely objective in its associations. Tradition regards this as the sign of hope.

Pisces ♓   **February 20 to March 20**

Twelfth sign of the Zodiac
Corresponds naturally to the twelfth horoscopic house

Ruled by Neptune

Zodiacal quality: mutable
Zodiacal element: water
Complementary sign: Virgo
Jungian type: introverted intuitive feeling
Psychological opposite: Gemini
Gender: subjective yin
Relates to: relief, sympathy, self-sacrifice, seclusion, hidden things, latent abilities, imagination, dreams, mystical feelings, charity, retirement, pilgrimages.

Other keywords: aid, compassion, devotion, repose, rest, refuge, convalescence, serenity, veneration, subtlety, alleviation, permeation, introspection.
Lower expressions: deception, seduction, secret enemies, self-undoing, obliquity, perplexity, shyness, inert will, melancholia, cowardice, masquerade, intrigue, mystery.

Positive Pisceans or individuals who have a preponderance of strong planets in Pisces are able to understand, transmute, and transcend emotional problems. In Cancer, personal emotional/sexual problems are either contained at the subconscious level or repressed; in Scorpio, the next water sign, one has to learn to deal with them, to release them from the instinctive control of the unconscious; in Pisces, one has to either sink or swim. It becomes the sign of suffering and bondage only when the individual fails to rise above his negative passions, selfish emotions, possessiveness, neurosis, and other shortcomings which are essentially unconscious in origin, and which cause trouble in one's relationships with others. The Pisces person who has gone through some personal suffering or sacrifice is in a position to feel sympathy for others;

hence, Pisces is said to be the sign of compassion; here is a broad understanding and an ability to lend aid to those less fortunate.

Pisces is sensitive to emotional nuances in others, and highly developed Neptunians can combat unconscious forces with considerable power of penetration. The idea is to mitigate, give relief, and help others, especially in some capacity behind the scenes. Some Pisceans may need to develop more objectivity in their character and judgments, the ability to pay attention to important outward details, and a more direct and warm manner. Too much secrecy is negative in this case, as is undue concern with intangible forces through which one may attempt to escape (because he cannot relate to others) from the responsibilities of daily life. Weaker Neptunians are easily beguiled by these hidden forces. Some may turn to dishonest practices, habit-forming drugs, secret societies, or another self-depreciating area of experience. Some personal sacrifice and/or expression of humility and sacrifice for the benefit of the world as a whole is required of nearly every Pisces person.

On a more esoteric level, this sign symbolizes the attendant-priest of the temple who guards its secrets with his life. Pisces also stands for the great marketplace where caravans come from all lands; it includes traders, buyers, and pilgrims alike. The position of Neptune in the chart will reveal the last word about the Piscean individual, showing his Achilles' heel as often as not. Any planets which may happen to be in the twelfth house are also significant in this respect. In solitude, Pisces comes to understand itself, and learns that there is no end which is not followed by a new beginning.

CHAPTER IV

THE TWELVE
HOROSCOPIC HOUSES

A horoscope is a diagram of the solar system in relation to a specific time and place of birth. It is made up of twelve sections called *houses* and is a two-dimensional representation of the celestial sphere surrounding the Earth as it is defined by the Sun's ecliptical path. The cusps of the four angular houses—the first, fourth, seventh, and tenth—correspond roughly to 6:00 A.M., midnight, 6:00 P.M., and noon, respectively. Every four minutes of time brings a new degree of the Zodiac to the cusp of the first house, the *ascendant*, and in twenty-four hours all three hundred and sixty degrees of the Zodiac will have risen on the first house cusp. Looking at the horoscopic wheel, the four directions are the reverse of what one is used to: the first house represents the eastern horizon; the fourth, the northern sector; the seventh, the western horizon; and the tenth, the southern sector. The seventh house cusp is referred to as the *descendant*; the fourth house as the *nadir* (Imum Coeli, I.C.); and the tenth house cusp as the *midheaven* (Medium Coeli, M.C.) or zenith. The intermediate house cusps also hold degrees of the Zodiac on their cusps, but due to the curvature of the globe they contain unequal amounts of the Zodiac in higher latitudes.

The signs are reckoned by the Sun's annual transit as defined by the four seasons, while the houses are traditionally figured on the basis of the daily rotation of the Earth on its axis. The planets transit the signs, and the signs and the planets are placed inside the houses of the horoscope. There is a natural correspondence between the twelve signs and the twelve houses. Aries, the first sign in the sequence, corresponds to the first house, but because of the daily rotation of the Earth, Aries will correspond to only about two hours of first house influence. A new sign will "rise" on the cusp of the first house every two hours, and in twenty-four hours each sign will pass over every one of the twelve houses.

Classification of Houses

The twelve houses can be classified in various ways. The wheel can be divided into four hemispheres analogous to the zodiacal hemicycles: eastern, western, southern, and northern, each containing six houses. Or it can be considered on the basis of four quarters or quadrants. The first, fourth, seventh, and tenth houses are called *angular* houses, and they correspond to the cardinal signs. The houses following the angular houses are called *succedent* houses—the second, fifth, eighth, and eleventh—and they find the most affinity with the fixed signs. The third group of houses is the *cadent* houses—the third, sixth, ninth, and twelfth—which correspond to the mutable signs.

Another way in which the houses can be studied is according to how they correspond to the four zodiacal elements. The first, fifth, and ninth houses are associated with the fire signs; the second, sixth, and tenth with the earth signs; the third, seventh, and eleventh with the air signs; and the fourth, eighth, and twelfth with the water signs. A person with many planets in Cancer as well as in the fourth house would have a strong emphasis in the cardinal water mode. If these same Cancer planets were in the ninth house, due to that individual being born earlier in the day, they would acquire some of the fiery attributes of the ninth house because it has an affinity with Sagittarius, a fire sign.

As the newcomer gets to know more about these basic factors he will learn how to determine, weigh, and synthesize the sometimes seemingly contradictory patterns in a chart. Generally, the zodiacal sign a planet occupies dresses it, so to speak, in its own special apparel (function), while the stage or theater (spatial circumstances) is best described by the house in which that planet is found. The drama is itself determined by both the sign and house; but the greater part of the action is indicated by the planet through the aspects it receives from other bodies in the horoscope. Each house is an existential arena, and each planet therein is a challenge or an opportunity, according to the basic meaning of the house, the planet itself, and the sign it occupies. Houses are tied together through aspects between the planets. For example, a planet in the seventh house of marriage in close aspect to a planet in

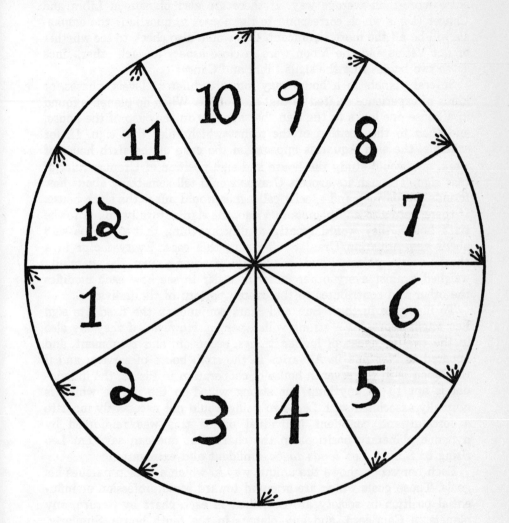

Fig. 8. The twelve houses of the horoscopic wheel.

the fourth house of security will unite these two areas of experience in some more-than-average way. If there are also planets in Libra and Cancer (signs which correspond to the houses in question) the emphasis will be all the more significant. One would also check to see whether or not Venus and the Moon were in close aspect to each other, since these two bodies rule the signs Libra and Cancer.

Several planets in a house may indicate different levels, phases, or kinds of experience related to that area of life. When no planet is found in a house one looks to the sign that appears on the cusp of the house, and then to the position of the planet which rules that sign. If, for example, the sign Aquarius appears on the cusp of the sixth house of work, one would study the house and sign position of Uranus, ruler of that sign. Through its aspects Uranus would tell something about how friends (Aquarius) and special colleagues would affect the sixth house. If there were also any planets in Virgo, the sign naturally linked to the sixth house, they would greatly modify anything that could be said about the Aquarian/Uranian effects in this case. Every factor in a chart—every pattern and planetary position—must be carefully weighed against every other factor in order to see how each modifies the other and contributes to the overall pattern of the individual.

To illustrate further: Sun and Mars conjunct in the fixed fire sign Leo *might* represent a strong willed person. However, if they are also in the twelfth house of hidden things, seclusion, and retirement, and opposed to Neptune in Aquarius in the sixth house of service; and if the Moon is in the seventh house of cooperation in Pisces, the individual is apt to be anything but strong willed to the degree which is normally associated with Leo. Leo rising would not necessarily indicate a forceful and confident individual unless this was reinforced by dynamic planetary positions in the chart. But one can say that Leo rising or Sun in Leo *tends to be* confident and extroverted.

Each horoscope shows the unique way in which a person pursues his goals. Those goals which are oriented toward some profession or influential position in society are described in each chart by Saturn, any planets in Capricorn, and any planets in the tenth house. Similarly, Venus' position and any planets in Libra or the seventh house reveal how we find partners who complement us and aid us in achieving our goals. Jupiter, Sagittarius, and the ninth house indicate how we acquire special knowledge (including the ideas of the partner) toward achieving those goals. The position of Uranus and any planets in the eleventh house or Aquarius help to define what kind of objective relationships will best reinforce our aims, especially those of a professional or publicly significant nature. The eighth house, Pluto, and Scorpio together provide additional clues as to what kind of material support we will need in achieving these greater successes. In studying the houses, one has to learn to associate them with the other basic factors: the signs and the ruling planets. Mars' energy is most like Aries. Aries' energy, the need to impress, lead, and activate, is similar to the individual needs denoted by the first house of the chart. How each of these needs are met, however, is determined by the time of day one is born. Any of the signs can appear on any of the houses in a twenty-four hour period.

The signs of the Zodiac which are placed on the cusps of the twelve houses are found in convenient *tables of houses* for every geographical latitude from the Arctic Circle to the equator.

Four Hemispheres

The hemispheres of the horoscopic wheel are similar to the four hemicycles of the Zodiac discussed in the previous chapter, so that by reviewing them, one can get additional ideas about the meaning of the four hemispheres. The *eastern hemisphere*, which includes the tenth, eleventh, twelfth, first, second, and third houses, symbolizes the individual's projection of himself into objective public situations that bring personal rewards and effective exchange and communication with others. This might be called the universal-personal hemisphere because it requires both a broad and impartial relatedness as well as a definite exercise and expression of individual free will and open participation with others. A majority of planets in this side of the chart indicates a tendency to manifest along these highly involved lines.

The opposite half of the wheel, the *western hemisphere*, includes the fourth, fifth, sixth, seventh, eighth, and ninth houses. This hemisphere relates to the familial-social spectrum where the emphasis is on the need to harmonize family instincts and one's basic sense of security (home, children, work) with the immediate problems arising from one's partnerships, marriage, and formal social ties. This implies a need for cooperation and tact in achieving one's aims, a need to work through others, and adaption to their ideas (ninth house) and practical needs (eighth house). This has to be done without losing one's own security (houses four, five, and six). The western hemisphere is one of give and take, of the need for balance between personal feelings and attachments and those social necessities and requirements of partnership which must be attended by reason and cooperation. In this sector of the wheel personal aggressiveness and assertive self-interest are not as fitting as they might be in the opposite hemisphere.

Houses one through six below the horizon of the wheel make up the *northern hemisphere;* they represent activities and concerns which might be called personal-familial. A strong emphasis of planets in this hemisphere indicates the necessity of integrating skills and values acquired early in life from one's family (clan, tribe), playmates, classmates, and peers with one's own needs and abilities for creative self-expression and productiveness. The role of the mother or early family life and setting may in some way be emphasized; or some instinctive or unconscious yin factor will be stressed in the formation of one's character. At the root of all actions is the subconscious need for security (fourth house); all work and creations are meant to contribute to security in this sector of the wheel. In the eastern hemisphere the emphasis is on the expression of individual will; in the western half of the chart it is on the importance of cooperation and objective unions with others on a face-to-face basis. In the northern half the individual is guided by the common sense faculties that deal with the ephemeral aspects of life, the subjective feelings that protect and ensure his foundations for survival. In this bottom half of the wheel he meets what comes to him in the form of useful things and relationships.

The last hemisphere, the *southern,* involves less subjective situations than the northern hemisphere; it is social or public rather than personal and familial. The individual who has a majority of planets in the seventh, eighth, ninth, tenth, eleventh, and twelfth houses may be thrust into the limelight in some way. Any prominence here is apt to follow upon well-defined roles, objectives, and alliances. Arriving at some significant achievement in this case depends upon suitable partnerships, additional resources, the right kind and degree of formal education (travel experience counts too), sponsors, friends, and often upon hidden supporters or followers as well. The goals defined by this half of the chart are not simply goals of sustenance or the successful rearing of children, nor are they necessarily the goals one's family wishes one to obtain. The center of the goal-seeking in the southern hemisphere of houses lies in the individual's drive for power, honor, recognition, and influence, whether this is for constructive or destructive purposes, fame or infamy. In either case, it is the hemisphere where the individual is the most visible and most vulnerable in the eye of the public. Here the things of the father (career, law, authority, and honor) are the fulcrum, in contrast to the more insular matriarchal concerns of the opposite hemisphere where the keyword is nourishment.

The planet which most effectively symbolizes the southern hemisphere is Saturn; the eastern hemisphere, Mars; the northern hemisphere, the Moon; and the western hemisphere, Venus. These are the natural rulers of the four angular, or seasonal, houses, the tenth, first, fourth, and seventh, respectively; and which form the basic framework for the other houses of the horoscope. The quaternary principle represents the best means man has of ordering reality: four seasons, four angular houses, four directions in space, four elements, four psychological functions, four sides to a pyramid. From the four points rise the intermediate points or functions, in this case, the succedent and cadent houses. But the mandala of experience is most easily identified at the angular, or cardinal, points and by the four planets with which they correspond. The cardinal cross represents the points of initiation in the act of becoming psychologically whole (which Jung called the process of "individuation"). The four hemispheres provide clues about how each person creates order and meaning in his life.

The planets and the signs they occupy in any hemisphere will show what struggles an individual must go through in order to realize his best potential. The hemispheres of houses change every six hours of every day, much as the seasons repeat themselves endlessly. A new sign appears on the eastern horizon approximately every two hours, shifting the overall picture. Thus, a person born about twelve hours away from you, on the same day and place, would have the planets in the opposite hemisphere. His life, although similar to yours in many respects, would be subjectively inclined, whereas yours would be more objectively oriented; or vice versa, depending on the time of birth in both cases. The hemispheres may contain fairly even numbers of planets; or the Sun and Moon together in one hemisphere could greatly outweigh the other eight bodies in the opposite half of the chart, these two luminaries being the strongest of the "planets."

Further study and experience will make clear upon what the deeper meaning of the four hemispheres rests. However, each generalization has to be tempered by a detailed analysis of the chart. In many instances a majority of planets in one or two halves of the chart will not be as significant as certain strong aspects between key planets elsewhere, especially the Sun and Moon. Aries rising, with Mars in Aries in the first house, and the Sun, Mercury, and Venus on the eastern side of the horoscope—all of this would greatly outweigh a majority of six planets on the opposite side, the western. Another chart, with Aries rising and Mars again in Aries in the first house, but with all the other planets in the western half of the chart, including the Sun, would indicate an emphasis—though perhaps one which is frustrating—on the western half of the chart. In effect, the need for cooperation would probably dominate a very strong desire for self-assertion, as denoted by Aries rising and Mars in Aries in the first house. Countless other examples could be cited to illustrate how the astrologer must carefully weigh the various factors in order to see what motivates the individual.

If there are no planets in the eastern hemisphere, the astrologer would study the position and aspects of Saturn and Mars in order to gain insights into that phase of experience. Similarly, for the western hemisphere one would study the Moon and Venus; for the northern hemisphere, Mars and the Moon; and for the southern hemisphere, Venus and Saturn. Through their affinity with the eighth and ninth houses, Jupiter and Pluto relate to the social phases of experience outlined by both the western and southern hemispheres. These two planets represent modifications in the values, resources, and ideas of the individual as he begins to orient himself to less personal or less strictly familial situations. Each new phase of experience requires new adaptions and a reshaping of earlier values, ideals, and aims. Neptune and Uranus represent further refinements of social urges, extending the person (if he is ready and willing) into the more universal concerns of life symbolized by the eastern and southern hemispheres.

The hemisphere in which the Sun appears in a chart is likely to be the hemisphere which, in the final analysis, holds the things closest to the individual's heart and sense of purpose. Specifically, this applies to the exact house and quadrant the Sun occupies. The closer he can get to aligning his energies, feelings, relationships, and goals to this area of experience, the happier he is likely to be. Of course the sign rising will count to some extent in describing the ease or difficulty of his adjustment, and the Moon always acts as a reflector of individual will as it is denoted by the Sun. Every position in a horoscope signifies something to which we must at some time direct our attention. Nothing this side of death goes unnoticed by the laws of change (karma); every planet in the solar system forms part of the pattern of our spiritual and physical reality. Each of the hemispheres of the chart is like a cup which is either being filled or emptied of its contents.

Quadrants of the Horoscope

One can also divide the wheel of houses into four *quadrants*. The quadrant consisting of the first, second, and third houses is analogous to spring and the emergence of individuality; here one can best determine what characteristics in his personality will enable him to communicate his values and ideas to others. It is here that these basic ideas and values are formed, personal resources defined, and the essential mentality determined through early contact with others besides the parents, namely siblings, neighbors, playmates, classmates, and other chance acquaintances. What this quarter of the horoscopic disk represents is the early activity and attitudinal posture which precedes in significance any conditioning by one's parents, mate, or later social relationships which are essentially formal in nature. It is the quadrant of greatest spontaneity and individuality, an area where native intelligence, informality, and adaptability in communication all work for the best interests of the individual himself. In this quadrant, the *individual decides* what he wishes to produce in life.

The next quadrant, which includes the fourth, fifth, and sixth houses, shows how the individual goes about producing those things which will bring security to his family as well as himself. This usually requires him to acquire additional skills and values, either through his family or through his work. His workshop as well as his creations (children: procreations) are found in this quarter of the chart. The keyword is security.

In the third quadrant this security is extended to include the individual's mate and all those with whom he forms partnerships for reasons of mutual advantage. In this quadrant, which includes the seventh, eighth, and ninth houses, the products of his efforts are presented to the public or combined with those of his partner. Within this autumnal quadrant lie the seeds of fulfillment found through a suitable complement to one's own talents, resources, and desires, both physically and intellectually. Union and cooperation are required before one can go any further in obtaining public recognition. Achieving success here often requires some degree of regeneration of the individual's basic attitudes, values, and aims. Personal powers are tested in what may seem to be alien situations or places (the ninth house, for instance, represents foreign matters). This quadrant, then, is the direct complement or opposite of the first quadrant.

The cusp of the tenth house, the midheaven, begins the last quadrant. Theoretically, this marks the highest individual achievement one can have, the greatest degree of influence in the world as a whole, and the broadest responsibilities. By this point in life our ideal, astrologically defined individual has understood his basic aims and talents (first quadrant), acquired additional skills from his family and through any necessary apprenticeship (second quadrant), and has combined this with new insights and the values and resources of others (third quadrant). In the fourth quadrant he is on top of the world, so to speak; this is where the Sun would be at noon, at the zenith. In this quadrant the only thing left to do is to form objective relationships which will further one's standing (Aquarius and eleventh house: colleagues) and to extend one's success as widely as possible (Pisces and twelfth house). If the individual's achievement (tenth house) has not been arrived at honestly, if he has made short cuts that go against natural development, he will have a short-lived or painful success, even perhaps making secret enemies (twelfth house) instead of self-sacrificing supporters or followers.

Mars is most like the first quadrant in effect, the Moon like the second quadrant, Venus like the third quadrant, and Saturn like the fourth quadrant. The rule is: first of all we realize what most closely corresponds to our individual identity, what we can actually call our own; then we seek nourishment from those close to us, selectively adopting some of their ways to further our own welfare; then we find a complement, usually in a mate, through which we can test and develop ourselves; and finally we reach the zenith, as symbolized by the last quadrant. This zenith, the midheaven, is the mountain which every sage climbs in order to receive the more divine truths of human experience.

In the first quadrant we have an idea of individual will and liberty. In the second quadrant we anchor this liberty to that which will most effectively sustain us and give us shelter. In the third quadrant we give this liberty substance in the social realm by defining (or redefining) its boundaries; we learn to give and take in the true sense. In the fourth quadrant we make liberty a fact—ensuring our individual liberty—by taking on duties and responsibilities that affect the entire community or world as a whole. Crops are planted, cultivated, harvested, and then utilized: spring, summer, autumn, and winter. This chain of experience has four complementary sides.

House Types: Angular, Succedent, and Cadent

The *angular* houses—the first, fourth, seventh, and tenth—represent the beginning of the four different phases of human experience discussed above: personal or individual, familial or tribal, social or public, and universal or cosmopolitan. Following each angular house is a *succedent* house—the second, fifth, eighth, and eleventh—in which certain things and values are defined, realized, transformed, or aligned with the tools and materials necessary for the person's growth in each particular quadrant. The final stage in each quadrant is described by the *cadent* houses, which include the third, sixth, ninth, and twelfth. The succedent houses organize and adapt the impulses of the angular houses to satisfy some immediate need, whether it be related to material gain, pleasure, sexual release, or friendship. The cadent houses are a further extension, sometimes even a reorganization of these values and impulses along less personal lines, although they are still significant for the individual himself. The cadent houses relate to such matters as communication of ideas and values, the acquisition of practical skills which aid creative self-expression, travel to foreign lands, and compassionate endeavors which affect people less fortunate in some respect than oneself. The highest output of energy usually takes place in the angular houses. The most fixed or centralized expression (for instance, one's personal possessions, children, legacies, membership in a club) is found in the succedent houses. And the most resilient, diffuse, and mutable energy is associated with the cadent houses (such as in matters dealing with travel, communication, health, occupation, hidden endeavors, and education).

At the level of the angular houses, decisions must be made rather swiftly in order to meet the various challenges and crises which are likely to arise. The immediate effects of these decisions are felt in the succedent houses which follow: increase in resources, rewarding recreational activity, gain through close cooperation with another, or realizing the fruits of friendship, to give but a few of the many examples of positive change which can occur. If failure, rather than success, is transmitted from the angular houses to the succedent houses there might be such manifestations as material loss, trouble in rearing children, divorce, estrangement from friends and colleagues, or some other shock or setback. The cadent houses show how we review our actions and analyze the rewards (or losses and failures) obtained in the previous houses. They represent opportunities at various stages, through which one can learn new ways to avoid further disappointments if these have occurred; the cadent houses also indicate where we can extend earlier successes into new or different realms. It is here that new ideas, skills, ideals, and empathies can be acquired; consequently, by the time the next angular phase is activated—the cadent houses preceding the angular houses—the individual is ready to test newly acquired powers or knowledge according to the environment or circumstances in which he finds himself. This might be his own immediate environment and interests, his family, tribe, or nation, his marriage, or his career.

The cusps of the four angular houses represent the points—corresponding symbolically to the seasons—in each quadrant where these new changes first become apparent, even though an individual may choose to ignore them and suffer some unwanted consequences later on in the succedent houses, or even further on in the cadent houses. If he has not applied himself correctly he may experience unnecessary strife or loss. The abuse of human freedom and willpower results in bad effects at some future point. Here there is no moralizing about good and evil; what is implied is that those out of tune with time are out of tune with nature and therefore with the deeper self.

Harmony is needed. When there is inner harmony (positive first house identity) we can relate to the outer world objectively and form positive relationships (seventh house). On the way toward forming such relationships the individual needs something tangible to which he can root or anchor himself. This attachment is largely instinctive and unconscious, providing each person with the things and conditions necessary for his protection, nourishment, and general security. This is the meaning of the fourth house and the nadir. The first house and the ascendant outwardly define the individual himself; therefore, the seventh house and the descendant are the "contra-self," the mate, or the animus/anima. Everything which is tenaciously yin is found at the fourth house cusp: the mother, family, clan, ancestral memories, heritage, emotional attachments, sentiments, and one's home.

At the midheaven, or cusp of the tenth house, the individual consciously meets the yang: the father, authority, established laws of the land, elders, superiors, and whatever one conceives to be his God. This is the point of conscious self-actualization of goals in the widest practical sense. The zenith of individual experience is arrived at, but only when a person is strong in the other three phases. He needs to be strongly individual, self-aware, and properly decisive: the first house. He also must be firmly rooted in whatever sustains him emotionally and physically: the fourth house. He must know which lessons of give and take are necessary in order to find harmony in relationships: the seventh house. Without dynamic individuality, emotional security, and harmony in relating to the ideas and things of others there can be little lasting success at the tenth house level. The intermediate houses, the succedent and the cadent, tell the story page by page, experience by experience, relationship by relationship. The requirements of each moment of time are announced through the angular houses, utilized and developed at the succedent level, and modified further in the cadent phase of experience.

Houses and Zodiacal Elements

The angular, succedent, and cadent houses correspond to the cardinal, fixed, and mutable signs, respectively. The houses can also be studied in the light of their affinity with the four zodiacal elements: fire, earth, air, and water. The first, fifth, and ninth houses correspond to the fire signs, denoting expression of will power and the search for personal identity. In the first house, the individual identifies his main creative powers, desires, abilities, perceptions, aims, and attitudes, everything which directly affects his outer personality. The fifth house represents the creative self-expression or extension of this power and ability into such forms as children, private enterprises, recreation, creative projects, and various avocations. Play and amusement, hobbies and pets, all of these things teach important lessons about how to apply personal ethics in dealings with one's family and co-workers. The ninth house relates to the further expansion of individual will power into areas where familial-personal motives and acquired talents can be expressed on a wider basis. Added at this point are contacts with foreigners, the ideas and beliefs of partners and competitors, formal education, and a rejuvenated sense of sociability or gregariousness that is essential in achieving one's higher ambitions. The ninth house person, like the Archer, should know what he's aiming for.

The second, sixth, and tenth houses, which correspond to the earth signs, represent matters that have to do with one's livelihood. The second house contains all things which could be called the resources of the individual, his materials for personal gain, possessions, tools, and those developable talents and abilities of a practical nature which bring him personal contentment. The sixth house indicates how he acquires and practices additional skills, undergoes an apprenticeship, perfects his skills and materials, and also how he shares his resources with his family. From fellow craftsmen and members of the family or tribe he learns new techniques which make his work more productive or profitable. The sixth house also has to do with the analysis and perfection of personal traits, methods, and resources. After a person has perfected himself in a practical way he is ready for the more professional concerns denoted by the tenth house of honor and career. The intern becomes a full-fledged doctor, the apprentice carpenter hangs out his shingle as a journeyman woodworker, the disciplined enlisted man is promoted to an officer's commission. The eventual achievement and recognition denoted by the tenth house follows a considerable amount of preparation and hard work at the second and sixth house levels. Only after the individual has inventoried his resources and proven himself does any diploma he might have obtained become a license of profession. Such true success in the practical world is based on diligence and self-regulation.

The third, seventh, and eleventh houses, which correspond to the air signs, have to do mainly with nonparental and non-authoritarian associations with others in the community. In the third house are the acquaintances, peers (pals, playmates, and classmates), neighbors, and siblings with whom one can compare ideas, mental processes, and natural sense of communication. As a social animal, man needs this Mercurial ability to converse with his own kind. In the exchange of ideas and perceptions he learns new things, hence the association of the third house with education. Without this intelligent exchange there would be no civilization. The third house is the point in our development where we begin to realize that we are citizens of the human community, and that we must make choices, define terms, illustrate our intentions or purpose to others, adapt to the customs of neighbors, and account for the needs and interests of our brothers and sisters.

At the level of the seventh house, we compare our aims and abilities with others: close comrades, opponents, the opposite sex, counselors, and others with whom we are in close face-to-face contact. Waiting here are the things and qualities we need to complement our own energies, aims, and desires. Here too, we often get recommendations that further our progress in society. If an individual is effective in presenting himself to others (positive seventh house approach) he will have a better chance of finding love, justice, peace, and harmony. But if he is overly selfish or aggressive (negative first house approach) he drives people away and can even make open enemies. It is no accident that the eighth house of death and divorcement follows the seventh house of marriage and cooperation. Many people never get far past this point. Of all things, nothing is more difficult to accomplish or maintain than cooperation. For one thing, the seventh house, like Libra, has to do with formal contracts, including marriage. If, as enlightened and reasonable individuals, people could trust each other and subdue their self-interest, there would be no need for such licenses and rituals.

Where there is communication (third house) and cooperation (seventh house) there is more room for the objective relationships described by the eleventh house of friends. These broader associations can take many forms: fraternal groups, spiritual brotherhoods, communes, special interest clubs, leagues, and other social relationships where the individual's specific interests and needs are subordinated to those of the group as a whole. Looking back on the first two air houses, it seems reasonable to say that success at the eleventh house level depends to some extent upon how well one gets along with his siblings and neighbors, and how well he can share responsibilities with his spouse and the opposite sex in general. Many relationships which are labeled "friendship" are more like the third house (acquaintances) or the seventh house (comrade-competitors).

The fourth, eighth, and twelfth houses correspond to the last of the archetypal elements, water. They represent the idea of integration, that is, the operation of feelings and unconscious elements binding together the acts and products of the conscious self. The fourth house shows the influence of the family, tribe, and nation on one's emotions and instincts for survival and nourishment. Here too, resources are stored—in the individual's own special manner—to be used as needed. The more that is properly stored, the better the chances one has in attempting things outside of the personal and familial environment; the deeper the roots of security, the less likely the individual is to be blown over by the vicissitudes of marriage and career. However, he must also be cautious, for the closer he has to operate to the family or tribe to achieve his wider goals, the more he is likely to offend their expectations, taboos, customs, and sentiments. To lose contact with one's roots (provisions) is to invite disaster.

The eighth house is where the resources of one's partner are stored, and here again, one must be sure to tread carefully so as not to be caught in some fatal web: a person will defend what he regards as his own if one threatens to abuse it in some way. The eighth house is also the point where both familial and personal resources are transmuted or redefined so that they can be combined with the resources of others (those of the opposite sex, for instance) toward some mutually satisfying end. To pass through this stage is to experience the "death" of purely selfish or personal needs and to awaken to the beginning of universal values. Foreigners and alien concepts (ninth house) seem less threatening when a person has, with good reason, yielded his possessions to a more just purpose (seventh house). The ego death or *satori* awakening described by the Zen Buddhists characterizes the transformation of the eighth house. In order to be reborn at a new level of awareness one has to die, even though this release may only be emotional or psychic rather than physical. In order to transform the ego and the things to which it clings some people have studied yoga, taken psychedelic substances, or used some other method through which they can obtain this cathartic experience. Such personal regeneration is easier where healthy feelings and attachments exist from childhood onward (fourth house) and where one's relationship with the opposite sex (seventh house) is governed by intelligence. The blissful sexual release associated with the eighth house follows such a development.

Integration of the individual with his roots is seen in the fourth horoscopic house: mother, family, heritage, ancestors, tribe, clan, and nation. The eighth house demands that he integrate both the personal and the familial with the things held by the mate, partner, and, generally speaking, the opposite sex. In his everyday dealings with others he has to learn to distinguish between different influences and interests. This requires powers of penetration, empathy, and clarity, for the dangers attendant upon involvement with the possessions and ideas of others can be very great. The individual must beware of destructive human entanglements; it is no partnership asset that hurts either party.

The twelfth house of "self-undoing" and hidden things also holds dangers. When a person has failed to integrate himself with the more universal aspects of experience he runs the risk of isolation. The twelfth house is also the house of retirement, rest, and review of individual achievements and relationships. In the eighth house he releases certain of his possessions to the partner or comrade; in the twelfth house he releases a great deal more, that is, everything he has accumulated which might be of some value in relieving the suffering or woes of others. In this regard, the twelfth house is considered to be the house of compassion, charity, and self-sacrifice. What he relieves here, what he has to offer, is not simply for the benefit of all mankind (eleventh house), but for the world as a whole. Not to release these things, to cling to the narrow illusion of ownership, is to create suffering, sorrow, and disappointment at the same time one becomes isolated from the mainstream of life. It is folly, as every good Buddhist knows, to hide one's treasures for his own use when he has outgrown his need for them. In this case one's own secret enemies are those of his own making. In the twelfth house we truly judge ourselves, and any cross we may have to bear is really our own burden. This house of the horoscope also represents necessary retreats of all types. In solitude and privacy there is often peace of mind; however, solitude can also be imprisonment, confinement to a hospital bed, a jail cell, or the crib of a dope addict or alcoholic. There are two sides: welfare worker and person on welfare; poetic sublimity or degrading burlesque; hidden supporters or treacherous enemies. This house associated with Pisces and Neptune holds many mysteries.

In the last quadrant of houses there is no house corresponding to the fire element. In that section there is no need for the individual to willfully assert himself. A successful career (tenth house) comes more from careful preparation than from aggressiveness and ambition. In associations and friendships (eleventh house) the individual (fire) is de-emphasized, in that he relates to others in some way that helps to fulfill a group purpose or function. In solitude or in acts of charity (twelfth house matters) there is little need to display power or to prove oneself a hero or saint in any way. The third quadrant of houses has no house corresponding to the earth signs. In the more psychologically and spiritually rewarding partnerships of long duration (seventh house) the main emphasis is not on material things, but on communication, intellectual rapport (ninth house), emotionally satisfying modes of reproduction, and the harmonious mingling of talents and resources (eighth house). Religious and intellectual understanding, even the acquisition of formal education, is not dependent upon practical skills. In this sector, real understanding cannot be either bought or sold.

The second quadrant has no house corresponding to an air sign. Logical abstractions are not so essential in dealing with family and personal feelings (fourth house), in instances of dramatic self-expression, or in the acquisition of purely practical skills for survival (fifth and sixth houses, respectively). In this case, the power of objective communication is of less importance than the impressions of sincere feelings, sentiments, and an awareness of the habits of those with whom one is in close daily contact: the child with its mother, the lover with his fiancée, or the doctor with his patient, to mention only a few examples.

The water mode is lacking in the first quadrant of houses. This may help to illustrate the need for directing the individual will and basic life aims (first house) along lines which are free from distorting feelings, emotions, and the taint of unconscious forces. Direct action is effective only when, following a spontaneous intuition, it is not encumbered by excessive worry, subjectivity, or changing sentiments, all of which are identified as characteristics of the water element. A water influence would not befit the second house of personal possessions either, because here concern over these belongings might become a clinging and dangerously narrow possessiveness. In terms of the third house of communication, a water influence would slow the individual down, perhaps causing him to be overly subjective or emotionally sensitive to situations or people who actually require only passing attention. From all of this one can see that the horoscopic wheel, like the Zodiac, can be studied in various ways, but always with the idea of its wholeness and the interrelatedness of the houses. Both the general and the specific have to be considered when studying an individual horoscope.

The Individual Houses

Man is like the four seasons: his selfhood is realized in four distinct phases or modes, each beginning with an angular house (or cardinal sign). As has been pointed out, here are four quadrants, each divided into three parts: angular, succedent, and cadent. The first quadrant, containing the first, second, and third houses, is the individual in action, his method of operation, and the power of his personality in communication with others. It also represents his natural abilities (originality in the purest sense of the word), tools, and materials, as well as his native mentality, and self-awareness in adapting to the ideas and goods of others. The first quadrant contains everything the person needs for survival which he can actually call his own.

The second quadrant of houses—the fourth, fifth, and sixth—describes the means by which the individual secures more permanent foundations, establishing connections in his tribe, family, or with co-workers. It is here that resources are gathered and stored (fourth house), acceptance and love found (and given, as in toward one's own children), and new skills acquired (sixth house) which augment the natural abilities and inclinations symbolized by the first quadrant of houses. The mother and early childhood are important formulative factors: nourishment and love at any point in life touches the memories of our younger years. It is impossible to sever the connection one has to his past, as every psychologist has observed. The second quadrant is the home and the workshop of the individual, his base of operations, and the place where he feels the most security. The tools and materials described by the first quadrant are used in the second quarter of houses to create something distinctive; this creative impulse can also manifest as recreation or procreation. So far, the individual has no major obligations outside his immediate family and job, no formal contracts, dealings with foreigners, membership in a special interest club, or involvement in anything very universal which is hidden from the changes and experiences of everyday life. Even marriage (seventh house of contracts) is not a fact here, in the sense that it represents a socially justified formal arrangement (legal union) between parents for the protection of the children. In primitive societies the idea of husband and wife is not quite the same as it is in a more cosmopolitan world; marriage then and there is defined more as a clan or tribal matter rather than as a voluntary agreement between two adults.

Formal encounters, alliances, and relationships of cooperation begin with the third quadrant: the seventh, eighth, and ninth houses. Having defined his resources and aims (first quadrant) and established the roots of security (second quadrant) the individual is now ready to form complementary relationships, meet new challenges on the other side of the horizon, align his aims with higher ideals, and expand into new or foreign areas of experience. He steps onto a path which may even take him away from his homeland. He meets the extra-personal and befriends it, or it becomes his open enemy; so much depends on his adaptability and what he has already learned at earlier stages of development.

In the last quadrant of houses, which includes the tenth, eleventh, and twelfth, the individual hopes to realize his highest aspirations and needs, his most conscious goals. Objective relationships and experiences are more important here than strictly personal or familial associations. The summit is in sight. Some reach only for fame or honor, prestige or recognition in the community, while others genuinely work for universal values that benefit the entire world. This is also the sector relating to the tribal gods and spirits, the laws of the land, and the shadow or image of authority, whether it is one's father, an elder, or someone else.

First House

The first house is the point and the means by which a person begins to define his reality. The cusp of the first house—usually identified with the ascendant—is an especially sensitive point in the definition of the basic attitudes, temperament, likes and dislikes, and the personality of an individual. Self-interest is most readily identified by the sign which happens to be ascending. The first house is generally said to represent one's physical appearance to some extent, particularly the head and upper part of the face. It can be observed that the eyes and other sense organs guided by the brain are the primary fact of experience, that through these faculties we satisfy our personal desires, tastes, and impulses for experience. One's sense of power emanates from this angle, particularly through the exercise of personality as it is projected in one's own self-image or identity.

The sign which is rising helps to describe the outward disposition of a person. Also important in this respect are any planets within the first house, as well as the position of Mars (due to its natural affinity with the first house). In contrast to the things of the persona indicated by the first house, Mars, and the rising sign, the Sun's position is a signature of the deeper will or sense of purpose. The Moon serves as an important modifier of the selfhood outlined by the Sun's sign and aspects (inner self) and the rising sign (outer self). At the first house level, instincts and intuition are more important than feelings of empathy (a fourth house matter) or reason (a seventh house function). The first house is a beginning, the early childhood of personal experience, yet is primary in importance, for what is formed here at the innermost personal level is in time expressed in the outermost sense (ideally, at the tenth house). Any traumas experienced in the early part of the life through the first or fourth houses can adversely affect the individual's broader relatedness later in life (seventh and tenth houses). Conversely, the same is true for early joys and positive assertions of self.

Second House

The borderline between the first house and the second house is defined by whatever things close at hand that a person naturally adheres to, especially those things which determine his ability to gather essential materials and tools. In those things and values to which he attaches himself without suggestion or interference from others the individual will find the most constancy. The second house also shows one's earning capacity, what he can transfer into other forms of wealth as needed. Because they form an integral part of his personality, the things of the second house are often called "movable resources." Wherever he goes in life he should be able to take along his most personal possessions. This is the second house of the first quadrant. The second house of the following quadrant, the fifth house, also has to do with resources, but here it is the wealth of the mother, family, clan, or heritage, and in a sense, the wealth and contentment each person finds in his children and creations. The fifth house relates to the seeds of the individual's creative and procreative ability. Its wealth is usually more pleasurable and less essential to the immediate survival of the individual than are those things associated with the second house.

The second house of the third quadrant is the eighth house, which has to do with the resources, possessions, and practical abilities of one's partner, mate, competitor, or whatever person with whom one is on a face-to-face basis. The eighth house can also be a source of additional income, materials, or resources useful to the individual as he seeks broader horizons; it has to do with such matters as wills, legacies, treasures, and taxes. The things which complement the wealth and materials of the individual himself are found in the eighth house, and ideally these are found in the opposite sex, specifically in one's spouse or mate.

The second house in the fourth quadrant is the eleventh, which represents the resources of friends, colleagues, and professional associates. In a more spiritual sense, the eleventh house is the collective wealth of a brotherhood, the wisdom, talent, abilities, and products of their intelligence and creativity. Only the second house of the first quadrant applies strictly to the individual himself. At each stage of development he adds new wealth or resources. Life is always a reinforcing of one's own possessions and talents with those of others: family, mate, and friends. Any planets in Taurus will reveal additional insights into this section of the chart, since that sign corresponds in nature to the second house. The same is true to some extent for Leo, Scorpio, and Aquarius; and the fifth, eighth, and eleventh houses, respectively. When a person has grasped the right things and values denoted by these succedent houses, and knows what is expected of him (the angular houses) he is ready to pass through the cadent phase of experience described by the third, sixth, ninth, and twelfth houses.

Third House

The third house of the first quadrant signifies the basic opportunities the individual has in which to learn the essentials of communication and exchange with others. This educational house is also related to brothers and sisters, childhood pals, playmates, acquaintances, neighbors, and other seemingly "accidental" or "side-by-side" relationships of an informal nature. Having established his identity at the first house level and determined his basic tools and resources at the second house, the individual is ready for new information and those experiences in communication with which to test and develop his native intellect and perceptive faculties. Every chance encounter will give him a new mental building block, a bit of knowledge that will prove useful at some later point, perhaps when he has to make important choices, such as in voting, instructing others, or guiding his own children toward the best educational environment. The more adaptable he is with people he meets early in life, the greater his role as an active citizen later on will be. The third house is where we first try out our tools and materials.

The third house of the second quadrant, the sixth house, is a further extension of this idea; here we combine the materials and tools acquired early in life (our own innate talents) with those of our family and our co-workers, testing them further in a routine practical setting. This produces the idea of craftsmanship and skill. In the encounters of childhood, in our play and natural curiosity, and with our peers, we learn what will work for us and what will not. If all goes well we are able to combine these ideas with the more pragmatic and essential needs denoted by the sixth house.

The third house in the third quadrant is the ninth, which has to do with the ideas of others, it being a complement to the individual's own third house. At this point, the abstract and innately individual perceptions and ideas of the third house and the acquired practical skills and concepts of the sixth house are combined with a more expansive intellect. New ideas are assimilated from those outside of our family, especially those of our mate or the opposite sex. A foreign language can be learned, a college degree obtained, or the individual may wish to travel afar with his suitcase as his textbook.

The third house of the last quadrant is the twelfth house. In this sector of the wheel the abstract intelligence or logic of the third house, the practical empirical intelligence of the sixth house, and the speculative idealism of the ninth house are made to join the more poetic and unifying emotional aspects of human thought. If, by this time, the person has acknowledged the need for objective data, practical facts, and inspiring ideals, he will be able to find peace of mind and a breadth of understanding that identify him as a true person of knowledge: *Homo sapiens.* Any failure to synthesize these different yet complementary forms of perception will result in the woes and doubts so readily identified with the twelfth house. The ideas of one's family (sixth house), one's partner or mate (ninth house), and one's own ideas and mental makeup—all of this must be clearly differentiated and at the same time unified before one can experience the universal intelligence and spiritual unity promised by the twelfth house.

Any planets in Gemini, plus the position of Mercury, will add insights into the third house. Any planets within that house, as well as the ruler of the sign appearing on its cusp, will also help to determine the nature of the native mentality and the primary experiences of communication, information, and learning. In effect, the third house (and Gemini and Mercury) represents the hands; it shows where one will achieve the greatest degree of dexterity and adaptability. The other cadent houses refine what is indicated in the third house.

Fourth House

The second quadrant begins with the fourth house. The closer a person is to his family, shelter, source of nourishment (mother), traditions of his clan, national sentiments, or his private workshop, the more he will be under the influence of those things denoted by the fourth house. This house contains the currents of the personal unconscious, deeper sentiments, and those emotional attachments which form part of the roots of our security. These ties are essentially hereditary and all-pervasive. Even when a person has left the protective fold of the family or mother to make his own way in life there is a deep connection to the past and to the surroundings of early childhood. Not to know one's roots or to have experienced a difficult childhood is to have emotional problems that require adjustment later on as one begins his own family.

Some people must relate more to the nuclear family or clan ways for survival and meaning rather than relying solely on their own initiative (first quadrant orientation) to procure the necessities of life. In many warmer latitudes near the equator the urgency for clan cooperation in obtaining food and shelter is of noticeably less importance than it would be in polar regions. Personality (first house) is less important to an Eskimo hunter or his wife than are those basic things that are acquired from the family's experience (fourth house). The Eskimo's major personal aim is nourishment and shelter, things which are denoted by the fourth house rather than the first house. When an Eskimo takes a mate he or she brings not so much his own unique resources to the eighth house (partnership assets) as those things—tools, methods, customs, and materials—handed down to him by the parents. These are all things represented by the second quadrant of houses, the fourth, fifth, and sixth. What is really his own—in the first quadrant sense—is how well he handles these very standardized items of survival. Of course, this is stretching the point a bit; a person born in the more benign latitudes of the globe also inherits customs and tools from his ancestors, but he probably will not starve if he loses them.

The Moon is a great modifier of the fourth house, as are any planets that happen to be in Cancer in a particular chart. The ruler of the sign appearing on the fourth house cusp is also a significator of the affairs of that house, but it is less important than the Moon's position or any planets which may happen to be in the fourth house. Shelter and nourishment are the main factors in self-protection. The needs of the fourth house are essential to all men. Some may feast in mansions while others cook meager meals in hovels. The reason for this apparent inequity is not clear, but those who believe in karma and reincarnation say that the roots of one's present environment lie in one's past deeds.

The fourth house tells much about where and how a person lives. It also indicates how he is affected by his immediate surroundings, how his feelings and moods affect his home setting, and to what extent he is attached to his tribe or nation. The fourth house contains the things necessary for survival. Even after one has married (seventh house) or reached some degree of recognition (tenth house) he will find that he is still affected by the natural attachments denoted by the fourth house. To be rich in ability, resources, and adaptability (first quadrant of houses) and to be at the same time careful in their collection, storage, and use (fourth house) is most important. The fourth house provides a key to the common sense management of the individual's personal affairs. To collect unnecessary items is folly, and so is the hoarding of personal resources for strictly selfish ends, although some things must be put away for later use which cannot presently be shared with others. Too much first house vitality can be wasted on maintaining fourth house trivialities, even exposing the individual to enmity rather than helping him to form broader associations where everyday resources can be shared or utilized for greater advantage. The fourth house is no less important than the first angular house, even though its effects may seem less apparent: a tree's roots are not easy to perceive, yet they are essential for the tree's survival.

Fifth House

When definite needs and limits for survival have been established and satisfied through the fourth house, one can relax and enjoy the pleasures associated with the fifth house of the horoscopic wheel. Good examples set by parents in one's own childhood help toward creating healthy attitudes toward one's own children. In the fifth house the heart expresses itself through love or through some creative means. Here is the child in all of us which invites us to play and find joy, to find release from the toils of life. Early in life we learn to portray our desires and feelings in some dramatic way. This self-assertion can take the form of play, good humor, and consideration for others, but it can also be distorted, so that later in life one continues to be a little bully, tyrant, or egotist who wants everyone else to play according to his rules and needs. But joy that is based on such purely selfish desires does not last long.

The fifth house is also the house of courtship and romance. Attitudes formed early in life have much to do with individual self-expression and procreation. No real love comes from a heart which is egotistically centered upon itself. In courtship there has to be some degree of deference paid to the other party. In the fifth house there is no true union of the sexes (this takes place in the seventh and eighth houses). In courtship one discovers what one wants to conceive in love, this most often being an ideal image of one's children-to-be.

Another thing associated with the fifth house is private enterprise, that is, some endeavor where there is gain through the individual's own initiative, creativity, and sense of speculation. Any such concern would be influenced by the fourth house, particularly by the resources, values, and attitudes of one's own family and childhood environment. The highest expression of the fifth house, as one of the four succedent houses related to wealth, would be to release joy and creativity in some inspiring manner. As the house of ethics and character, the fifth house would also tell something about the development of a person's moral worth and sense of integrity. Avocation is followed by vocation. Work follows play, as can be seen in the sequence of the fifth and sixth houses. Every festival has to consider the harvest which made it possible. The boy on the circus merry-go-round may be an apprentice in the workshop where the animals for the carrousel are carved tomorrow. Any planets in Leo will strongly influence this part of the chart.

Sixth House

The limits and concerns of practical intelligence as it is exercised for personal advantage are defined by the sixth house. The individual can adapt himself to the ideas of his family, clan, and co-workers to the extent that it proves to be fruitful. The swift personal activities of the logical native intelligence described by the third house are given additional form and meaning in a more concrete sense in the sixth house. A person is employed, works hard at his craft, learns to be efficient, acquires new skills, observes the effect of his ideas and work on others, analyzes things, and otherwise learns to be thorough and discriminating at the sixth house level.

Health and hygiene are associated with the sixth house. Where the individual is able to integrate himself with his immediate physical environment and the daily tasks which he must perform he increases his chances for enjoying better health. Where there is order he can refine his nature, distributing and utilizing the necessities of life effectively. In becoming more proficient, he may have to be subordinate to others for a time. He digests what is most essential, avoiding the superfluous, for at this point there is an awareness of bigger things ahead. One may be an apprentice, assistant, or servant today in order to be a leader or master tomorrow.

The sixth house teaches the lessons of humility. There is purification in the sense that the individual's tools, materials, and capacities, as denoted by the five earlier houses, are regimented along the most practical lines. Realistic attention to detail now means security in the wider experiences to follow: marriage, career, and social associations. Here any undue subjectivity and unnecessary attachment to one's roots or family comes to an end, and the way is paved for the more objective experiences and relationships symbolized by the six remaining houses. In essence, one has passed through spring and summer, and autumn is on the threshold. Whether or not the final harvest will be good depends upon how well one has tended the crop. The storms of childhood may have proven to be too difficult for some, but for others these hardships only strengthen character and make a person a better opponent of fate. Any planets in Virgo will influence the sixth house. Wherever these may appear in the chart one must be thorough, realistic, hardworking, serving but not servile, analytical, and clean in every respect. The sixth house is also the house of betrothal: the fifth house relates to courtship and the seventh to marriage. What one brings to any partnership or comradeship and the essence of his resources at the time of union is determined largely by the sixth house.

Seventh House

If the sixth house is the final stage in putting together resources and skills at the personal-familial level, the seventh house represents the beginning of the more objective social-universal phases of experience. A mate is taken and formal arrangements or contracts are made. The ideas and things of the individual have to be carefully weighed against the ideas and possessions of others. Sometimes there can be an opponent or a competitor of some kind, a person whose own aims, desires, and impulses are opposed to one's own. The seventh house also reveals something about how one reacts to his or her opposite sex. Two magnets are thrust together: now they attract each other, now they repel as their poles are reversed. Back and forth the individual goes, trying to determine which course of action or which ideas will work best. The scales can be tipped two ways: will it be companion or opponent, open enemy or partner, love or hate, peace or war? The seventh house is like one end of a seesaw. The fulcrum of this teeter-totter, or lever, lies in the fourth house; that is, it is found in personal feelings, attachments, instincts, and the personal unconscious. At the other end of the seesaw, opposite the seventh house, is the first house, denoting individual self-interest, desires, and aims. The pressure of the first house is all that the individual must confront in order to find harmony and balance. The outcome of this active balancing can be seen in the tenth house which is directly opposite the fourth house.

Any planets in Libra, and the position of Venus, will provide important clues about this process of synthesis, objectification, and development of social skills. The mate *is* Venus, regardless of whether or not the partner is male or female. One's own conscious sexual drives are denoted more by Mars in the horoscope than they are by Venus. The seventh house cusp, the descendant, is the contra-sexual counterpart to the ascendant, or first house cusp. Here, in zodiacal terms, one can catch a glimpse of what Jung termed the *animus/anima:* this might loosely be called an ideal mirror image we hold of the opposite sex, and to which we are unconsciously or naturally attracted. The things of the descendant attract us because they seem well formed, interesting, beautiful, compelling, or are in some other way appealing. There is a longing for wholeness through union with one's opposite; yet the conditions of time suggest that it is a rare instance when someone really obtains all that he or she desires in a mate. The position of Venus is usually a better indicator of one's partner than the seventh house cusp, unless there happen to also be planets contained within that house.

The lessons of communication and relatedness which are learned or expressed through the third house are now put to the test in the comradeships formed at the seventh house level. Can we learn to cooperate, yield, share, exchange, complement, even compete, if necessary, without loss of individuality or decorum? Can we at this point give ourself to new causes and relationships without alienating our family, tribe, or earlier companions? What will it be: mutuality or contest? Is one's comrade actually one's competitor or open enemy? The scales have to be balanced in the seventh house before further growth and commitment are possible. We may desire close union with friends, communion with our gods, or we may wish to obtain influence on a wide scale, but none of these hopes will have any substance if we cannot objectively and intelligently manage well enough in face-to-face relationships in the seventh house. There seems to be no end to the questions which can arise regarding the forming of partnerships. Have we chosen the right partner for the right aims or purpose? To what extent can we compromise our personal and familial ties and instincts in order to acquire a mate whose background is apt to be quite different from our own? Finding harmony means that one has to see as much beauty and meaning in dusk and autumn (seventh house) as in dawn and spring (first house).

The weights and measures of justice in human relationships are endless in their number and variety. Each person has a different set of circumstances and relationships with which he has to learn to harmonize. Without this harmony life is merely a dull and frustrating routine with only momentary flashes of joy or mutual recognition. Harmony can best be arrived at through a kind of reason which, although maintaining its own sense of independence, defers to others. A deeper intuition knows when one has to yield in order to avoid conflict that can harm important goals, especially goals which may be of importance to both parties. The seventh house requires conduct that makes life an art. For those who must cooperate with others, the learning of this art—tactfulness—may be more important than the pursuit of strictly personal ends, especially those symbolized by the first house and by Mars.

In most every horoscope one or two of the four angular houses will dominate or lead the individual through the experiences most suitable for him, whether or not they are painful or rewarding. The seventh house is the experience of finding the appropriate complements, the task of becoming an objective person of the world. The fourth house person is oriented more to the roots of his being, and this can include his family, particularly the mother and the home setting. Those things related to security and to the home are important in the fourth house. The first house denotes a more independent kind of self-expression, often describing the pioneer type who leaves his mark through conquering various obstacles. The ambitions of the tenth house, the last of the angular houses, are directed to the world as a whole. Any prominence sought in this angular house should ideally transcend any purely personal motives for gain or influence.

Eighth House

The eighth house of the horoscope is one of the most difficult to understand. It is associated with such diverse matters as sexuality, death, partnership assets, extrasensory perception, and taxes, among other things. Occult tradition calls it the vessel of spiritual (or psychological) transformation. The most obvious thing about this part of the horoscopic wheel is its capacity to transform, reform, or regenerate (and demolish) values and things of the individual just at that point when he forms a close union with another person. As the second house from the seventh it represents the abilities and resources of the partner; and, ideally, it symbolizes everything the person needs to complement his own natural materials and tools (denoted by the second house). The death which is symbolized by the eighth house can be the death of selfishness. If, in the seventh house, the individual has not learned to give and take to the right degree, coming to a suitable agreement with his comrade or partner, the eighth house may indicate a serious catharsis, or even a violent purging, of the egotistical qualities and attachments that have caused him to contribute to the failure of a good union. If, on the other hand, he has cooperated toward building a suitable union or partnership, the treasures and rewards of his partner in essence become his own, and vice versa. He inherits things of inestimable value. In a successful marriage (seventh house) union finds its deepest expression through the release of the eighth house. Specifically, this applies to sex, where sperm and ovum unite, forming a fetus. Nine months later, in the last part of the fourth house (womb, mother, fecundity) the child of marriage is born into the fifth house.

As the house of wills and legacies, the eighth house is the fifth house from the fourth house of the individual's family (not the family he himself creates, but the one into which he is born); what is shown in the eighth house is the connection between blood relationships and wealth of an ancestral kind. As the third house from the sixth house, the eighth house describes the power of investigation, analysis, and realistic views in penetrating and overcoming personal problems. The general medical practitioner becomes a surgical specialist. He must go deeper to purge the body of its afflictions, and in doing so he must use unusual techniques such as X-ray and acupuncture. The bad part (the psychological problem, if one is viewing this psychologically) has to be treated by some unique method. The treatment can be, and usually is, a painful process; perhaps it may even be dangerous, because in dealing with deep personal problems one has to walk the very limits of human knowledge. This can be in the unconscious or the very part of reality from which the seeds of life arise from the depths of sexuality. Self-destruction can occur here, or a person can become obsessed with some part of the web and forget the spider who always lurks there in complete indifference: death seems quite impersonal.

If the individual, with well-chosen partners and comrades, can pass through this purgatory of selfhood—if, for example, the user of psychedelic drugs can escape (understand) his own hallucinations and the terror of having his ego transformed, he will come out on the other side truly baptized, cleansed, and ready for a new view on life (denoted by the ninth house of self-understanding). Psychologically, he will now be ready for an introduction into the more universal, spiritual aspects of human experience, especially those shared with others. The person who passes through this phase of experience is in a position to better understand the ideas of his comrades and mate, as well as those beliefs which are associated with the ninth house. At the tenth house cusp he meets his personal God and highest aspirations. Any planets in Scorpio, as well as the position of Pluto, will modify the eighth house influence. In this sector of the horoscope one can experience both great terror

and sublime joy. The rattlesnake strikes out just as the eagle lifts its
wings.

Ninth House

The ninth house relates to orthodox or formal religion and philosophy, higher education, idealism, speculative thought along intuitive
lines, sports in general, travel, foreign countries, law (judgment), international matters, and the natural impulse to teach others. Arriving
here, the individual needs a suitable vehicle to go any further. This
can be some form of education, a philosophy of life, or a credo. He
borrows some of the concepts of his close comrades or partner to
strengthen his own views and means of communication. Knowledge is
no longer personal at this juncture; it is something which is shared
and which can stimulate the minds of others. A ninth house person
learns and then teaches others, learning all the more, but he must
avoid becoming an evangelist, zealot, or fanatic. Religion can inspire
people to high deeds and ideals, but there is still a higher level to be
reached than that indicated by the ninth house, which is only the
beginning (fire mode) of this higher level of intelligence. Universal love,
spiritual brotherhood, and self-abnegation are still to be encountered
after one has traveled down the road of self-understanding to find his
God or highest principle (tenth house). A college degree may show that
one has applied himself to learn some important higher skill or body
of knowledge, but it is not in itself the experience of a career which
must follow any such fine learning.

The ninth house reflects the vitality of the adolescent in each person.
It is the youth learning sportsmanship through contests; this sportsmanship is later translated into the ability to be adept in meeting
others with views and customs unlike one's own, this often being people
from other lands with whom something must be shared in common.
Every true explorer is a ninth house type: somewhere in his chart
Jupiter or planets in Sagittarius are helping to organize expeditions,
whether geographical or intellectual in nature. The creative experiences
and impulses of the first and fifth houses are guided to broader expressions in the ninth house. Intuitive insight and personal energy are
combined with the ideas of others in order to imbue one's own ideas
with added depth or breadth. One is still, as always, an individual, but
now his orientation should be more worldly than personal. The flag
of his homeland is not the only flag he sees. The international view of
the ninth house recognizes genuine differences between people, and

from this comes the more universal or cosmopolitan viewpoint symbolized by the tenth, eleventh, and twelfth houses. The beginning of this universality actually lies in the ninth house, just as the first and fifth houses mark vigorous points of concern in earlier phases of experience. The fifth house, for instance, ties a person to his mate through children; or, looking at it in another way, the fifth house shows how the creative impulses of an individual are brought to bear on the social realm (denoted here by the sixth, seventh, and eighth houses). The first house through the fourth house is the area where he establishes connections between his own sense of self and the deeper subconscious roots of experience, especially those symbolized by the mother and the shelter of early childhood.

In the ninth house we can expect to have our ideas judged fairly by others. The keywords are truth and expansion. Without truth and genuineness, without honesty and courage, one can not expect to get past the imposing cusp of the tenth house: Jehovah and the other religio-mythical figures whom one supposedly must regard as High Authority are waiting there. Many of these old (and new) gods are barriers which can be a threat to the individual who wants to grow spiritually and intellectually: in order to reach the eleventh house one has to climb the summit symbolized by the tenth house, and this can be most dangerous when one is not prepared for such an undertaking. Wherever he becomes attached to dogma, the searcher stops. He says that there is only one vehicle appropriate for his journey: one truth, God, religion, way, means of meditation, or trail up the mountain, even though he may not have considered all possibilities. Those who mechanically go to church or evangelize a doctrine are apt to stay in the ninth house. However, it is necessary that the universally oriented person seek out something higher than dogma and worn-out rituals. He must be forward-looking, for at the ninth house level he has to transcend or cast away every narrow affiliation with the past, every false enthusiasm, every crooked arrow, if he is to go forward in understanding.

Tenth House

The cusp of the tenth house, the midheaven, can be the zenith for an individual, both materially and spiritually, but only if he arrives at that point himself. What Moses should have said—and perhaps he did— is that every person has to climb the mountain of responsibility himself in order to make a covenant with life. Once one arrives he should find that the same laws that governed Moses, Buddha, and other sages of the past apply to himself as well. This should be so because the tenth house is the very pinnacle of the universal phase of experience. The important thing is that we arrive there by our own power, even though we may have been guided toward our goals by some wise person symbolized by the ninth house. Our teacher or guru bids us farewell as we enter the tenth phase of experience. To get there we have to project our aims clearly and with great perseverance (first house), lay appropriate foundations (fourth house), and find the necessary reinforcements and recommendations (seventh house) for the ascent. In the tenth house we become fully responsible for our deeds, words, and goals. If we are wise we soon find others to whom, in mutual trust, we can attach ourselves, since the heights can be perilous and lonely. With friends (eleventh house) we make a lifeline as we reach the upper slopes. If a person is not inclined to climb he is apt to be more influenced by one of the first two angular houses, the first and fourth. Not everyone is meant to climb perilous peaks at a particular time.

Also associated with the tenth house are such things as government, management, authority, elders (the father), superiors, self-esteem, and honors. Fulfilled here are those essential conscious aims which begin at the ascendant or first house, which are modified (or repressed) at the nadir, or fourth house cusp, and which are appraised, reinforced, and promoted (or vanquished) at the descendant, or seventh house level. After a person has reached the peak symbolized by the tenth house he has to descend—this is a law of life. Greatness is both preceded by and followed by humility. Again, one has to pick the right time, route, and company for the descent. He still stands on his heritage, family roots, co-workers and assistants, as well as his close comrades, business partner, and mate. As he comes down, carrying his honors, he needs to know which route to take or he may be caught in inclement weather (karma). Even the agile mountain goat can slip and fall. When a great person does fall he is sometimes made a martyr by the masses, but serious and reflective people will wonder if he could not have done better in order to avoid a tragic or bitter end.

The eleventh and twelfth houses have to do with this descent. The best and only reasonable path to take at this point is the one blazed by friends and helpful colleagues, the one which leads to a peaceful retirement (twelfth house) in which one's actions can be studied in retrospect. Such a person follows the way of the ancient hero or sage. From life to life he sets a positive example. His superior is always the drive for excellence in his own heart and actions. He is foursquare and ever aware that he is still becoming and will always be becoming a person of knowledge (eleventh house). His authority and influence last beyond his own time because they rise not from personal motives alone, but also from the natural capacity to help others. The tenth house person, the public person, has to be the very epitome of intelligence and receptivity in order to gain this power. Nature will not sing along with the aggressive, self-seeking person as readily as it will with the person of good faith who follows its will. Any planets in the tenth house are apt to have a great deal to say about these higher responsibilities. One should also study carefully the position of Saturn and any planets that may happen to be in Capricorn.

Here, at the zenith of individuality, the boundaries of responsibility are extended, and they cannot be ignored without dire consequences. Saturn, the natural ruler of the tenth house, is not malefic by nature; it is simply time reminding the individual to stay on the correct path as he proceeds. For each person there is a special path, one that others may traverse or use for awhile, but which is largely his own. If the tenth house is not active, that is, if it contains no planets; and if Saturn is not prominent and there are no planets in Capricorn; then the metaphor of the mountain will not be so important for an individual. Such a person usually is better off not making the climb and should remain in a less ambitious, conspicuous, or dangerous position. There is always a need for other functions on an expedition or project. Only a handful will be able to reach the top of the mountain, the depths of the forest, or the bottom of a sea, yet tenth house success can be shared. The achievement is typically centered on one person, but it is also very often, if not usually, the accumulation of the talents, resources, and efforts of others as well. A good leader or manager of an enterprise finds good helpers who share a common aim. A president (a nation's manager) is only as effective as the quality of his agents and advisors (seventh house) and his relationship with the people of the land (fourth house). There is no true fame that belongs solely to an individual. The tenth house is the beginning of the universal phase of experience as it becomes manifest; but of course their spirit is ignited in the ninth house. In the tenth house the individual is promoted as a public focal point even though this recognition may be in complete harmony with the personal aims symbolized by the first house. However, fame is not often well understood by those whom it visits.

Eleventh House

Having reached the zenith the individual is in a powerful position to align himself with friends who can further his conscious goals, spread his ideas or goods, or increase his efforts in some manner. Informal yet well defined alliances are made. Any such friendships are made for higher purposes rather than simply for gaining some personal advantage. Humanitarian causes are able to utilize the best of that which each one has worked so hard to achieve. In turn, each individual is able to experience the joys (and sorrows) of a broader relatedness; ideally, this is expressed through universal love and communication. The intellect, rather than the emotions, legislates the actions which will be taken here. The future is what counts most. The community is more important than the family per se; but the family is not forgotten as being an important basic factor in individual development. Nor should we ignore our old comrades, partners, or mate (seventh house relationships) who have helped us arrive at a better place in life.

Open relationships are favored, particularly those where there are objective, socially significant aims. Each individual does what he is best suited for. To secure this freedom and love, he must be able to impose voluntary limitations on himself. Giving at this level becomes a rich experience. Any planets in Aquarius or an emphasis of the position of Uranus in the chart increases the power of the eleventh house. This sector of the horoscope represents our highest hopes and wishes as they might be affected by others.

Twelfth House

The twelfth house is the "final" house of the horoscopic wheel. It shows how the person of great deeds (tenth house) and altruistic concern (eleventh house) can be imbued with a broad, penetrating, and compassionate intelligence. Piety, a poetic sense of the unity of life, contemplative solitude, intuitive feeling, and a sense of self-sacrifice arise from the twelfth house. As a house corresponding to a water sign, Pisces, the twelfth house is thought to hold the seeds of the next incarnation as symbolized by the first house. At this point the whole is somewhat more important than any of its constituent parts, and it is cared for tenderly: the old woman adds a hem of fine lace to the already carefully sewn garment; the spirit of the concert hall is perceived as being both the orchestra and the audience, and something, in addition, which is less tangible but truly pervasive. A person can have reached the zenith, acquired friends, and done much to prove himself worthy of emulation, but somewhere in his psyche there is a single doubt, a haunting mystery, the vestige of some unresolved karmic experience. Buddha drops out of public life to meditate on the meaning of life, only to be pulled back inexorably by the sighs of the world. Here, in the twelfth house, are the secrets the individual has never mentioned to anyone, the small (or large) things that both tantalize him and make him feel guilty. Who could understand such a thing? he might ask, for such things are rarely spoken of. Perhaps he has given his heart to others (eleventh house), but has he left enough for himself with which to begin a new phase of experience, a fresh expression of individuality (first house)?

The twelfth house is very difficult to understand. It represents both hidden support and self-undoing. Self-judgment also takes place here. Success or failure at the earlier stages of life, in previous lives perhaps, add up to the twelfth house. As the old octopus quietly sits at the bottom of the sea it pulls its arms in one by one: to each is attached something which will give him a sense of satisfaction or quiet release; or there might be some kind of danger or impediment to which he fatefully clings. If a ghost from the past could haunt us it would be at this point. All things which are considered evil and subversive to life are associated with the twelfth house. It can be the chamber of horrors, psychosis, imprisonment, deformity, sorrow, destitution, bondage, loneliness, or any of a great number of things of earthly existence to which one can be unhappily fettered. The twelfth house may also be the place where a person of good will and charity helps those unfortunates who cannot help themselves for some reason or another. He may still be in the chamber of horrors, a therapist in the asylum, a guardian in prison, or a welfare worker, but he is there more by choice than by fate. The ascetic, nun, welfare worker, and hermit alike are ruled by the influence of the twelfth house, by Neptune, and by any planets in Pisces. The criminal, liar, spy, talebearer, cheat, narcotics addict, alcoholic, wastrel, and the deviantly submissive are all caught up in the net of Neptune. Great joy and great sorrow can be found at the twelfth house level, from chart to chart, and from life to life.

Some degree of self-abnegation is often required of the individual at this point. Only through self-contemplation in solitude can a person reach a total awareness of the unity of life. As long as he is striving, competing, worrying, and otherwise devoting his energies to strictly worldly things and achievements, no matter how noble they may be, he will not have quite reached the depths of universal understanding. How long he should be in seclusion and how this should be done varies according to each chart. A lack of planets in the twelfth house or in Pisces, might be an indication that in the present life solitary contemplation is less important than direct action and participation at some other level of experience. Solitude is not necessary at the level of the first quadrant of houses, and at the second quadrant it is not likely to be conducive to the learning of new practical skills from one's relatives and co-workers. Even at the third quadrant phase solitude could work against the stability of a partnership or marriage where active cooperation and participation are required.

Solitude becomes really important in the last quadrant of houses. The great responsibilities and pressures of the tenth house require rest and relaxation more than ever. Involvement with friends, associations, and special interest groups can also cause one to lose his individuality within those groups, and this is unfortunate, even dangerous, because an effective group must first of all be made up of strong individuals. The individuality described by the first quadrant, nourished by the second quadrant, and furthered by the third quadrant must not be smothered at any point along the way of its development, because from it, from all that it accrues, comes the seed (good or bad karma) for growth in future times or levels.

The best way to get to one's heaven, nirvana, or next life—whatever one's concept of the future may be—is to be true to oneself at every moment in the present. Suffering can result at the twelfth house, for it is despair, rather than bliss, that awaits the person who willfully avoids the wise dictates of his own inner self and conscience. This has nothing specifically to do with good or evil; what matters in every case is a person's motive or reason for his actions, as well as an awareness of their immediate effects. In the final analysis (which is what the twelfth house means) he judges himself on the basis of how well he has passed through the seasons of human experience. The more fully conscious person decides for himself the path his feet will travel. The individual who lacks this kind of willpower is always in doubt as to whether or not he is on the correct path; he does not realize that he forges the trail himself.

Chapter V

The Sun, Moon, and Planets

 Man belongs to one species of a particular life form on a small planet that orbits around one star out of an infinite number of stars. A biopsychic organism with specific needs, characteristics, and activities similar to other animals, he nonetheless regards himself as the intellectually and morally superior life form on this planet because he is capable of modifying the geography, climate, and evolution of life on Earth. Having the greatest degree of mobility and freedom of any species of animal, a human being is able to control natural terrestrial conditions to a large degree. However, this ability does not include control over extraterrestrial forces.

The planets in the solar system modify the actions of man by acting as "force fields" or reflective agencies of various types according to their geometric relationships with each other at any given moment of Earth time. The recent discovery of Uranus, Neptune, and Pluto suggests many new variations in the development of the collective psyche of man, as well as in his collective karma and biocultural evolution. In the course of time he has come to "know" (through his own devices) about the presence of other bodies in the solar system. Through the telescope, microscope, and other tools, he has come to better understand his place in the scheme of things. At least specific individuals have perceived these truths, even if most have not.

As man evolves he continues to learn about his role in Nature. He moves away from instinctual modes of behavior toward the technological, but he does not yet seem to realize that he has incurred a responsibility as overseer of the world. Not yet a wise custodian who furthers other creatures as well as himself, man is presently a derelict spoiler of the environment. If he does not realize his duty as steward of the Earth, modern man may, by his own design, go the way of Tyrannosaurus Rex. If, like the Amerindians and others of the past, he can learn to treat other creatures ecologically as his "little brothers," he may survive for some time to come. Man will also have to control his unusual inclination to murder himself in war. Such willful cruelty and indifference must somehow be curbed. I am not moralizing here; I simply want to briefly establish why I believe astrology is so valid as a tool to help in understanding human differences which, poorly communicated, create the hate, fear, and greed that make the future look less hopeful than it might otherwise. Mankind is an evolving wholeness in itself. Self-understanding means integration at all levels of experience, and the study of astrology, particularly of the planets, contributes very greatly to this understanding. As our culture becomes more complex it is of the greatest importance that we make peace with ourselves and learn to use natural resources wisely.

Other unique life forms or forces could possibly be at play on the other planets of this solar system. There might, for instance, be forms of life or manifestations of consciousness on Venus or Mercury that are more (or less) advanced than human beings. It would certainly be typical of our biopsychic conceit not to admit that such a possibility could exist. The fact that Uranus encircles the Sun lying on its side might provide a necessary condition for consciousness or life quite different from our own, some phenomenon associated specifically with that planet. Does every intelligent force or being need to respire oxygen, feed at a mother's breast, or have the ability to perceive visible light? Saturn's rings are not there simply for our enjoyment through telescopes. To every body in the solar system there is a purpose and a unique place in the dimensions of time.

Many centuries ago, the sages of China were intuitively aware of the importance of the planets in influencing life on Earth. They too, were careful scientists, noting the solar seasons and the phases of the Moon as well as other changes in nature. From their observations came the commentaries in the *I Ching*, which I have already mentioned. We can make the shift from the wisdom of King Wen and Confucius to modern astrology without any great break in the inherent meaning of their knowledge. Scientific knowledge of the laws governing the solar system will not dramatically change the insights they obtained intuitively. What *is* different at any time is the prevailing world view or spirit. The precession of the equinoxes has brought a new age with new demands and ways of solving basic human needs. The *I Ching* is a product of the age of Aries; its use, along with other ancient bodies of knowledge, has to be adapted to the coming time, the age of Aquarius. The planetary bodies, the wanderers of the sky, have to be discussed in terms appropriate for the time, and this includes the practice of borrowing terms and concepts from psychology and other social sciences. Evil is now called "unconsciousness," and the solar God is equated with the deeper sense of individuality and "freedom" for which modern man strives.

In the Aquarian age, the planets and their aspects are especially significant in pointing out how well each person associates with others. There are many people in the world now and many new adjustments to be made. Singular actions (Aries) may still be admired to a point, but group action and communication are what the Sun dictates as most beneficial for the kingdom of man at this time. The old individual heroes and sages of earlier ages may not be reborn, at least in their previous roles, for many ages to come. Little in this new age is hidden, and all men and women can drink from the same cup if they are careful. The waters of Aquarius are not its own waters, but the spirit of equality and love born (but not realized) in the previous age of Pisces. In Aquarius, individuality is realized within diversity. The cup belongs to no one in particular; the television has many channels from which to choose; the airplane can reach any land, and it can bring both the missiles of destruction and the offering of peace and cooperation. What good does it do to study astrology, in this case the planets, unless one can put oneself in the right place in time?

For instance, one can see where Uranus is located in a chart. That planet is an important key to understanding friendships and contributions in this life to the things of the future, especially those of the age of Aquarius. In another position in the horoscope one will find Saturn: that is where the individual has to be dutiful and patient with tradition; and there is Neptune, quietly giving its warning to avoid self-deception while at the same time it requires some degree of self-abnegation before it will reveal its secrets. Pluto's position in a horoscope suggests an area of essentially unconscious regeneration or transformation, an area where the individual is linked (like it or not) to the rest of humanity. Venus is not far away from Mercury: cooperation and love are not far away from communication and objective intelligence. Neither of these two planets is ever very far away from the Sun, which is the symbol of the most essential and heartfelt things with which the individual constantly identifies. In another sign and house, Mars attempts to energetically assert some conscious desire or aim; Jupiter is in another position, or perhaps even in the same sign and house. This largest of planets is the principle of expansion and encouragement, an area where one should be able to take advantage of some opportunity. The Moon's position is extremely important because it shows how daily experiences affect individual moods and feelings. In some ways, the Moon is the most sensitive point in a horoscope.

After the position of each planet has been noted, by sign and house, one can study more about its basic meaning in terms of astrological analysis. One will then begin to see how to approach the chart. The wheel can be viewed as a personal mandala for meditation. For some, the horoscope may be a compelling web of karmic entanglements. The sign rising and the position of the body which rules that sign will provide additional clues about the nature and quality of one's life. Each planet and its geometric aspects point to an area of experience that must be satisfied along definite lines. No two charts will be the same, if an identical aspect occurs between planets. People have different karma (lessons to learn), so that even if they come close to having identical charts, as with twins, there will be subtle differences in what they experience. One of the great ideas of astrology is that of learning to recognize that each person needs a particular kind of freedom and environment in which he can best express himself and develop. No two people, however much alike, will obtain the same benefits from the same curriculum, menu, laws, values, sentiments, contract, religion, friends, program, itinerary, or plan.

Before studying the individual planets in more detail, it would be helpful to note that in no case does a pure manifestation of the qualities associated with each planet occur. At every moment of time each body is not only in a compelling position with respect to the Sun, but it forms aspects of varying strength and meaning (effect) with other members of the solar system. There is also the Moon to consider, since it acts as an intimate reflector for the energies denoted by the Sun and planets. Certain archetypal qualities are associated with each body, but these are constantly being modified by the positions of the others. The natal horoscope is to some extent like a photograph of the heavens at a specific point in time, but even after the first breath, for which the chart is set up, the planets continue to move, forming aspects as they transit around the natal positions. As these aspects are formed they trigger or synchronize with changes experienced by the individual. Looking up these transits in planetary tables called "ephemerides" is an important part of the astrologer's job.

The physical characteristics of the planets and the laws by which they are governed are not the main concern of this book. Any popular

Fig. 9. Symbols for the main planetary bodies.

almanac will provide such basic astronomical data. However, the time
is approaching when astrologers may begin to refine their science by
noting the various characteristics of the planets, their actual and relative distances from the Earth, and details about their mass, motion,
and other astronomically significant data.

The Luminaries: Sun and Moon

The Sun and Moon are of primary importance in astrological analysis. In any chart the Sun shows the deeper motivations and needs of
the individual. It represents the protagonist in the personal drama of
existence, the vital force that provides each individual with a feeling
of conscious purpose and self-expression. As such, the Sun denotes the
deeper character and convictions that affect his main experiences and
obligations. It is the heart of selfhood. In the course of a year the
Sun appears, from the geocentric view, to transit the twelve signs of
the Zodiac. The other luminary, the Moon, revolves around the Earth
in twenty-seven days, seven hours, forty-three minutes, and eleven and
one-half seconds, with a daily average motion of thirteen degrees and
twelve minutes of zodiacal longitude. Thus, it moves through the Zodiac
in slightly less than a month, while the Sun goes through one sign in
about a month's time. The Moon's rapid motion reflects the rapidly
changing or fluctuating moods and feelings one is subject to, those
emotional tides that come and go daily. Some astrologers see the Moon
as representing the weaker side of human nature because it is the
threshold of the subconscious, a place where one is especially vulnerable
to emotional whims. Others see in the Moon the feminine or yin principle: mother, nourishment, fecundation, shelter, security, and the family tradition. The Sun is then associated with the yang principle, the
father, consciousness, and radiance, but Saturn is also a complement
to the Moon through its association with the father and masculine goals.

The Moon reflects the solar energies more readily than do the other
bodies in a horoscope, particularly where it is in close aspect to the
Sun. Through the Moon, success and failure are felt in personal terms.
It also has to do with inherited traits, survival instincts, emotional attachments, sentiments, and the general sense of empathy a person has
with his environment. The Sun's position and aspects show how,
through the exercise of will, we seek to shape this environment; it is
the principle of active volition. The Moon is the receptive principle
which instinctively embraces that which is essential for survival. The
rhythm between the two "lights," that is, the signs and houses they

occupy in a chart, determines the main course of a life (of course, this is strongly modified by the rising sign and planetary aspects).

A poorly placed Moon can imply either a lack or an excess of receptivity, while an effective Sun position can indicate a dearth or excess of vital energy. The other planets give clues as to how this energy is broken down, distributed, utilized, or directed. A weak Moon might suggest repression of feeling; an overbearing Sun can burn the individual out in excessive or ill-timed displays of power or will. The Sun shows how we move out and forward in time and space, whereas the Moon pulls us back to our roots, downward to the past and the unconscious. It might be that the two forces are about equal in strength, astrologically speaking. After all, they are about the same size to the naked eye at various times and at different points on the celestial sphere. When evenly balanced, the solar and lunar forces imply a life of peace and well-being.

A general rule is that where a person is emotionally unstable, his horoscope will also reveal a weakly placed Moon. Where the person relates to his family realistically, provides good shelter for himself, and has some control over his emotions, he is apt to be using the lunar powers more effectively. We grow most familiar with those daily things symbolized by the position of the Moon in our birth chart. This is true even if our deeper aims, as symbolized by the Sun, are in contrast to this. The cord of the lunar womb is cut at birth, but the mother unconsciously continues to affect our habits, feelings, and sense of security until our dying breath. It is for our own protection that much of what we do is learned in early childhood and held in readiness at the level of the personal unconscious (memory). But it is also for this reason, owing to their tenacity, that these things are so difficult to modify in our personality. The more conscious an individual becomes of his purpose or place in life, as described by the Sun's position and aspects, the better his chance is for rising above the fetters of the emotional part of his nature. The apron strings of the unconscious *can* be cut, but the individual must be ready to apply free will if he is to survive. To be a free soul under these conditions is no easy task: all that one can do is to ride out the lunar tides; one cannot really control them.

In Buddhist and Hindu philosophy the conscious sense of purpose is called *dharma*, the law for living and developing one's own character through fulfilling the right duties. A person's entire horoscope is a key to understanding and defining these duties; however, it is the Sun that dictates the exact nature or the heart of this conscious and mature relatedness. The planets which form aspects to the Sun show exactly how this is carried out. Naturally, this refers mainly to a person who has

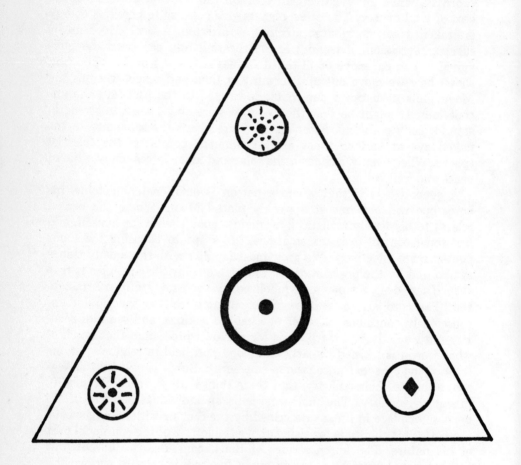

Fig. 10.   Solar symbols.

developed self-awareness to a degree where he can determine many of the conditions of his present, as well as future life. In the *I Ching*, he is called a "superior man." Astrology, as it is being discussed here, would have little meaning for someone who is not assiduously seeking the truth about his being. The solar individual is enlightened to the degree that he can utilize, direct, and project his energies and his will toward the lunar phases of experience; that is, his daily life. It is precisely there that life has the greatest meaning and value. The conscious person (solar self) is ever more receptive (lunar self) so that he can continue to learn the laws of life that make his survival easier while he develops himself spiritually. On the other hand, the egotistical or ignorant person is unwilling to accept those limitations of time which are marked off by the positions and movements of the luminaries and planetary bodies. In each horoscope it is the solar/lunar relationship which best illustrates what each person's limitations will be. It is in knowing these limitations that a true sense of freedom and success can be obtained.

Astrological tradition has it that the Sun rules Leo and the Moon rules Cancer, and the fifth and fourth houses, respectively. Therefore, in any chart planets in these signs and houses are apt to reveal additional insights about the solar/lunar relationship. Perhaps in time an intramercurial planet may be "discovered" and found to more closely correspond to the sign Leo than does the Sun, but until then it is necessary to make the traditional association. The Moon, however, does seem to find correspondence in Cancer. In a general sense, the Moon in a chart represents women, especially the mother, and to a lesser extent, the wife. The Sun signifies men, the father (along with Saturn), and the husband, in addition to one's children. The Sun is the most masculine (yang) force and the Moon the most feminine (yin) force. Keywords for the Sun are vital force, spirit, and will, all of these having to do with the processes of conscious self-expression and actualization. The supportive unconscious forces of the Moon relate more to soul, instincts, memory, and habits, all of those things which make survival possible. To distinguish between the effects of the two luminaries is one of the major steps in astrological analysis.

Many questions can be asked. How does the Moon reflect the energies denoted by the Sun's sign and house position? Which aspects from other planets modify the basic relationship? Do any planets closely aspect both the Sun and the Moon? What is the condition of the planet that rules the sign the Sun occupies? And the Moon? Which planets are also in the same sign or house occupied by the Sun and the Moon? What is the influence of the ascendant? In which of the four quadrants of houses are the luminaries placed?

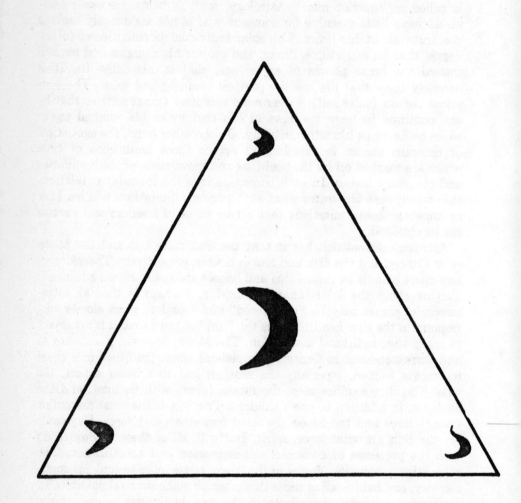

Fig. 11. Lunar symbols.

Planets Near the Sun: Mercury and Venus

Mars, which is the first planet *outside* of the Earth's orbit, symbolizes individual assertion and independence. Both Mercury and Venus are *inside* the Earth's orbit, closer to the Sun. A yet undetected planet (Vulcan?) may lie even closer to the Sun, so close in fact that it cannot be seen from Earth. If such a body exists, and some feel intuitively that it does, it may be found to rule Virgo, which for the time being shares the sovereignty of Mercury with Gemini.

Mercury moves around the Sun in about eighty-eight days and it is never more than twenty-eight degrees, zodiacally speaking, away from the Sun; therefore it is never more than one sign removed from the Sun sign. Being the most neutral of all planetary vibrations, Mercury is affected mainly by the sign it occupies, the Sun sign itself, and the aspects it receives from other planets. This small planet symbolizes the basic mental makeup of a person, his innate ability to communicate what is represented by his Sun sign, his capacity to learn facts, and the general way in which he correlates and articulates ideas and perceptions. The degree of adaptability and dexterity a person has is also shown to some extent by Mercury. At its best it is an objective extension of a person's individuality. The higher the degree of objectivity and power of logical analysis, the more effective communication and exchange with others will be. Mercury is also said to relate to acquaintances, siblings, neighbors, peers, and other side-by-side or "accidental" relationships. As ruler of Virgo, it is associated with powers of observation, cultivation, digestion, instruction (how-to-do-it), empirical thought, assistants, co-workers, one's sense of order, efficiency, and craftsmanship. Through Gemini or the third house, Mercury relates to designs, short trips (traveling lightly or swiftly), translation, communication, educational habits, information, collaborative ability, and logical thoughts of an abstract nature. Mercury is rather like an antenna which brings in the different signals of the other planetary bodies.

A weak Mercury can signify a weak mentality which has little power of discrimination or composure in times of crisis. A strong Mercury indicates the capacity for quick perception, clarity, and mental detachment. When it is poorly responded to it is indecisive, impulsive, or unduly conforming to the intellectual habits and ideas of others. Mercury also has to do with language. The words a person speaks and writes tell you something about that person. When there are serious difficulties in communication and learning, in reasoning and concentrating on or illustrating details, Mercury is apt to be poorly placed; or planets in Gemini or in the third house of the chart may be contributing to the problem. The same is true if there is serious trouble through siblings, neighbors, and chance acquaintances. Any kind of vacillation will be reinforced by a weak Mercury, just as intellectual perceptions are enhanced by a vigorous position of the planet.

When it is in the same sign the Sun occupies, Mercury's importance is increased in terms of what that sign represents. This is even more so if Venus is also in the Sun sign. In most cases, except for the first two and the last two degrees of a sign, Mercury will be in one of three signs: the Sun sign, or the sign just preceding or following it. For example, one could have the Sun at fifteen degrees Aries, while Mercury could be in Aries, Pisces, or Taurus. It is not any wonder, then, that popular generalizations made about the Sun signs seldom hold true in every respect for a particular individual. In addition, any of a great number of possible aspects from planets in various signs and houses can modify the basic Sun/Mercury/Venus pattern. No two minds are exactly alike, although they may share certain things in common, due to the fact that the two people may both have Mercury in the same degree of the zodiac.

Venus, the other planet inside the Earth's orbit, is traditionally regarded as the ruler of Taurus and Libra, although close study might find that the larger asteroids (denoting resources and talents of a personal nature) affect Taurus in some way. I have personally never been able to find a strong connection between Taurus and Venus; this, however, may be due to the fact that in my own chart Taurus planets are located in the seventh house, the house corresponding with Libra, the sign I have rising. As ruler of Taurus, Venus relates to resources, rewards, talents of a practical nature, favors, profits, construction, concentration of wealth, and the various processes of qualifying and evaluating (valuing) things essential to the individual himself. In this light it is the principle of contentment, especially with material things. Since I favor Venus as sole ruler of Libra, I might suggest a rule of compromise: if in doubt, read Venus primarily as the ruler of Taurus if the Sun is in a feminine sign (water or earth), and if the Sun is in a masculine sign (fire or air) give precedence to Venus as ruler of Libra. In all cases interpret Venus as the main significator of an individual's partner, mate, competitor, open enemy, or opponent. All face-to-face relationships where two people are involved can be studied by noting the position of this planet in the chart. A similar thing could be done with Mercury regarding its dual rulership.

As ruler of the seventh house, and the seventh sign, Libra, Venus acts as a pivotal point in one's relatedness to others. Everything preceding the seventh house is more or less personal and oriented to one's past,

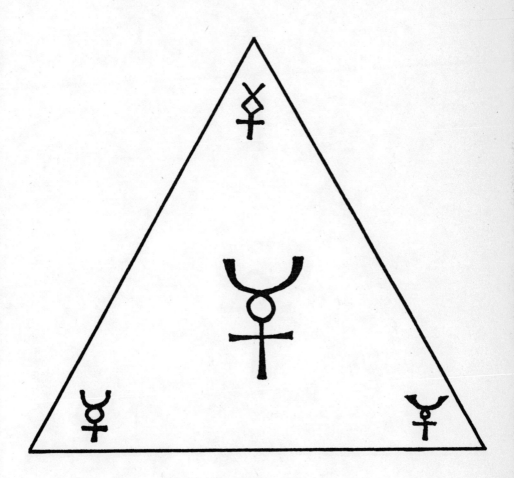

Fig. 12. Symbols for Mercury.

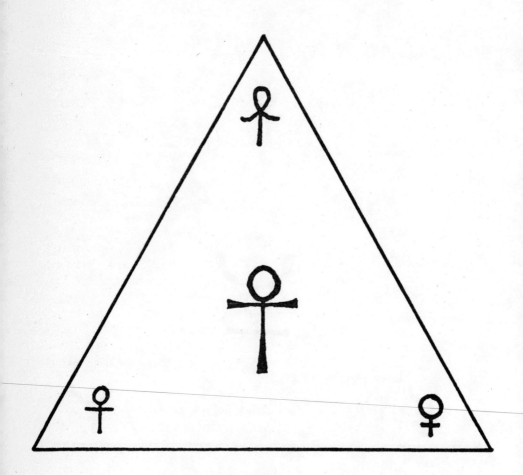

Fig. 13.   Symbols for Venus.

family, and instincts for protection and nourishment. With Venus and the seventh house the social or public realm begins—the area of experience where objective matters require new kinds of responsiveness and relatedness from the individual. Venus shows how we can best harmonize in relationships, hopefully finding justice and peace. It gives clues to a person's sense of propriety, poise, grace, measure, tact, affectional posture, and ability to cooperate. Mutuality is the keyword. Venus indicates what is needed in a partner to best complement the desires and aims described by one's Mars and the first house. Rather than harmony and an easy complement, the Venus position may indicate contests, contention, unhappy alliances, or even lawsuits and open battles. To say that Mars represents men and Venus women is a great oversimplification, and it is probably not particularly true in the Aquarian age, where sexual distinctions are changing to a more androgynous view (psychologically speaking).

Mars symbolizes one's own conscious drives, aggressiveness, exercise of power, and obvious sexual drives. Venus, in the chart of either sex, is a key to that to which one is magnetically drawn, often whether one likes it or not. It is the animus-mirror-anima which projects an image determined largely by the aspects Venus receives from the other bodies in the chart. Venus is also associated with the appreciation and definition of art and beauty, that is, with aesthetics. A well-placed Venus is very effective in helping one to achieve any kind of public or social success. A weak Venus may expose a need for developing thoroughness, reflection, and reason before one defines ends to be obtained. Some trouble in dealings with the opposite sex can be expected, according to the sign and house position of a Venus that receives strong frictional aspects from other planets. If Mars is essentially a point of subjective and necessary self-interest, Venus is that point in the chart which requires objective involvement in addition to subjective concerns, as in marriage. With Venus there has to be an agreement, contract, or formal arrangement in order to make sure that the scales are balanced.

Mercury and Venus are close to the Sun: communication and cooperation are necessary before anything else for man to exist as a socially civilized animal. Without this responsiveness we might be less successful than our fellow primates. Human love (Venus) requires a certain ability in the exchange of mutually understood symbols, gestures, or language (Mercury). The next body out from the Sun, astrologically speaking, is our own Moon, and this is symbolic of the need for shelter and protection, as well as nourishment. Love and language mean little without food and shelter. In the tribe each individual (Mars) has his own function or place. Customs, even taboos, exist for his own protection and for the furtherance of the tribe, family, or clan (even the nation). The Sun sign represents one's deeper function, whereas Mars is apt to show how this is actively or immediately carried out in a way appropriate for the individual. Indeed, the actual individuality and independence symbolized by Mars necessarily follows the lessons of social responsiveness (Venus) and maturity learned while securing the goods necessary for survival (Moon). Individuality could never precede social sophistication: Mars would not be closer to the Sun than Venus. Mercury gives clues about the dexterity one has in communicating with others. Venus shows how we can enlist their aid and talents in achieving our broader aims. The Moon, situated between Venus and Mars, helps one secure the habits of survival. Everything that is strictly personal is located between the Sun and Mars. With Jupiter, the more ideal phases of life begin, although these, as represented by the large outer planets, nevertheless touch upon the everyday life of the individual.

Mars

In one year, three hundred and twenty-one days, and twenty-three and one-half hours (about 22 months) Mars transits all twelve signs of the Zodiac. It is the first planet outside the Earth's orbit, and thus it appropriately symbolizes the urge to personal power, strength, energy, willed action, impulses (personal intuitions), as well as one's general capacity to initiate things. Words which relate to Martian activity are spontaneity, stimulation, forging, impetus, exploration, discovery, command, courage, intention, and passion. Other words are agitation, prematurity, violence, anger, impulsiveness, and narrowness (of views and attitudes). Some of the more obvious or dynamic features of an individual's personality and temperament are expressed through this planet, regardless of the sign that happens to be rising. This is true because Mars has a natural affinity with the first house through its rulership of Aries. The Moon may show how a person protects himself, but Mars indicates how the offensive is taken, and it is for this reason that Mars is often equated with anger, war, and violence.

The first reaction one has to things is generally indicated by Mars, and it shows as well, where one seems to be "headed," even though the deeper will (Sun) and instinctive feelings (Moon) may try to dictate otherwise. Man is a social creature who must procure the goods of life for mutual benefit and security (Mercury, Venus, and Moon), but what makes him actually evolve is an equally strong sense of individuality

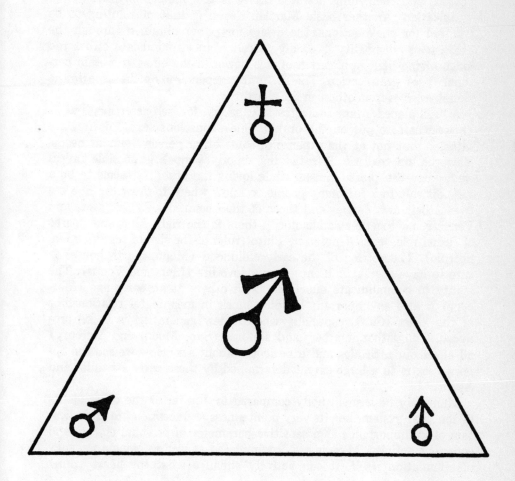

Fig. 14.   Symbols for Mars.

and the need for personal satisfaction within the family or group. This is the meaning of Mars, although the satisfaction of these personal desires or aims can take many forms, both positive and negative. The most obvious and compelling of these drives is the one for physical sexual gratification. Another basic Martian desire is that of wanting to be admired for one's actions, the desire for power obtained through the exercise of personality. A badly placed Mars can indicate either too much or too little application of this power in the effort to obtain personal (ego) gratification. This naturally depends upon the aspects the planet receives from others in the chart.

A well-placed Mars indicates a capacity for self-assertion, but it knows where to put on the brakes. One's conscious sexual desires are satisfied, but not at the expense of some other person's similar needs. However, no realistic or satisfying union (Venus) is possible unless each party can please himself while loving the other. It seems to be a very difficult task for many people to know where to draw the line between their own desires and those of their comrades. Where Mars and Venus come together satisfactorily there is the right kind and degree of sexual release, as denoted by Pluto (ruler of the sign of reproduction, Scorpio). The setting of the early childhood (Moon, fourth house) is sure to have a great influence on our love life (Mars and Venus). The ability to communicate effectively with others at an early age (Mercury) is also an important building block in meaningful relationships of the heart (Sun), especially when a new generation is to be produced. The father, mother, and siblings (Sun, Moon, and Mercury) all affect our attitudes and experiences about sex. How we see the opposite sex is to a large extent determined by these early attitudes and lessons.

Mars may be a small body compared to Jupiter or the other giants of the solar system, but its very pointedness and location are an indication of its importance as a sensitive barometer of personal change and conscious activity. Mars is easily stimulated as well as being an agency of stimulation itself. It can actively enhance what the heart (Sun) desires.

Jupiter and Saturn

Jupiter and Saturn are sometimes thought of as being opposites, the former representing expansion and all those forces that extend the individual into higher realms of understanding and relatedness, and the latter, the principle of contraction and limitation. Jupiter moves slowly around the Sun in eleven years and three hundred and fifteen days, remaining in a sign for about one year. Saturn revolves through the signs in twenty-nine years and one hundred and sixty-six days. Jupiter rules Sagittarius and the natural ninth house. Saturn has its greatest affinity with Capricorn and the tenth house of the chart.

Wherever Jupiter appears in the horoscope there is an area of potential improvement and expansion, an opportunity to test or demonstrate one's higher ideals and philosophy of life. This can take many forms, such as involvement in international affairs, travel abroad, religious quest, exploration of new lands, higher education, or athletic achievement. If Mercury, ruler of the sign opposite Sagittarius, reveals something about the native intelligence and mental abilities, Jupiter shows how these abilities are put to use in a broader sense, especially in some socially significant matter. Mercury represents the basic ability to communicate with others, whereas Jupiter is a further extension of this, showing how new languages and concepts are acquired that expand a person's horizons beyond that of his family or nation. A positive Jupiter placement denotes a search for truth, frankness, optimism, good judgment, joviality, gregariousness, and an ability to reach for new or greater goals of a more universal nature. If it is poorly placed, Jupiter can contribute to pretension, exaggeration, excessive evangelism, rashness, gullibility, boasting, undirected wanderlust, and wasteful speculation (gambling). In a spiritual sense Jupiter represents revelation and the imparting of wisdom and knowledge. A person who is born under its positive influence is not easily fooled by the promise of questionable rewards or advantages. At the root of his deeds is the earnest need to seek and demonstrate (teach) truth and to encourage others. The weaker Jupiterian tends to romanticize his existence, and he is usually characterized by restlessness and an arrogant and unfruitful self-righteousness.

It is an error of traditional astrological thought to make Saturn out as the villain or "malefic" and Jupiter as the planet which always denotes "good fortune." Both positive and negative expressions of these and the other planets are possible. The beauty of Jupiter can be Venusian beauty magnified or amplified many times, but Jupiter can also increase the arrogant self-interest of an egotistical Mars position to disastrous proportions. Likewise, Saturn can give great depth and stability to whatever planet it contacts, and it can also denote situations of congestion and restriction. Saturn tends to draw things toward itself, containing and polishing them; Jupiter gives something out, extending itself.

Saturn is said to be the principle of crystallization; that is, wherever

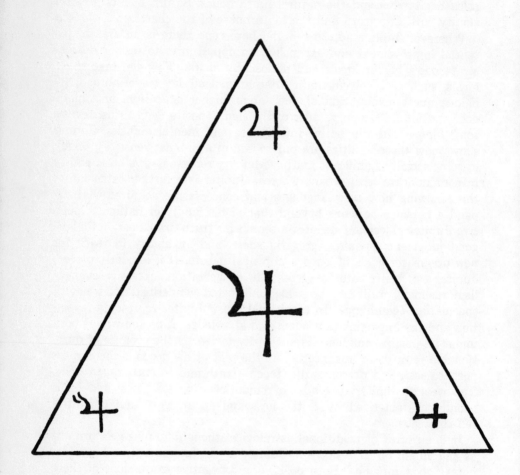

Fig. 15. Symbols for Jupiter.

it occurs it signifies a situation where the individual has to consolidate his energies toward some very real responsibility or duty. This may entail some degree of worry, apprehension, sense of disappointment, and restriction, or the feeling that one has been bound by fate itself. The greatest trouble arises when the individual fails to concentrate the necessary energies, as defined by the house and the sign Saturn occupies, and thinks he can cheat the dictates of time. Such an individual is apt to experience a larger than average number of falls, setbacks, burdens, obstacles, and delays, all of which can make him sullen and unhappy. But Saturn need not mean coercion or contribute to a feeling of unrelenting opacity and density if one comes to understand its meaning in the chart. Normally, it represents some necessary barrier where reliability, regulation, management, and respect for some superior force (rules, standards, tradition, and authority) is required. As the significator of the experienced person, the professional, Saturn shows the value of composure, organization, apportionment, loyalty, perseverance, and thoroughness in achieving success and acclaim. The main lesson taught by this planet might be that of learning the necessity for patience and dignity in some particular phase of experience where responsibility is emphasized.

When it is poorly responded to, Saturn can and does indicate disaster and sorrow; but this is usually attributable to some instability, lack of caution, or lack of thoroughness on the part of the individual in seeking his goals. Occultists suggest that, karmically speaking, this misfortune has arisen from previous lives. Perhaps this is so. Saturn is associated with the past and with tradition, but this is somewhat misleading, although true enough. The eyes of Saturn are always turned toward the universal, toward the future (symbolized by Uranus), and the medium through which it sees or focuses upon the future is the past itself. Saturn wisely knows the limits of experience. Jupiter may enthuse or stimulate the individual to reach toward the intellectual and spiritual heights of Olympus, to reach for his god or his deeper self, but Saturn is the top of the mountain. One can probably go no further on this plane of existence in terms of individual accomplishment. Uranus and Neptune are further refinements of the Saturnian achievement since they distribute the rewards (and pains) of success. Uranus describes the friends, even disciples, which the enlightened (Saturn) person acquires as he comes down from the summit of his achievement. Neptune represents his compassionate works, which are always of universal value. It should be apparent that few people are able to tune into these higher manifestations of the extramartian planets.

Jupiter is the impetus to energetically reach toward something

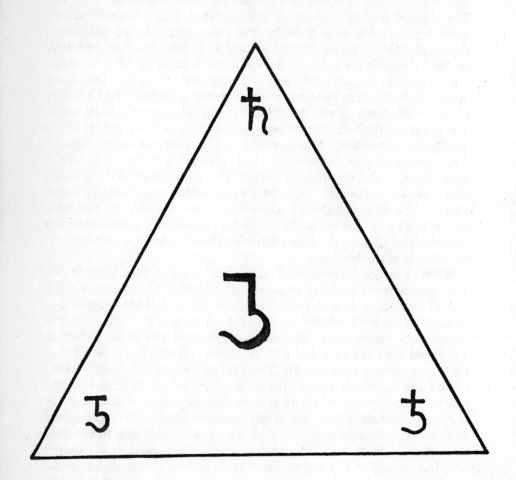

Fig. 16. Symobls for Saturn.

higher; it is the big booster. Saturn defines exactly what this shall be for each person. To some extent, Saturn represents practical universal values and things in which all men can share, such as the regulatory standards and laws of the community. As the planet that has to do with established and recognizable authority, Saturn produces the more important rules of life that make civilization possible. In connection with Jupiter it forms the general regulations for society. Along with Venus it seeks to preserve traditional mores and culturally significant standards of justice. Through Mercury and Saturn the laws affecting communication and commerce are born; and with Mars Saturn gives us strict laws to punish criminals. The Moon, in contrast, has more to do with tribal mores, ancestral taboos, and family rules or standards: it is the mother and Saturn is the father. These two bodies are astrological opposites, to some extent, yet they complement each other functionally, just as do Mercury and Jupiter, or Venus and Mars.

The Outer Planets: Uranus, Neptune, and Pluto

The journey of Uranus around the Sun takes eighty-four years and four days; it stays in one sign for about seven years. Neptune takes one hundred and sixty-four years and two hundred and eighty-nine days, staying in a sign for about fourteen years. It will return to the position it held at the time of its discovery in the year 2011. Today, most astrologers associate Uranus with Aquarius and the eleventh house, and Neptune with Pisces and the twelfth house. Pluto, which was discovered in 1930, is generally considered to be the new ruler of Scorpio, at least, it should have established itself as that sign's ruler by the time it returns to the position it held at the time of its discovery. This will be in the year 2178, since it takes Pluto two hundred and forty-eight years and one hundred and fifty-seven days to go around the Sun. Owing to its eccentric orbit, Pluto stays in one sign for anywhere from eleven to thirty-one years, the average being twenty-one years. At times, it is even closer to the Sun than Neptune; in fact, it is thought by some that it may be an escaped moon of Neptune. Pluto is more like the planets closer to the Sun in its size and physical makeup than it is like the gaseous giants which precede it.

Uranus' discovery in the late eighteenth century and Neptune's in the early nineteenth helped to clarify certain ambiguities in astrology, namely the rulership of Aquarius and Pisces. These signs had previously shared rulership of Saturn and Jupiter, respectively, with Capricorn and Sagittarius. Today Neptune is usually assigned to Pisces, and Uranus to Aquarius, although there are a few astrologers who still hold to the old rulerships. Mars used to rule both Aries and Scorpio until Pluto was discovered. Now most astrologers have given Mars solely to Aries. A very small number of astrologers think Aries is ruled by Pluto and that Mars rules Scorpio, although their reasoning seems questionable when one considers what these planets and signs symbolize. Mars is the conscious drive for power and sexual gratification; Pluto is the deeper unconscious aspects of sex which has to do with the actual genital release of the sperm and ovum. Pluto has to do with the mysteries of reproduction itself, aside from any conscious sexual desires. As human consciousness and understanding evolves we need new symbols and a broader language in which to interpret our changing biopsychic reality. Still, that which is visible and attainable will continue to be described by Saturn. It stands at the threshold of the more universal values that man aspires to: freedom, humanitarian love, and altruistic service. At the same time, Saturn includes what is actually obtainable as one approaches these higher goals and hopes.

With Uranus, the individual can begin to express higher values through meaningful and objective relationships and associations of friendship which have goals that extend to the welfare of all people (Neptune). Uranus shows how and where a person looks to the future progress of his own kind. Such an insightful view requires a spirit of optimistic experimentation, reformation, transformation, intuitive thought, applied science, cosmopolitan ideals, inventiveness, and an attitude of openness with others. Narrow, anthropomorphic views have no place to root themselves in the realm of Uranus. Unexpected shocks upset such views or relationships. Objectivity, as well as tolerance, is required in all Uranian associations.

The less positive side of this planet may be seen in the person who is anarchistic, foolishly bizarre, dissonant, rebellious (without good reason), and who lacks direction in relationships. This diffusive, willful, and eccentric person is easily estranged from others he tries to befriend. The positive Uranian, on the other hand, gets along well with his carefully chosen friends and colleagues. He does not try vainly to become everybody's friend. What counts most to him is the effect of an objective relationship, what it can reproduce that will be of value for the betterment of mankind as a whole. This altruist is not simply a do-gooder; he gets things done by associating with the proper people for the proper reasons.

In Uranian (eleventh house) situations a person's personal feelings and desires often have to be subordinated to the wishes and aims of the group as a whole. Universal cooperation and peace would follow

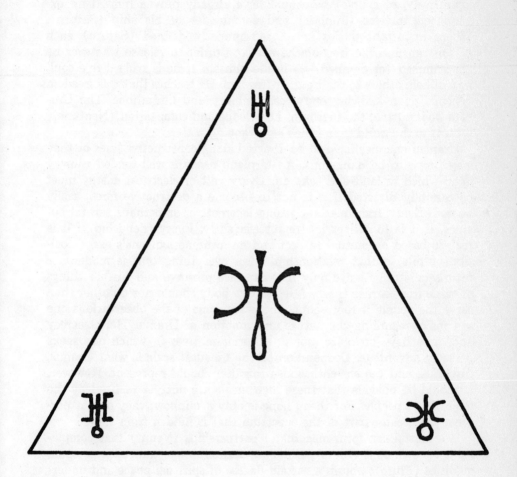

Fig. 17. Symbols for Uranus.

if all people could do this. Knowledge can be shared most effectively when these conditions prevail, especially when there is no need to compete or prove oneself. By the time one lands on Uranus (I mean this figuratively, of course) he should have already proven himself an experienced traveler (Jupiter) and commander of his ship (Saturn). Where important duties have been properly defined (Saturn) each person can find the freedom he needs in order to release whatever he has dammed (or damned) up inside himself. If he is truly a free soul, he will help others to realize their freedom. He teaches that this freedom depends upon knowing one's responsibility and limitations. The Uranian *bodhisattva*, the person of knowledge and compassion (Neptune), returns to the world from which he sprang.

Uranian energies have to be directed along constructive lines or they may prove to be dangerous. An airplane needs a well-tended runway upon which to land and take off. Every volt of electrical energy must be carefully directed if it is not to become a destructive force, easily wasted. Every train needs a strong locomotive, or perhaps several engines, if it is to deliver its freight efficiently. Every friendship, if it is real, is based on mutual respect and an awareness of one's exact position or role in that relationship. Also, everything that is modern or futuristic is progressive only if it can also preserve and further things of value from earlier times. A legislative body should not do other than serve the people it represents. These are some of the observations one can make regarding the nature and function of Uranus. Here, secrecy and guile have no place, nor do ulterior motives in which one seeks personal advantage. Cooperation on the broadest scale is what Uranus, Aquarius, and the eleventh house together should represent. However, it should be obvious that these high ideals are not yet realized by the majority of people. For them, hope is only a rainbow; they do not perceive the greater part of the spectrum that is hidden from view.

If a person can form meaningful partnerships (Venus) that complement his own aims (Mars); eliminate undesirable or unneeded personal qualities (Pluto); obtain a certain degree of spiritual peace and understanding (Jupiter); achieve some degree of constructive influence in the world (Saturn); and make good friends and associations (Uranus), he is ready to walk the path used by the masters of the past. This is the trail of Neptune, a complicated path upon which only a few can travel safely and without getting sidetracked. The positive aspects of this path are humility, self-sacrifice, renunciation, sympathy, charity, awareness of inner unity, and meditation. On either side of the path are the sorrows and dangers of life, the many failings that man is subject to, especially those rising from his own ignorance, desires, and selfishness. To lose sight of the path is to run the risk of self-deception, seduction, imprisonment, loss of vital energy, the making of secret enemies, or any of the many negative things Neptune can symbolize.

Any degree of uncalled for self-prostitution becomes one's own self-undoing. Some degree of submissiveness and sacrifice is required by Neptune, but not a masochistic surrender to fate. Neptune's effect is deceiving. What may appear to be a puzzle, maze, or muzzle from which there seems to be no escape may in fact be an opportunity for self-enlightenment. Glamorous and tantalizing things may also be offered up, but these can prove to be dangerous. What seems substantial one moment may in an unsuspected turn reveal itself as translucent, evasive, or unattainable. Neptune can confuse, dissolve, debase, and take away a person's last sanctuary when it is poorly responded to. It amplifies our imperfections and congenital weaknesses. It makes us dishonest and causes us to cheat, or rather, it symbolizes our dishonesty, for no planet is in itself the cause of our actions.

Neptune shows where an individual has to be alone or at least be hidden from the flow of the normal business of society. This solitude can be sublime meditation or it can be the jailhouse, depending upon who we are and what we are doing in a particular life. Saint and criminal alike bear the imprint of this planet. To be able to accept defeat or poor health, or to live in isolation, is required of many of those who come strongly under its influence. Neptune seems to gather up all kinds of forces from the deeper strata of the unconscious. These can contribute to poetic imagination and to psychoneurosis as well. The average person is probably to some degree aware of both manifestations. He may have some seemingly unresolvable problem, some secret fear or vice, that he can share with no one else, but which, fortunately, does not dominate his life all of the time. A psychologist might call this a complex. Certain phobias are also associated with Neptune, depending upon the sign involved and the aspect the planet receives from other bodies.

In the intellectual sphere, Neptune can denote a broad understanding and intelligence which is much influenced by intuitive feelings, as well as by a deep empathy for the desires and feelings of others. The study of symbolism might come under Neptune because it deals with hidden things and qualities, such as those found in poetry, art, and music. Neptune is also associated with rest, seclusion, retirement, and other matters which require the haven of privacy. It does not seek salience, but is content with actions behind the scenes. It might require some rather large degree of introspection from the individual, some of which can be painful or frightening, and occurring at what may seem

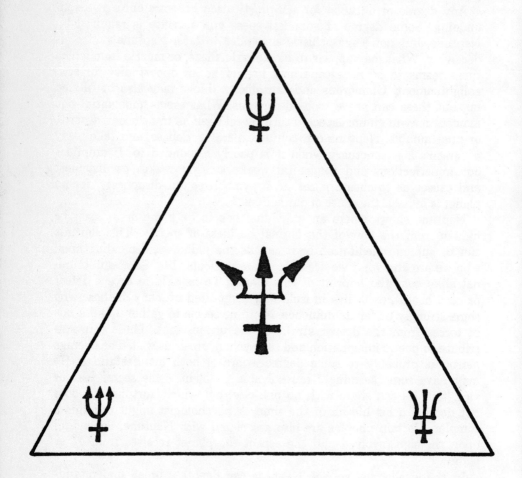

Fig. 18.   Symbols for Neptune.

to be the worst of times. The person who has traveled down these thorny roads knows what it is like to be sick, humiliated, frightened, turned back, left alone, or defeated. But it is his own hardship which enables the pilgrim to compassionately regard his fellowman. If a person would remove obstructions for others he must first of all have encountered them himself in some manner, even if only for a moment. Adversity, viewed in this way, is more of a teacher than a punisher. People respect one who overcomes or intelligently deals with personal defects, whether they are psychological or physical.

The person who is unable to overcome his shortcomings, or at least meet them halfway in good humor, is apt to turn to habit-forming drugs, excessive use of alcohol, deception, secret activities, or some other self-depreciating Neptunian practice or situation. His efforts to achieve something constructive and meaningful are only a burlesque of the real thing. He is quite unable to channel his energies and abilities into something of value created in unison (Uranus) with others. The person who is caught in the net of Neptune is apt to be attracted to things which are nebulous, and even to sinister things. Some try to escape through the practice of some secret rite or cult that emphasizes hidden forces and self-mastery through some unearthly means. They cannot find the way of the individual who blazes (Mars) his own trail. Others with Neptune in a poor position become the victims of lies, treachery, thieves, and strange illnesses, among other things. Or, they may be humiliated or slandered in some way that damages their position in the community. Much of this suffering could be avoided in many cases.

Neptune, like Uranus, requires a view of life that is broader than average, a frame of mind that is aware of the larger cycles and currents in society and the historical development of mankind. Something larger than personal gain compels the Neptunian to continue down the path of self-sacrifice ("dropping out"), a path which he has to travel alone. Buddha reached his nirvana, but he turned right around to find his friends and student-disciples coming down their own paths of contemplation, merging at the same point of universal understanding and love. Christ, too, made his sacrifices. The person who intelligently yields to others is chanting the songs of Neptune. There is always a time in the future, even if a person is presently constrained, or has to retreat, when his knowledge or talents will come to bear (Mars) on the collective conscious of man. Any Neptunian accomplishment will take at least two lifetimes to arrive in full force—the length of the orbit of Neptune is almost exactly double that of Uranus, the latter planet symbolizing the altruist—and few people today live beyond eighty-four years.

There is little lasting satisfaction in glamour, self-deception, or adherence to those inferior people and things that reinforces one's desire for a premature success or position. Thoroughness and devotion will always be ready to unmask that which is superficial, stolen, false, and acquired through guile. Evil, that is, excessive self-interest and subjective entanglement in unconscious forces, goes against the things that make human existence successful. One cannot fool a Nature which insists that each creature act according to the laws which best suit it. Human beings differ from other life forms on this planet in that they are forced to use reason to survive. Where this enlarged power of reason fails is in those instances where conscience and compassion are ignored. Then, the pain of Neptune's trident will most likely be felt.

The most remote known planet in the solar system is Pluto. There is some agreement that it relates to forces which control the collective unconscious of mankind (along with Neptune perhaps), that it has to do with deep biosexual drives for reproduction, and that it signifies extrasensory perception. Negative Plutonic manifestations appear to take the form of compulsions, genocide, destructive death wishes, propaganda, manipulative states of mind that induce terror, bereavement, and lessening of an individual's resources. Pluto seems to have an effect in mass movements where destructive forces are unleashed on a grand scale (for example, Nazi Germany). Death appears to be quite content riding in the carriage of Pluto.

This distant planet is also regarded as the principle of regeneration, catharsis, elimination, and transformation. Through Pluto, egoic self-interest is transmuted into something higher. The individual who has enough courage and understanding can enter into the forbidden realms of the unknown, gathering insights and spiritual resources from the divine repository that Carl G. Jung referred to as the collective unconscious, and which the Buddhists call the *akasic* records: nature's memory. This is the kingdom of the mythical bird known as the Phoenix, which destroys itself on a pyre to become the ashes from which it is born again, at each cycle supposedly at a higher or more refined level. The idea that the ego must die or be transformed (one has to "let go") in order to reach the deeper levels of consciousness and being is seen in this eternal process. Each life and death cycle is a purification of self. The process is very risky for some; the seeker must learn how to correctly interpret the "omens" (today called "synchronicity"), visions, or whatever Plutonic transformations and images occur. Regenerative forces can all too easily become destructive. Radioactivity, a Plutonic phenomenon, has to be approached with caution. Pluto is small, but a little goes a long way.

To glimpse the secrets of the universe is not the same thing as learn-

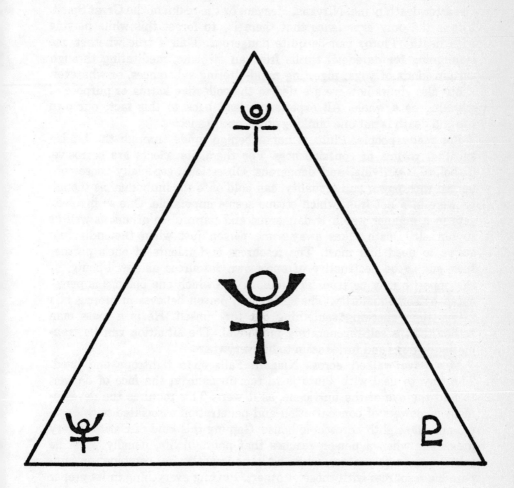

Fig. 19. Symbols for Pluto.

ing how to use the knowledge obtained wisely. Pluto can give a person an experience or view of the transcendental states that lie beyond corporeal life and death; this may be that great void which some call the after death plane, Nirvana, Heaven, or the realm of the Great Spirit. Life is the only *experience* that there is: to forget this while playing with death (Pluto) can be quite dangerous. This is true whether one is jumping for daredevil thrills from an airplane, meditating through certain kinds of yoga, ingesting mind-altering substances, or whatever. Pluto also shows how we are tied to the collective karma or purpose of mankind as a whole. All experiences lead back to this fact; our own life and death is but one blinking of the entire species.

For many people, Pluto is not a benign guide through the hidden spiritual realms of consciousness. For them, its effects are corrosive, diabolical, terrifying, and dangerous. Obsessions, especially those connected with power and sexuality, can hold onto the individual as though he were in a net from which escape seems impossible. One so involved acts in a manner which is dangerous and harmful to others as well as to himself. Death takes away some person just when the individual seems to need him most. The resources and talents of one's partner turn out to be destructive of one's own resources and well-being, or the opposite may be true. The minority to which one belongs is persecuted by some majority. The spellbound person believes in propaganda rather than checking something out for himself. He is a mass man rather than a self-regenerating individual. The situation can be traumatic: demons and furies seem to be everywhere.

Men have walked across Niagara Falls on a tightrope and lived. The way to deal with Pluto is to remain calm in the face of danger, to find the eye of the hurricane, as it were. This requires the development of powers of concentration and penetration associated with Scorpio and the eighth horoscopic house. Gaining this kind of clarity is very important when a person reaches that point in life, usually when he takes a mate or partner, when he has to synthesize, combine, or compare his resources with those of others. Putting everything in its proper place at the right time demands a certain eagle-eyed attention to detail. Nothing should be overlooked. Unless a person can do this he will not find the support he needs in order to reach the greater heights of human experience denoted by the houses which follow the eighth house. When there is a suitable sexual union and release there will be less chance for hidden neuroses to spoil one's higher aspirations. A person in a high position (Saturn, the tenth house) who is obsessed by some serious unconscious sexual difficulty is a tragic figure. His power of influence can too easily become infested by destructive unconscious motivations

(Adolf Hitler seems to have been such an individual). One should not underestimate the effect of the prominent Pluto-dominated person on the course of human history. Christ was another person apparently touched by Pluto; his crucifixion was a great statement about life and death. Pluto seems to favor such extremes.

Planetary Rhythms

Each member of the solar system moves in a different orbit and represents, in itself, many facets of experience. Each has its own dimensions, effect, and levels of activity, these synchronizing with events occurring in terrestrial human experience. Throughout his study of astrology, the reader should keep in mind the fact that pure astrological manifestations are rare. The Sun in Pisces, for instance, can be in any of the twelve horoscopic houses depending upon the time and place of birth; and it can be in aspect to any of the planetary bodies. The new astrologer has to develop his own intuition and ability to synthesize the various factors. Until he has absorbed the meaning of each planet he will not be able to interpret a horoscope as it should be. No textbook can list the effects of the planets through the signs and houses in such a manner that everything which is said actually applies. Subtle differences have to be noted by the astrologer himself, especially those created by the planetary aspects. To try to interpret a chart using a textbook alone is to render a superficial and stiffly narrow reading.

Chapter VI

Astrological Categories and Correlations

Astrology invites one to attempt to classify any-thing and everything according to the zodiacal signs or the planetary bodies. This includes such things as colors, musical notes, gemstones, and parts of the body—the list seems endless. In some of these classifi-cations there is as much disagreement as there is agreement, and every author seems like an authority. What I have done, without being able to avoid doing so, is to join in this, hoping that my ideas and observa-tions are sound enough to be of some use to the reader. A good portion of the material included in this chapter is not controversial, such as the correspondence between the signs and the parts of the body. Other areas are largely speculative. Almost everything in this section could stand further elaboration, but space does not permit comprehensive discus-sions in a book such as this. The reader is urged not to be hasty in ac-cepting zodiacal classifications and correlations wherever they appear. He should read widely, compare, and then make up his own mind on what is symbolically correct.

Zodiacal Symbols and Images

There are many things which in some way seem to express a truth about a particular sign. A brief list of symbols and images associated with the signs is provided below, but it is by no means complete; there are hundreds of other terms which one might add. Also, there are many things and situations which are better symbolized by two or more signs.

A barber might be symbolized by Aries (the head, cutting instruments) and Virgo (a service commonly provided). In its various forms, the sphinx would seem to represent combinations of various creatures; for instance, the great Sphinx in Egypt is thought to be a combination of Leo (lion) and Virgo (human being). Many other examples exist. Astrology is, after all, a symbolic language that describes how different factors—signs, planets, and houses—combine to produce meaningful wholes. Few things or situations can be associated exclusively with one sign or planet, since pure zodiacal or planetary types are not likely to occur.

Each horoscope is a complex combination of factors, a graphic picture of a particular moment in time when the bodies of the solar system line up in a unique pattern. The art of astrological analysis lies in knowing how to intuitively synthesize these relationships, to create a true and congruent picture out of all the various factors in the chart. The symbols of astrology are fairly simple and few in number, yet the complex meaning in each chart requires specific attention. One has to keep in mind the interrelationships between certain planets, houses, and signs, as well as the difference between these three basic factors. The sign Sagittarius, for instance, is naturally related to the ninth house and to Jupiter, and all three can share to some extent in the same symbols and images. The difference between the three is that the signs are archetypal divisions of the four seasons; the houses are divisions of the celestial sphere based on the daily rotation of the Earth, and they show circumstantial matters; and the planets and their aspects are the dynamic symbols for the solar system forces that affect life on Earth.

ARIES: early spring, dawn, thunder and lightning, volcano, fireman, policeman, warrior, javelin thrower, pharaoh, hat, headdress, helmet, ax, battering ram, sword, rifle, scissors, scepter, wand, trumpet, rocket, forge, flame, torch, candle, key, door, ram, lamb, bighorn sheep, cock.

TAURUS: midspring, hill, Zen garden, boulder, monolith, stock exchange, geologist, lapidarist, surveyor, sculptor, earthen objects, candle holder, personal possessions, bank vault, purse, wallet, treasure chest, the dollar sign, chest of drawers, yoke, bull, cow, buffalo, bison, yak.

GEMINI: late spring, a breeze, library, wandering teacher, vagabond, mailman, trapeze artist, singing duet, messenger, twins, hermaphrodite, typewriter, quill, newspaper, telephone, roadmap, wooden flute, concertina, lyre, dictionary, bicycle, hare, chameleon, parrot, roadrunner, lyrebird, mockingbird, gibbon, monkey.

CANCER: early summer, running stream, rainstorm, fountain, shelter, tent, home, kitchen, hearth, pantry, laundry, tiled bath, banquet, mother nursing her child, tribal chief, basket, loaf of bread, safety pin, silver objects, drum, town bell, things from the seashore, crab, lobster, snail, porcupine, turtle, hen, badger.

LEO: midsummer, rainbow, castle, amphitheater, fair, carnival, circus, ballroom, playground with children, king, clown, vaudevillian, minstrel, film star, golden crown, trophy, solar disk, jewelry, cosmetics, perfume, aphrodisiacs, heart, ancient brass lamp, painter's palette, lion, tiger, jaguar, housecat, peacock, pheasant.

VIRGO: late summer, valley, granary, manger, closet, virgin, family doctor, shepherd, farmer, craftsman at work, servant, broom, dust mop, pruning shears, funnels, sieve, thermometer, medical caduceus, tailor, woven fabric, sheaf of grain, cornucopia, almanac, ledger, blackboard, beaver, squirrel, dungbeetle, gerbil.

LIBRA: early autumn, dusk, sky, government building, art gallery, diplomat, juggler, men fencing, teeter-totter, wedding, Adam and Eve, scales, mirror, belt (girdle), chess board, Ping-Pong, podium, faucet (hot and cold), gyroscope, flying saucer, copper objects, flower bed, embroidered objects, dove, swallow, cicada.

SCORPIO: midautumn, tornado, snowstorm, glacier, deep cool lake, swamp, mud spring, hot spring, geyser, deep well, iceberg, laboratory, operating room, surgeon, mortician, alchemist, occultist, shaman, hypnotist, microscope, whip, nuclear armament, scorpion, spider, serpent, eagle and other birds of prey, vulture, crow, lizard.

SAGITTARIUS: late autumn, college campus, fortress, gambling casino, race track, scholar, judge, matador, hunter, archer, cowboy, cross-country runner, explorer, airplane pilot, mounted knight, chariot, carriage, religious vestments, manuscript, incense burner, lantern, gavel, telescope, cartoon, horse, zebra, impala, wapiti, deer, gazelle, dromedary, elephant, centaur.

CAPRICORN: early winter, mountain, pyramid, monument, skyscraper, bridge, patriarch, tycoon, executive, political leader, governor, hourglass, grandfather clock, old objects of lasting value and quality, finished wooden things, cube, pipe organ, pewter objects, briefcase, goat, giraffe, ibex, peccary, penguin.

AQUARIUS: midwinter, waterbearer, inventor, gypsy, bohemian, quilting bee, football team, fraternal group, tribal council, political party, legislative body, orchestra, ballot box, crazy quilt, Holy Grail, calumet (peace pipe), airplane, electronic computer, electrical or nuclear power plant, flock of birds, ant colony.

PISCES: late winter, sea, cavern, market place, oil refinery, museum, monastery, asylum, hospital, prison, gallows, pawnshop, seance, sorceress, wizard, nun, monk, hermit, Red Cross worker, pilgrim, poet, cobbler, spelunker, dwarf, mummy, ghost, harpies, trident and net, ark, ship, veil, labyrinth, amphora, crutch, encyclopedia, fish, octopus, dolphin, hippopotamus, bat.

The Thirty-six Decanates

Since the time of the ancient Egyptians the signs of the Zodiac have been subdivided into thirty-six minor sections called *decanates*. This means that each sign is divided into three equal sections of ten degrees each. There are different interpretations for each of these decanates, and some astrologers assign planetary subrulers to them. One popular method is that where the first decanate of a sign is considered to be ruled by the traditional (regular) ruling planet; the second decanate by that planet which rules the following sign of the same element; and the third decanate by the planet which rules the preceding sign of the same element. Thus, the first decanate of Aries would be ruled by Mars, the second by the Sun, and the third by Jupiter. Leo's first decanate would be ruled by the Sun, the second by Jupiter, and the third by Mars, while Sagittarius' first decanate would be ruled by Jupiter, the second by Mars, and the third by the Sun. Familiarity with the four zodiacal elements and the rulership of the twelve signs should make it easy to see which planet subrules each decanate. Even though one uses the subrulers it is important to keep in mind that the regular ruler of the sign as a whole—as with Mars for Aries—is still given precedence.

Another view, the one I feel is more accurate, holds that the center of a sign—the fifteenth degree to be exact—represents its purest expression. Therefore, the regular ruler is associated with the second decanate, with the rulers of the following and preceding signs of the same element ruling the other two decanates. Table II gives the subrulers for each of the thirty-six decanates. Both of the approaches mentioned here could be supported by good arguments. The reader should study both before making up his mind which seems most appropriate for his needs. The use of the decanates is convenient when figuring aspects between the planets: those bodies which are placed in a sign's first decanate will aspect planets in the first decanate of all the other signs; the same is true, appropriately, for the other two decanates. A planet at 2° Aries will be in aspect with one at 2° Gemini and one at 9° Capricorn, and with other bodies located between 0° and 10° of a given sign. The second decanate covers bodies between 10° and 20°. The third decanate includes those between 20° and 30°. The third decanate will be influenced by the sign which follows, and the first decanate will have some of the coloring of the preceding sign. This line of reasoning will not appeal to those who believe that the first degree of a sign is its strongest and most characteristic manifestation, with each following degree diminishing in its effect. In that case, the first, not the second decanate, would be the most powerful expression of a sign, and the first of the two systems discussed above might be used.

Astrological/Anatomical Correspondence

There is a system of classification which equates certain parts of the body to basic astrological factors. The branch of astrology which treats disease dates back to at least the time of the Greek healer Hippocrates. Since that time astrologers have viewed the human body as a microcosm of a greater whole, the signs and planets having been found to relate to certain disorders, according to their nature. There are several texts available on this rather specialized facet of astrology, and there may be some disagreement on certain points, but the correspondences given here are generally accepted. The first house is often regarded as being an index to the individual's general vitality, along with the position of Mars, Sun, and Moon. The sixth house is the main indicator of health and practical curative methods; the eighth house has to do with special techniques and surgery; and the twelfth house represents hospitals and convalescence. It is generally considered to be favorable to have the Sun and Moon in good aspect to other planets as well as to each other. A planet receiving frictional aspects might incline one to have problems in several areas. For instance, in a chart where there are "afflictions" to Jupiter (several squares, oppositions, and quincunxes) there might be problems with the hips, liver, or possibly accidents through horses or automobiles. All of these things are associated with Jupiter. Also, any planets in the ninth house or Sagittarius might reveal similar effects. Transiting planets seem to trigger or correspond to certain problems one has in terms of health. The beginner should not

TABLE II—THE THIRTY-SIX ZODIACAL DECANATES

DECANATE	APPROXIMATE DATE	PLANETARY SUBRULER	KEYWORDS
Aries 1	3/21 to 3/30	Jupiter	identity, inspiration
Aries 2	3/31 to 4/9	Mars	innovation, activation
Aries 3	4/10 to 4/19	Sun	stylization, formulation
Taurus 1	4/20 to 4/30	Saturn	production, construction
Taurus 2	5/1 to 5/10	Venus	contentment, acquisition
Taurus 3	5/11 to 5/20	Mercury	evaluation, definition
Gemini 1	5/21 to 5/31	Uranus	adaption, education
Gemini 2	6/1 to 6/10	Mercury	correlation, illustration
Gemini 3	6/11 to 6/21	Venus	communication, exchange
Cancer 1	6/22 to 7/1	Neptune	empathy, impression
Cancer 2	7/2 to 7/12	Moon	memory, containment
Cancer 3	7/13 to 7/22	Pluto	protection, nourishment
Leo 1	7/23 to 8/1	Mars	entertainment, creativity
Leo 2	8/2 to 8/12	Sun	self-expression, romance
Leo 3	8/13 to 8/22	Jupiter	enterprise, direction
Virgo 1	8/23 to 9/2	Venus	discrimination, craftsmanship
Virgo 2	9/3 to 9/13	Mercury	utilization, analysis

		Saturn	
Virgo 3	9/14 to 9/22		perfection, efficiency
Libra 1	9/23 to 10/3	Mercury	order, harmony
Libra 2	10/4 to 10/13	Venus	comparison, justice
Libra 3	10/14 to 10/23	Uranus	combination, cooperation
Scorpio 1	10/24 to 11/2	Moon	clarification, adjustment
Scorpio 2	11/3 to 11/12	Pluto	intensification, penetration
Scorpio 3	11/13 to 11/22	Neptune	regeneration, purification
Sagittarius 1	11/23 to 12/2	Sun	exploration, judgment
Sagittarius 2	12/3 to 12/11	Jupiter	speculation, encouragement
Sagittarius 3	12/12 to 12/21	Mars	expansion, enthusiasm
Capricorn 1	12/22 to 12/31	Mercury	achievement, honor
Capricorn 2	1/1 to 1/10	Saturn	responsibility, regulation
Capricorn 3	1/11 to 1/19	Venus	capitalization, administration
Aquarius 1	1/20 to 1/29	Venus	association, circulation
Aquarius 2	1/30 to 2/8	Uranus	diversification, knowledge
Aquarius 3	2/9 to 2/18	Mercury	unification, friendship
Pisces 1	2/19 to 2/29	Pluto	sacrifice, aid
Pisces 2	3/1 to 3/10	Neptune	permeation, contemplation
Pisces 3	3/11 to 3/20	Moon	review, solitude

try to interpret health matters in a chart; even the experienced astrologer, unless he is also a medical doctor, should be most careful in this area.

ARIES/FIRST HOUSE/MARS: head and face, brain, eyes, ears, nose, sinuses, upper jaw, pituitary and pineal glands.

TAURUS/SECOND HOUSE/VENUS: lower jaw, tongue, uvula, tonsils, throat and neck, pharnyx, epiglottis, larynx, trachea, Eustachian tube, thyroid and parathyroid glands.

GEMINI/THIRD HOUSE/MERCURY: lower respiratory system (bronchi, lungs), collarbone, shoulders, arms, hands, upper ribs, nerves.

CANCER/FOURTH HOUSE/MOON: breasts, mammary glands, armpits, upper abdominal cavity, esophagus, stomach, pancreas, uterus.

LEO/FIFTH HOUSE/SUN: heart and aorta, back, spinal cord and column, thymus.

VIRGO/SIXTH HOUSE/MERCURY: upper intestines (duodenum, jejunum, ileum), spleen.

LIBRA/SEVENTH HOUSE/VENUS: lower abdominal cavity, lumbar area, lower ribs, kidneys, ureters, adrenal glands, ovaries, oviducts.

SCORPIO/EIGHTH HOUSE/PLUTO: lower intestines (colon), rectum, anus, sacral and pubic areas, buttocks, bladder, urethra, scrotum, testes, vas deferens, penis, prostate gland, vagina, vulva, appendix, sweat glands.

SAGITTARIUS/NINTH HOUSE/JUPITER: thighs, hips, liver, gall bladder.

CAPRICORN/TENTH HOUSE/SATURN: knees, joints, ligaments and bones in general, teeth, body hair, epidermal tissue.

AQUARIUS/ELEVENTH HOUSE/URANUS: lower legs (calves, ankles), circulation of blood.

PISCES/TWELFTH HOUSE/NEPTUNE: feet and toes, lymphatic system, fatty tissues.

Spiritual Symbolism and Astrology

Astrology lends itself well to religious concepts and metaphysical speculation. To illustrate: even at a glance, the biblical ideas regarding death and afterlife can be studied zodiacally. A person dies (Scorpio), is judged (Sagittarius) by the Almighty Father (Capricorn), and then his spirit goes either to heaven (Aquarius) or to hell (Pisces). Uranian angels or Neptunian demons are to be one's new companions. The signs between Aries and Libra would, in this context, represent the life of the individual, his basic physical and emotional needs, relationships, and experiences (karma). This could be equated to the houses as well as the signs. The first house would symbolize the birth or rebirth into a new incarnation and it would represent the most salient features and drives (persona, mask) brought over from a previous life. Houses two through seven would be the life itself. The eighth house, in addition to symbolizing death, could be associated with funereal preparations; the ninth house with the spiritual death ceremonies; the tenth with the burial or final resting place; the eleventh with the "resurrection" of the soul and spirit (etheric and astral elements), and the twelfth house with the after-death plane and universal womb from which one is born into a new incarnation (first house). I am not saying that I believe that this is what actually happens; it just seems interesting to think of these timeless concepts and metaphysical beliefs in terms of the zodiacal sequence.

Certain associations can be made between the zodiacal elements and spiritual symbolism. The fire signs correspond with celebration, joy, release, light, illumination, expression of spirit, glory, inspiration, purification, evangelism, and salvation. Keywords for the earth signs are devotion, confirmation, divine law, altar, and service. The air signs seem to correspond to communion, contemplation, transcendence, sacred knowledge, revelation, congregation, apotheosis, and priesthood. The three water signs could be associated with the sacrament, sacrifice, mysticism, compassion, initiation, baptism, libation, meditation, and solitude. Keywords for the twelve individual signs as they might relate to spiritual practices and settings are given below.

SAGITTARIUS: primary experience in the temple; the reason for being there.

CAPRICORN: ceiling, roof, and tower of the temple.

AQUARIUS: the gathering or congregation; spiritual brotherhood.

PISCES: initiation into divine mysteries; study, meditation, and solitude; awareness of unity.

ARIES: key and door or entrance to the temple; lighting therein.

TAURUS: foundation and steps leading up to the temple; outdoor setting; incense and botanical furnishings.

GEMINI: music, dance, and chanting.

CANCER: covering on temple's floor; fountain or pool; the sacrament.

LEO: the spirit of celebration.

VIRGO: the altar; articles of ceremony and essential furnishings in the temple.

LIBRA: form and procedure of ceremonies; walls and decor of the temple.

SCORPIO: sacrifices and offerings; arcane rituals.

Astrology as a Spiritual Art

Many phenomena of an occult or metaphysical nature cannot be "proven" in the terms of quantitative science. To a large degree, this is true of astrology wherever it touches upon these phenomena. The experienced astrologer recognizes certain patterns and cycles which correspond to changes in a person's life, and he realizes the value of astrology in helping to tie the parapsychological to the more observable occurrences of existence. It seems to me that no philosophical system or school of psychology is very penetrating if it does not have an understanding of astrological symbols and concepts somewhere near its roots. The zodiacal archetypes embrace all modes of human experience. The planets and their aspects give specific information about desires, hopes, and changes which are apt to occur. As a spiritual art—perhaps one could say spiritual science as well—astrology helps to determine what type of karma an individual has to work out. Of course, the horoscope does not tell at what *level* of spiritual development a person finds himself in the present life any more than a topographical map tells about the life processes and past history of a forest indicated on its two di-

Fig. 20.   Design inspired by an Indian Zodiac.

mensional surface. What is important is the involvement of the astrologer as a metaphysical translator at the moment of the reading. For example, in talking with a client he can determine how a prominent Jupiter will manifest. That planet could indicate intellectual wisdom in one chart, enthusiasm for horses in another; or an athletic interest in yet another, among many such possibilities or all three manifestations could be present. Each planetary position represents several facets of experience.

The astrologer can see those patterns in the chart which are inherently frictional or nonfrictional, but unless he is also very psychic, he will find it difficult to know in advance just how those energies will manifest. It is for this reason that most professional astrologers act as counselors who prefer to see their clients in person, while deploring the pseudo-specific, computerized interpretations so readily available to a gullible or uninformed public. One person with the Sun squaring Mars might be a bully, and another with the identical aspect might be a courageous and vigorous leader. Frictional aspects in the charts of highly developed people denote great ability: they need the ninety degree building block denoted by the square aspect because they have to accomplish a great deal in a short time. For those still struggling through the maze of complex desires created by the ego these same aspects can be very frustrating or painful, but this happens because they do not understand who or where they are in time. If squares, oppositions, and quincunxes dominate, the inherently favorable sextiles and trines will go unused. The egotistical person believes he can master, control, or cheat time, whereas the aware person flows with the changes of nature. He realizes that what is called "free will" actually arises from understanding and accommodation of these natural cycles and changes. Life may not be easy, even for him, but when he sees the hurricane approaching he seeks its calm center, travels along with it, and waits for the tempest to blow itself out. Where one lives with a spirit of honesty and innocence (by that I mean perfect and fearless openness to change) he probably does not need to worry about the patterns of astrology. However, such sagacious people are rare, and even they use astrology to teach others about the path to spontaneous free decision. The influences of the Sun, Moon, and planets are basic to all living beings in this solar system.

Astrology and Arcane Science

Most people unfamiliar with astrology immediately associate it with occultism and various mysterious practices. There is some validity in doing this, but for the most part astrology stands apart as a unique art and science which deals with definite and observable relationships. In discussing arcane things a materialistically oriented scientist is apt to quickly dismiss them as superstition. The majority of scientists who do not accept astrology have never studied the subject in depth, if at all. Superstition is a basically irrational expression of the ego's fear of being overpowered by "evil" (unconscious) forces which it does not understand. Oddly enough, modern science is to some extent an outgrowth of the ego's need to infuse conceptual meaning into these same hidden forces: it is felt that reason conquers all; yet the old doubts still linger and nag at the threshold of the subconscious of even the most empirical scientist. The more enlightened person, whether he is a scientist or not, neither fears nor tries to control these forces; instead, he seeks to use them in some creative and constructive manner. The great artist, mystic, teacher, psychologist, astrologer, healer, and musician alike use or channel these subtle energies for meaningful purposes. They have learned that there is much more than has been spoken or dreamed of in philosophy or science, although they may not be able to empirically prove many of the facets of their experience in scientific terms.

A number of people associate astrology with divination. To divine is to find out something by means of a deep intuition. The diviner is apparently able to communicate with or translate that which arises from a supernormal intelligence. Thus, some individuals are mediums or oracles for cosmic energies through whom others may obtain arcane information regarding their life. Until very recently, especially since the eighteenth century, science has pushed the diviners aside, claiming that only it is qualified to play the role of soothsayer. (To sooth means to show the hidden truth of something, to prove, or to confirm.) A soothsayer predicts the future. Modern science has the marvels of the greatly expanded technical sciences to help it in forecasting trends in the future. The electronic computer is a fabulous invention. The old soothsayer, lacking this equipment and science, relied mainly on his intuition, the signals from Nature, and his knowledge of solar system cycles and patterns as revealed in astrology. Today there seems to be a new interest within the scientific community in astrology, parapsychology, the I Ching, and other facets, of occult knowledge and wisdom. The Aquarian age ideal touches upon the idea that all types of knowledge can and should meet in a spirit of receptivity and flexible objectivity. Not everything which is occult or mysterious will qualify for objective study; there is still a strong current of superstition and

Fig. 21. Solar disk with astrological script: "astrology."

misunderstanding (as well as fantasy and wishful thinking) in the area of occult science. Astrology seems to offer a middle path upon which one can travel, with a certain amount of scientific interest (not so much that it smothers receptivity), in order to arrive at a better understanding of the cosmic forces that pervade the universe. What we can perceive with our senses and intellect is probably very far from the total of what there is to be perceived.

Music, Art, and Astrology

The ancients incorporated music, drama, art, and religious ceremony into their tribal celebrations. Primitive people (those living close to the soil) also do this. Astrology probably played an important part in this synthesis of the spiritually creative aspects of human nature, even if only through the observation of solar and lunar cycles. Many astrologers have found the spiritual-aesthetic side of astrology to be very rewarding. Music and solar system bodies were of great interest to Pythagoras, and in China, as elsewhere, music was regarded as something sacred in itself, a universal factor at the root of spiritual enthusiasm. Perhaps the future will see the reunion of music with astrology, possibly through sacred chants for the signs, dance, and compositions written by those skilled in the zodiacal arts. It is not inconceivable that in the nearer future, probably even now, great artists and spiritual teachers would appear to herald in the new age, using astrology as their main means of integrating the various arts and sciences with well-established spiritual disciplines. In the last age, that of Pisces, the rites and practices were essentially and necessarily hidden from the public as a whole; but in the Aquarian age reincarnated sages and artists (the *bodhisattvas* or *avatars* spoken of in India) might be expected to share their ancient knowledge and crafts with others, and thus many people would be exposed to new or higher levels of perception and experience. Religion for them would no longer be so much a church-oriented institution as it would be an experience joyfully and openly shared with friends.

The universal quality of art and music seems to be very close to the center of the zodiacal wheel. Through sacred music people of all signs are united, the zodiacal spokes fall away momentarily, and one can perceive that at the center all people are expressions of a Universal Self. It may seem dogmatic to say so, but I feel that the best astrologers are those who have a deep love or ability for music and dance. There is little else in life that can transcend simple categories, save the basic rhythms of music. The flute and drum are heard everywhere and through all time people have danced with the Sun, Moon, and planets.

It is very difficult to generalize about which astrological factors denote musical ability or the capacity for its appreciation. There is a difference between the performer and the artist. For some people music is entertainment, while for others it is a sublime experience. And there seems to be no limit to the kinds of music that can be heard. Some can create their own tunes, others can play only the tunes of others. Also, there are often striking differences between a composer, conductor, instrumentalist, singer, and dancer. The subject seems to be too vast and complex to justify any kind of astrological classification in the present work.

Identification of specific artistic ability in terms of astrology is also difficult because there are many different tools, techniques, materials, skills, and values (personal and cultural) that go into a work of art. Literature (another universal?) is similarly impossible to pin down to any particular astrological factor, although poetry seems to be influenced by Neptune. Drama involves other art forms as well as literature, so it is also difficult to identify in specific, regularly recurring patterns. One might be able to generalize in saying that fire signs incline to dramatic or colorful artistic expressions; the earth signs might be solidly associated with the more practical crafts and arts; water signs affect those creations where imagination touches upon pathos and other emotions; and air signs incline to art forms where intellectual design and order prevail, or where illustration and graphic portrayal are needed. Any artist or musician will be influenced by all of the planets and signs in his horoscope, regardless of any separate generalizations about a particular factor. The Sun, Moon, and rising sign will probably be most prominent in their overall effect.

Color Symbolism and Astrology

Traditionally astrology has been associated with the study of color symbolism, the various signs and planets being made to correspond to the colors of the spectrum. These associations may be more important than they appear. Color derives from the perception of light waves that emanate from the Sun along with other electromagnetic waves. These light waves constitute only a very small portion of this solar energy, which ranges from gamma rays to radio, or electric waves. There may still be undiscovered dimensions or effects related to this energy. Because color is an objective phenomenon subjectively experienced the astrologer can only suggest what colors he thinks go best with each astrological factor. Most astrologers would agree that red, the most advancing of colors, is related to Mars and Aries; gold to Leo; silver and grey to the Moon; light blues with the air signs, brown tones with the earth signs; Saturn with black; and turquoise with Libra or Venus. There is considerable disagreement among astrologers about which colors correspond to the signs. Listed below are classifications that seem valid to me.

PLANETARY COLORS

SUN: white, bright yellow, yellowish orange, gold, the rainbow.

MOON: grey, bluish grey, silver.

MARS: red, pink.

MERCURY: blue, indigo, azure, violet blue.

VENUS: bluish green, turquoise, light blue.

JUPITER: purple, magenta, violet.

SATURN: black, dark brown.

URANUS: emerald green, bright green, mixed colors, scintillating hues.

PLUTO AND NEPTUNE: see Scorpio and Pisces.

GENERAL COLORS FOR THE SIGNS AND HOUSES

ARIES/FIRST HOUSE: red, pink, rose salmon, garnet, bright warm colors.

TAURUS/SECOND HOUSE: reddish brown, cinnamon, copper brown, golden brown, tan, fresh earthen shades, beige, cream.

GEMINI/THIRD HOUSE: medium and dark blue, indigo, royal blue, azure.

CANCER/FOURTH HOUSE: shades of grey, silver, opalescent watery hues, bluish grey.

LEO/FIFTH HOUSE: yellows and golds, orange, rainbow shades and hues.

VIRGO/SIXTH HOUSE: white, off-white, pearl, ivory, lilac, lavender, violet.

LIBRA/SEVENTH HOUSE: bluish greens, turquoise, aquamarine, light blue, pale green, pastels.

SCORPIO/EIGHTH HOUSE: deep reddish orange, strong contrasting hues, especially with black. Also use for Pluto.

SAGITTARIUS/NINTH HOUSE: purple, amethyst, wine, magenta.

CAPRICORN/TENTH HOUSE: deep earthen shades, darker browns, solid hues, black.

AQUARIUS/ELEVENTH HOUSE: shades of green, mixed colors, electric shades, combinations of blues and greens.

PISCES/TWELFTH HOUSE: amorphous shades, olive, sage, chartreuse, somber yellows. Also use for Neptune.

Note: grey, black, and white can be used for contrast with any color.

Color preference is probably described for the most part by the ascendant, Sun, and Moon, with the other planets acting as significant modifiers through their aspects to the luminaries. According to the system of classification given above, Mars in Aries in the seventh house would relate well to some combination of red (Aries, Mars) and light blue (seventh house). Moon in Sagittarius in the fifth house might relate to some combination of grey (Moon), magenta (Sagittarius), and gold (fifth house), with white or black added if desired for emphasis. Precedence should be given to a sign a planet occupies and then its location by house. In all cases white, grey, and black can be used as needed. Shown below are certain things which are associated with each planet. This list can be used as a general guideline for making various articles or applying color in some way that reflects the planetary positions in the natal horoscope. For example, if a pennon or banner is being made, the position of Jupiter in the chart would be noted. If it was in Taurus in the seventh house one might use some combination of purple or magenta (Jupiter), cream (Taurus), and turquoise (seventh house). If one wanted to make a meditation rug, the position of Neptune would be noted. Imagine that Neptune is in Virgo in the second house; one could then choose some combination of olive (Neptune), off-white (Virgo), and copper brown (second house). Black might be added for general contrast. In these examples the classification for the planets and the general classification, just above, were used.

GENERAL COLOR GUIDELINES

SUN: birthday or Sun sign color (e.g., red for Aries); color of court-ship; the color of individuality and the when-in-doubt color; used in coat of arms and other emblems; best if combined in some way with the color for the ascendant.

MOON: colors related to the family or clan; objects related to dining and the home in general; planets in Cancer or in the fourth house may modify the lunar color.

MARS AND ASCENDANT: things that have to do with the head, such as hats, veils, jewelry, and cosmetical art; things that relate to the outer personality and appearance in general. The position of the ruler of the first house cusp should also be taken into consideration.

MERCURY: small but significant articles such as rings and bracelets; colors of communication and general mental posture; vests; shoulder wraps; small or simple vehicles.

VENUS: formal attire; dance outfits; necklaces; ties; belts; sashes; bags; purses; settings for face-to-face contacts; objects related to love. The descendant might also be considered as a modifier of Venusian aesthetic applications.

JUPITER: pennants, banners, devotional clothing ("Sunday best"); ceremonial and diplomatic attire or settings; riding outfits and articles; hunter's colors (e.g., for arrows); garters; large or ceremonial vehicles.

SATURN: uniforms; mature or somber articles; suits; walking sticks; timepieces; trademarks. The sign at the midheaven should also be considered.

URANUS: ankle jewelry; clothing or things that have to do with friendship; special occasion outfits such as club uniforms.

NEPTUNE: colors related to places of rest, solitude, or contemplation; color of pilgrimage; rugs; socks and shoes; cloaks; subtle usages.

PLUTO: funereal colors; those appropriate for arcane ceremonies or rites; planned psychedelic experiences.

Gemstones and the Zodiac

In the Middle Ages, during the time of the alchemists, there was considerable interest in associating certain gemstones with the signs of the Zodiac. In time this led to the idea of "birthstones." The birthstones defined by the modern jewelry industry often do not agree with those used by astrologers and arcane scientists. Astrologers themselves are not in agreement about which signs correspond with which stones. Color, rather than chemical composition or hardness, might be the best criterion when selecting a stone. In addition, it is felt that certain gems have vibrations that affect the wearer in some subtle way. Gemstones have been worn everywhere as amulets or charms, as well as decorations denoting royal power, wealth, and ecclesiastical pomp. Availability and cost should be considered when selecting a gemstone; a few can even be created synthetically. There is no definite rule that one can follow in determining which stone goes best with each astrological factor. Personal preference and one's own intuition might be a better guide than anything an astrologer could recommend. What might be suggested is the importance of the rising sign, Sun, and Moon, and perhaps Mercury, where rings or bracelets are involved. The stone associated with the Sun sign would probably reflect the most individual expression. The rising sign would be effective for overall use. Stones asociated with the Moon's sign may have some significance in an occult sense. Red stones might be found to relate to Aries or Mars; light blue, turquoise, or light green to Libra; yellow to Leo; and so forth with each sign. Several planets, including Sun or Moon, in one sign would be an indication that the stones associated with that sign are worthy of consideration. The following classification of gemstones for the signs is a reflection of my own feelings about which correspondences are most suitable. They are based mainly on ideas about color, aesthetic value, and the personal experience of having been an amateur collector of stones since early childhood.

ARIES: ruby; red gems of garnet, zircon, spinel, and tourmaline; rose and pink gems of topaz, zoisite (thulite), tourmaline (rubellite), and beryl (morganite).

TAURUS: onyx; sardonyx; marble; brown gems of sphene, zircon, garnet, and idocrase; tumbled pebbles.

GEMINI: lapis lazuli; benitoite; blue gems of tourmaline, zoisite, spinel, diamond, zircon, dumortierite, kyanite, and sodalite.

CANCER: agate; chalcedony; flint; chert; beach stones; opal; pearl; coral; moonstone; abalone.

LEO: golden topaz; orange zircon (hyacinth); citrine; tiger's eye; sunstone; yellow or golden gems of tourmaline, sphene, zircon, sapphire, and beryl (heliodor); colorless gems of tourmaline, diamond, topaz, zircon, rock crystal, danburite, and phenakite.

VIRGO: lavender stones; lilac kunzite; pale amethyst; fluorite; apatite; subtle combinations of various stones.

LIBRA: jade; turquoise; aquamarine; peridot; epidote; sillimanite; hiddenite; green sphene; chrysoprase; prase; chrysocolla; diopside; light blue or green topaz.

SCORPIO: carnelian; sard; bloodstone; obsidian; smoky quartz; sag' nite (rutilated or tourmalated quartz).

SAGITTARIUS: almandite garnet; amethyst; purple spinel; purple kunzite; blue (star) sapphire; violet dumortierite; iolite; blue-john fluorite.

CAPRICORN: jasper; petrified wood; jet; staurolite; galena crystal; black gems of tourmaline, rutile, and garnet; bone.

AQUARIUS: emerald; malachite; amazonite; dioptase; variscite; labradorite; californite; green garnet (demantoid); green gems of tourmaline and aventurine; conglomerate.

PISCES: bi-colored tourmaline; cat's-eye (chrysoberyl); andalusite; alexanderite.

Astrology and Occupation

Some astrologers specialize in counseling people in the area of employment. The earth signs and their corresponding houses are an index as to the means of livelihood, depending upon which planets occur therein, or which signs appear on the cusps of the second, sixth, and tenth houses. The rising sign and the signs which the Sun and Moon occupy are also strong indicators of conditions surrounding work or career. The second house describes the basic means and tools of livelihood, the sixth shows what additional crafts and skills are acquired on the job, and the tenth house has to do with one's calling or career. Planets in Taurus, Virgo, and Capricorn should be carefully noted because they will have something to say about how one makes a living. The tenth house is more of a professional area, whereas the sixth house is where one works for someone else or undergoes a period of apprenticeship. The sixth house has to do with menial tasks. If a person is in business for himself the fifth house or planets in Leo are apt to be active. Material gain is also possible through the eighth house of "partnerships assets," wills, and legacies, and through the eleventh house of friends and colleagues. The second house remains as the best means of determining the individual's own earning capacity.

Usually, no single planet or sign alone describes the type of employment that an individual will pursue, and such variables as culture, educational background, health, age, and sex must also be considered in each instance. Every single factor, that is, every planetary aspect and position, will in some way affect the choice (some people have little or no choice) of occupation. This is an important part of astrological analysis because it deals with activities that normally comprise at least one third of the average person's daily existence. The general categories listed a little further on should not be taken too literally. Not all journalists, for instance, will be born with the Sun in Gemini, but one could be almost certain to find some prominent planet or other factor involving Gemini, the third house, or Mercury. Similarly, not every world explorer will be a Sagittarian, yet one could expect to find some important planet in Sagittarius or in the ninth house, or Jupiter would be prominent in some way, either by position or through its planetary aspects. A fulltime housewife in today's modern society would usually have some strong emphasis through the Moon, the fourth house, or Cancer. A careerwoman would be better described by Saturn, Capricorn, and the tenth house (to a lesser degree, also by Virgo and the sixth house). Pisces, Neptune, and the twelfth house can sometimes indicate one who is not working in the usual sense for one reason or another; or these factors might signify work which is more behind the scenes.

Aries lends itself to some work where strength or leadership is needed; Taurus gives a sense of practicality and craftsmanship; Gemini denotes adaptability and speed; Cancer stores things or gathers them together; Leo enjoys directing, speculating, and creating something; Virgo increases one's sense of efficiency; Libra establishes powers of mediation and exchange; Scorpio penetrates and reveals hidden values and qualities; Sagittarius is effective in selling things and in dealing with foreign matters; Capricorn denotes management and the ability to capitalize on things; Aquarius shows the influence of sociability and friendship in one's line of work; and Pisces deals in hidden assets of all types. The rising sign modifies the kind of work one does, especially in the sense that it represents the effect of the outer personality upon one's immediate environment. The sixth house is apt to show how we work; it is also the method of operation and the setting. The Sun sign tells something about the purpose behind one's livelihood through the aspects it receives from other bodies in the horoscope. In looking at a chart the astrologer has to know something about the client's background, education, and conscious aims before he can counsel him in the area of employment. Without having first talked to the individual it is practically impossible (for most astrologers, at least those who deplore being called fortune tellers) to determine the level of his development, karmically speaking. The fruits of a strong tenth house can hardly be realized when a person, for one reason or another, is poorly prepared for a profession; yet, a person with less "positively" placed planets in the tenth house, might, due to his higher level of development (higher motivation and more experience in past lives) become successful in his chosen profession. Opportunity cannot be determined from looking at the horoscope alone. The astrologer must discuss these matters with the client in the capacity of vocational adviser.

What each person does in his hours of "occupation" is very important. The child plays, the monk meditates, the artist creates, the bus driver drives a bus, the actor acts, and the mother nurtures her family. What may be routine work for one may be something else to another. An Aquarian and a Taurean working in a bank are apt to see their customers, fellow employees, and the job itself in somewhat different terms. This does not even take into consideration the variables introduced by different rising signs, Moon positions, and planetary aspects. Similarly, two astrologers will have their own motives and unique abilities, and will interpret horoscopes within the limits of these abilities. Neptune in one chart may show one man a cobbler; in another it might be the signature of a winemaker or a burglar. What is meant by occupation is the main activity of the individual during waking hours aside from hobbies, social activities, or other duties. A retired person will be occupied mostly through the twelfth and fourth houses. The young person just making his or her way in the world is oriented toward the sixth and tenth houses.

A final point needs to be made: Pure zodiacal or planetary manifestations seldom, if ever, occur. In the geometry of astrology everything is colored to some degree by everything else. The planets operate in the horoscope much as the inner parts of a clock contribute to its overall function. All signs and planetary positions share in and are affected by a common center. Therefore, any kind of work will be described by a combination of astrological factors. To say that earth signs generally have to do with practical and business matters is true, or that the fire signs have the power of directness needed in salesmanship; but they affect each other and the other zodiacal elements (air and water signs) in such a way that any occupation is a mosaic of various zodiacal elements and planetary patterns. In the past, a man often (in some places, always) followed in the profession or craft of his father and male elders (Saturn) and a young woman learned the arts of the clan that affected the home and the rearing of children through her mother and her companions (Moon). Nowadays, any of a number of possible occupations are open to those living in the more technologically advanced (Uranian) part of the globe. New types of employment can be expected to develop in the future. At the same time, perhaps in a world of increasing leisure, some individuals will take up ancient arts, crafts, and skills.

SAMPLE OCCUPATIONS

ARIES/FIRST HOUSE/MARS: steel and iron industries, sheet metal work, metallurgy, tool and die making, machine tool operation, welding, munitions, gunsmithing, blacksmithing, fire prevention, law enforcement, logging, dentistry, optometry, combative athletics, prospecting, pioneering, barbering, beautician work, hat making (millinery), innovative jobs.

TAURUS/SECOND HOUSE/VENUS: finance, banking, purchasing, pawnbroking, business in general, economics, accounting, civil service, civil engineering, architecture, sculpting, basketweaving, woodworking crafts, lapidary, gardening, landscaping, natural and physical sciences in general, forestry, park range work, conservation, stonemasonry, bricklaying, surveying.

GEMINI/THIRD HOUSE/MERCURY: communications, television work, journalism and magazine work, printing, postal service, graphic arts, copywriting, bookbinding, drafting, cartography, receptionist work, secretarial work, typing, office equipment operation, stenography, writing in general, delivery service, personnel work, education, automobile industry, bicycle industry, local truck driving, taxi driving, school or city bus driving, library work, linguistics, manicuring.

CANCER/FOURTH HOUSE/MOON: food production (also distribution and preparation), home economics, services catering to essential feminine and domestic needs, hotel work, laundry work, shipping and receiving, storage, contracting and general construction (plastering, carpentry, painting, etc.), real estate, water utilities work, work in spas, catering services, adoption agencies, dam building, auctioneering.

LEO/FIFTH HOUSE/SUN(?): private enterprises, creative professions in general, executive and directing positions, royal functions, entertainment industry, film industry, drama, cartooning, work related to children, game making, toy manufacturing and sales, petshop work, jewelry, goldsmithing, cosmetology, fashion, modeling.

VIRGO/SIXTH HOUSE/MERCURY: business to some extent, vocational counseling, health and medicine (general), hygiene, herbology, acupuncture, chiropractic, public inspection (e.g., health), veterinary medicine, animal husbandry, agriculture, enlisted military service, serving positions (butler, maid, waitress, etc.), practical handicrafts, labor (unions), instruction (how-to-do-it), custodial work, cleaning occupations, detailed clerical work, menial work in general.

LIBRA/SEVENTH HOUSE/VENUS: fine arts, music, dance, interior decoration, display and advertising, florist work, calligraphy, public arbitration, diplomacy, public relations, marriage related industries, psychological counseling, work with weights and measures, lobbying.

SCORPIO/EIGHTH HOUSE/PLUTO: surgical medicine, X-ray technology, sexology, mortuary science, pharmacology, biological science, chemistry, scientific research, statistics, nuclear science, plumbing, air conditioning, refrigeration, sewage and disposal work, demolition, slaughtering, mining, parapsychology, occultism, marketing research, stock market work, insurance, taxation, investment.

SAGITTARIUS/NINTH HOUSE/JUPITER: travel industry, over-the-road trucking, inter-city bus driving, heavy equipment operation, navigation, astronautics, racing, exploration, hunting and trapping, athletics (team sports), cow wrangling, teaching and education, publishing, literature in general, astrology, religion and philosophy, humanities, astronomy, geography, translation, editing, traveling sales, gambling industry, adventurous professions.

CAPRICORN/TENTH HOUSE/SATURN: administrative and managerial positions, government work, urban planning, services catering to basically masculine needs, clock making and repair, elevator construction and maintenance, business in general, positions of honor and responsibility, paleontology, archaeology, gravestone manufacture.

AQUARIUS/ELEVENTH HOUSE/URANUS: electronics and electrical professions, computer technology, railroad work, aviation, electroplating, invention, legislative politics, cultural anthropology, group and encounter psychology, sociology, avant-garde professions, humanitarian work, work related to organizations and special interest groups.

PISCES/TWELFTH HOUSE/NEPTUNE: welfare work, charity, rehabilitation, criminology, prison work, detection, orphanage work, celibate professions (nun, monk, priest), hospital work, fishing, longshore work, maritime industry in general, oceanography, zoo work, circus and carnival work, petroleum industry, perfume industry, liquor and wine industry, cobbling, spiritual healing, locksmithing, photography, museum work, criminal pursuits, begging.

Chapter VII

Astrology and Human Relationships

Astrological analysis is concerned with personal relationships in all phases of experience, particularly those having to do with love and the rearing of children. This chapter discusses the role of astrology in determining compatibility between individuals.

In the early part of the Aquarian age in the Western world there seem to be five basic amorous relationships among men and women. The first is that of being single and "playing the field," a romantic involvement in which the Sun, Mars, and Jupiter are emphasized. The second kind of relationship is one where two people are living together without any formal or legal commitments. This noncontractual cohabitation is a lunar type of relationship augmented by the normal Venus/Mars attractions. It tends to be semipermanent. The third kind of relationship is that in which the alliance is formal, ritualized, and legally binding. This contractual alliance is the traditional marriage and it is characterized by the Moon/Venus/Mars attractions, with the addition of a Saturn influence, denoting loyalty and responsibility. The fourth type of relationship is rarer, and it might be termed "quadra-cohabitative" because it has to do with sexual union and cohabitation between two couples; another version of this type is "wife and husband swapping." The alliance between four people is essentially a Moon/Venus relationship, with the Martian sexual drives being affected by associative-experimental Uranian influences (in effect, this is a union of close friends). The fifth type is the communal group which consists of several couples loosely united. Uranian and Neptunian urges dominate the other urges to some degree in this last kind of involvement. All of these types may overlap each other to some extent, and there may be a bisexual theme in the latter two cases. Not included in this brief discussion are the polygamous and polyandrous relationships found in some primitive societies, which for the most part are disappearing. Also not included are homosexual alliances or triangular relationships.

As man continues to enter the Aquarian age he will experiment with new life styles that express new values and roles. This does not mean that a reasonable person would promiscuously investigate all possibilities. Only relationships based upon mutually satisfactory goals, aims, intimate affection, and spiritual love are apt to endure for any length of time. Altruistic alliances which have a practical basis and a great deal of freedom will be the most successful. Divorce rates prove that not everyone fits well into the third category, that of traditional marriage, but something like it will probably continue to be the main type of alliance between the sexes for some time to come. Hopefully, in the future, marriage will be a freer, more open relationship. Many new ideas in this important area can be expected to originate from astrology and related fields. The ideas discussed in this chapter are geared mainly to marriage or to the relationship where a couple lives together on a long range basis. However, the conclusions made could be applied, with some variation, to the other types of relationships. Regarding homosexuality: one should not underestimate its effect as a major current in the sea of human sexual drives. Even though one cannot equate it to heterosexuality, where children are reproduced, there are millions of quite sane and worthwhile people who prefer the affection and company of their own sex. Besides this, anyone who has studied the sexes is well aware of the fact that there are masculine women and feminine men and everything in between. This kind of preponderance by gender can be determined by looking for an emphasis of planets in either yin or yang signs.

The rising sign might denote either a yin or a yang outer personality at the same time that the positions of the Sun, Moon, Mars, and Venus represent just the opposite. This high degree of horoscopic variability accounts for many kinds of sexual makeup, and for this reason it is extremely difficult to analyze a person's sexual motivation in astrological terms. One, unfortunately, has to rely on the concepts of psychology and such terms as onanism, heterosexuality, homosexuality, bisexuality, and so on. So much is lost in the way of understanding when we overuse or misuse such terms and categories, although they may be correct up to a point. There seem to be as many exceptions as there are rules and standards in defining sexual roles and experiences. Nevertheless, certain patterns are observable astrologically, such as the tendency for a person to marry the astrological counterpart of his or her parent. One can note that in many cases, just considering the Sun, Moon, Mars, Venus, and the ascending sign, that a person will select a mate whose horoscope has one or more of these factors reflecting similar positions in the parent's chart. In one example, the wife's father had Sun in Gemini, and Venus and Saturn in Cancer; her husband's chart had identical positions. His mother had Sun in Aries and Libra rising; the wife had Mars in Aries and Venus in Libra. That is not to say that in such cases as these that the mate is a close double for the individual's parent; what is shown is the tendency for there to be an attraction on the basis of similar planetary placements.

Even in the choice of friends and close comrades we select people whose horoscopes in some way reflect those of our parents and siblings. This attraction is natural and to a large extent unconscious. Certain zodiacal vibrations constantly attract and repel each person. Any skeptic of astrology would soon find very convincing patterns that occur again and again, and every experienced astrologer can relate what may seem to be fantastic stories about the "coincidence" of attractions between individuals. It is in these attractions that one can sometimes catch a glimpse of the laws of karma. There are hidden forces at work which draw people together, as well as pull them apart. Astrology helps one to perceive what these forces are and how they can be dealt with.

The Signs and Love

Popular books on astrology and love sometimes go into great detail about the love life of each sign. Although they often disagree, most astrologers feel that signs of the same element are compatible. This will be explained later on. All of the signs play a part in one's love life, some in a way more obvious than others. Leo (and the fifth house) is the sign of courtship and love that emanates from the heart. Virgo (sixth house) is the sign of betrothal and grooming,[1] Libra (seventh house) is the sign of marriage and consummation, and Scorpio (eighth house) is the sign of sexual release and conception. Aries, Taurus,

---

[1] Virgo could also be identified with that aspect of affection which in lower primates is called *grooming*. The practical result is that it rids the individual of vermin while serving as a means of demonstrative affection. Human beings who live in antiseptic environments have lost much of this kind of mutual physical contact. Petting, massage, and bundling might also be identified with Virgo and the sixth horoscopic house; that is, all essentially sexual physical contact this side of coitus.

Gemini, and Cancer, and their corresponding houses, have to do with the early values and experiences through which the individual learns about love and defines in his own mind what he seeks and can give to a mate or lover. Sagittarius, Capricorn, Aquarius, and Pisces represent the more objective and idealized forms of love, what might be called spiritual or platonic love. They also affect the formation of attitudes about sex, love, and the responsibilities of friendship and union with others. Sagittarius, for example, has much to do with the sweeping romance of the teen years. Capricorn values loyalty in the period between the midthirties and the early forties.

The sign rising affects a person's initial sexual drives, along with Mars and any planets that happen to be in the first house. The strongest needs of the heart (deeper sense of self) are met through the Sun's position in the horoscope. The Moon acts as a sensuous emotional modifier. Venus shows what we are attracted to in a mate by its sign and house position. The twelve signs, the houses of the horoscope, and the four bodies already mentioned can combine in a large number of possible ways; and this is not even figuring the positions and aspects of the remaining six planets. For this reason, all generalizations about compatibility and individual sexual makeup have to be modified by a careful analysis of the unique patterns in each horoscope.

The Planets and Love

Even though the Sun sign expresses the needs of our deeper self, it is often the rising sign or position of Mars that describes the more obvious or conscious features of our sexual feelings and physical drives. The position of Mars is strongly modified by aspects it receives from other bodies in the chart. It represents sexual drives as they form a part of the individual's sense of identity and self-actualization; as such, it is a significator of strong likes and dislikes operating within the process of physical attraction. In fire signs (Aries, Leo, and Sagittarius) Mars tends to be bold and initiating, even romantically inclined; in earth signs (Taurus, Virgo, and Capricorn) the process of attraction is more deliberate and cautious, there being a tendency to evaluate one's drives or to control them in some way; in air signs (Gemini, Libra, and Aquarius) Mars is stimulated through the intellect and through a sense of communication, and it may have to reason or rationalize its attractions; the water sign Mars (Cancer, Scorpio, and Pisces) inclines to physical drives that are affected by emotions and feelings of empathy. Mars might be most effective when it is in the sign of the same element following one's Sun sign; for example, that would be Taurus for a person born when the Sun was in Capricorn.

The sign, house position, and aspects of Venus best describe the mate or person to whom one is attracted, this attraction being to some extent unconscious. Venus represents the drives of the partner just as Mars describes the individual's own conscious sexual drives and demonstrativeness. As the principle of cooperation Venus illustrates the manner and extent of one's ability to find harmony, especially with the opposite sex. What one desires through Mars and actually obtains through Venus are seldom the same thing. Venus will usually be in one of three signs—the sign the Sun is in, the sign preceding the Sun sign, and the sign just following the Sun sign. It is an interesting point that the planet which symbolizes the partner is closer to the Sun than the planet which symbolizes one's own conscious sexual drives. In the middle of this is the lunar force, just as Cancer is placed in between Aries and Libra. The limits of love on a practical scale are defined by Saturn, and Saturn-ruled Capricorn lies at the midpoint between Libra and Aries in the other hemisphere. That leaves only Mercury and Jupiter, not counting the outer planets or the Sun, to act as modifiers of both the small and great things that go into the making of an effective partnership.

Jupiter tends to idealize love and to create romantic enthusiasm. An exaggeration of this would be seen in the tendency to worship the lover by putting him or her on a pedestal: Don Quixote rides in this direction. Jupiter can also describe a more spiritual or intellectual form of love. In a general sense, it expands whatever it comes in contact with; in contrast, Saturn has a subduing effect. Jupiter's effect in one's love life may be more important than has been previously supposed. There may be a sense of excitement and adventure associated with this planet, especially during the period of adolescence (fourteenth to twenty-first years). Its transits through the Zodiac and the aspects it forms to the natal planets have a strong effect on a person's love life. In this context it is fruitful to study the transits of Mars at the same time one calculates those for Jupiter, for together they establish a rhythm that the transits of the other bodies readily respond to and modify.

Mercury has mostly a mental influence in matters of the heart, which in some cases is an important factor in overall compatibility. This small planet, so close to the Sun (self), relates to siblings. Almost everyone has learned basic things about sex and demonstrations of affection from a brother or sister. Mercury also describes contacts with playmates, classmates, and other acquaintances of one's childhood (and later as well), and from these associations additional ideas about sex are acquired. Early experiments and the innocent pleasures of childhood make up part of what Mercury teaches. Later on a person takes these concepts and experiences into his marriage. In some cases, in many perhaps, what has been acquired are misconceptions about love. There also may be some degree of incestual desire (a perfectly normal early attraction) that for one reason or another has been distorted, suppressed, or which causes guilt. The spouse cannot act as a valve for such attractions, hence one seeks an affair outside his or her regular relationship. Many such attractions can be traced astrologically back to a brother or sister with whom one shared an early (usually pleasurable) experience in the course of their education about love. Mercury shows the mental imprint of intense early sexual experiences, usually amounting to something less than sexual intercourse, with a sibling, playmate, cousin, classmate, or some other person in the neighborhood where one grows up. A weak Mercury contributes to fickleness. A strong Mercury demonstrates the importance of communication as a basic factor in partnerships of love.

Saturn's effect in matters of the heart is shown mainly through its aspects to Mars and Venus and by its position, should it occur, in the signs and houses related to love. Its influence is paternal and somewhat demanding. Negatively, it manifests as inhibitions, delays, obstacles, impotency, misanthropy, frigidity, and excessive caution. There may be a rather severe influence of parents, laws, or codes on the development of the individual's sexual attitudes and ideas about cooperation with the opposite sex. But Saturn can also be a steadying influence which has great value where loyalty and responsibility are emphasized. Saturn may tie the career to the marriage in some way, possibly through an aspect with Venus or through its placement in Libra or the seventh house. Sometimes it indicates a delayed marriage or involvement with an older person. With Saturn the attitudes of one's father (tradition) are apt to touch upon one's own ideas about duty and propriety in affairs of love.

The ascending sign is the persona or mask of outward appearance which has so much to do with the way others see us. It is an important factor in terms of attraction. However, the Moon is a more dynamic and significant factor because it shows how subconscious energies, sentiments, and feelings filter into consciousness, affecting the expectations of security one has with respect to a potential mate. The Moon also describes one's views about women, particularly one's mother, and it has to do with a number of things which strongly modify the love life. Among these are habits, protective instincts, moods, emotional attachments, domestic needs and desires, and one's kind and degree of empathy for the emotions of others. The Moon is the main means by which the solar energy denoted by one's Sun sign is reflected in the routines of daily life. In marriage it is important that there is not excessive conflict between these lunar rhythms and tides. A weak Moon signifies possessiveness and trouble with the emotions. A strong Moon can handle the emotional changes which always occur in partnerships. It is an important planetary body to study when comparing charts.

Pluto signifies those deeper biological sexual drives which are essentially unconscious and which have to do with reproduction. As such, it is that point in sexual union where the sperm and ovum are able to come together. Pluto is a small planet in comparison with the four planets preceding it in its orbit around the Sun—the seeds of life are small and obscure, and they are far removed from dictates of the conscious will as symbolized by the Sun and Mars. In its negative manifestation Pluto's effect can be identified by such terms as "compulsion" and "obsession"; it can intensify the sexual nature in ways which are destructively the opposite of the compelling drive for reproduction. Its position in one sign for a number of years affects the deeper instincts and sexual mores of an entire generation, and this is also true to some extent for Neptune, which stays about fourteen years in each sign. It is interesting to note that puberty comes to its full force about the fourteenth year. At that time the last corner of the veil of innocence is lifted from the face of the child and he is confronted with a sea of passionate feelings. Pluto's eccentric orb causes it to stay in one sign anywhere from eleven to thirty-three years, the average being twenty-one years. Neptune and Pluto together seem to affect the changing sexual attitudes from one generation to another in some way, although these two bodies have only begun to reveal their secrets to mankind.

Neptune's influence in sexual matters seems to be very subtle and often of a negative sort. One who is cut off from others, whether physically or psychologically, may show signs of a painful and negative onanism. Neptune may also contribute to secrecy, feelings of guilt, distortions of sexual feelings, unpleasant continence, seductive fetishes, and other confusing situations surrounding matters of love. On a higher level it is the planet of universal love and unity through which one can compassionately embrace all creatures. Mercury, Virgo, and the sixth house may have to do with voluntary continence, whereas Neptune, Pisces, and the twelfth house often show where one has to make a sacrifice of his passions for one reason or another. Obviously, a lack of sexual release through heterosexual union is denied those people who are confined in such places as prisons, asylums, hospitals, and monasteries. Masturbation becomes the main means of relieving sexual tension when one is isolated, unless, of course, a homosexual situation prevails.

Homosexuality seems to be best described by Uranus. In another sense, Uranus is the significator of altruistic love as it is expressed through humanitarian acts and associations. It is also the planet of friendship. Uranian love is inclined to be bizarre (by mass standards) and experimental. People living in communal environments are drinking from the cup of Uranus. Less developed people may experience estrangement from lovers and friends; they have a generally unstable love life which is subject to unexpected shocks and changes. Where Uranus is concerned, there is little room for the clinging, possessive kind of affection that characterizes many relationships. Instead, it celebrates that spirit of equality and sexual freedom (among other kinds) that is needed in every objective relationship. It stays in one sign for seven years and influences people born in that period through that particular sign.

No doubt the planetoids will some day have something important to add to the description of the forces that affect one's love life. Little things can be very important in an area where intense feelings prevail. They may be found to act like fuses that both ignite and prevent ignition. Much is yet to be learned about the intricate sexual forces which are at the root of our very existence.

The Influence of the Sun Sign

What our heart really desires in a mate and through our offspring is what is described by the Sun. Through courting those things which correspond to our deeper selfhood we experience the joy of self-extension. Often though, the combined magnetism of Mars, Venus, and the Moon, and the sober requirements of Saturn, overpower what the heart (Sun sign) desires, and one may be left feeling cheated. The Sun sign is the most important factor in the chart, but it seldom happens that it obtains the perfect self-expression, lover, and children, owing to its modifying aspects—the geometry of the will—and its house position. Any brief generalizations about the love life of the Sun signs can be shattered by the fact that the Venus, Mars, Moon, and Saturn positions, not to mention those of the other planets, in nearly every case modify the desires expressed through the Sun sign. There is also the strong influence of the rising sign (and therefore, descending sign) as well. Keeping these facts in mind, one might consider some of the following general statements about the needs of the twelve Sun signs:

Aries wants most of all to be admired by his lover or mate. Love is at its beginning an ardent need for self-realization through the loved one and through any children that come through the relationship. Some Aries people see love as conquest.

The Taurus person emphasizes the more practical things in a marriage and seeks comforts and rewards that are essentially constructive and helpful in increasing his own sense of productiveness.

Gemini desires communication and stimulating companionship. The individual looks for a companion who is more like a brother or sister to him, and who is at the same time adaptable. The search is for a "twin" or counterpart.

Cancer looks for security, nourishment, and empathy. It needs a person who can tolerate its moodiness and its tendency to collect and store things.

Leo people need someone with whom they can share their creative designs. Some Leo natives seek an audience in their partner, while others simply want a playmate. Children play an important part in the life of many people born with the Sun in this sign.

The Virgo person takes pride in a working relationship where order and common sense help the parties involved establish a smooth running partnership. Some Virgoans serve the aims of their partner.

Libra seeks mutual appreciation and an equal commitment. Tactful concern for the partner has to be tempered by respect for one's own aims and interests. Cooperation is not something Libra is born with; rather, it is the basic aim toward which the sign must direct its energies.

Scorpio people find gratification in sharing and mixing resources with the partner. At the same time they expect the mate to be able to accommodate any rather intense changes that may occur.

The sharing of an ideal or some enthusiastic idea is at the center of what many Sagittarians seek in a mate. There also may be a spirit of adventure and desire to travel. The partner should be able to accept the Archer's candidness and its sometimes impulsive gregariousness.

A steady person who can further his career or standing in the community is what the Capricorn individual desires. The partner has to be able to make his own way and be able to accept responsibility. For this sign, loyalty may be more important than passion.

Aquarius needs a partner who is as much a friend as a lover; it is disappointed when its partner turns out to be too insular or lacking in social adaptability. Some Aquarians are experimental in matters of love, and a good number of them place a value on intellectual rapport in relationships.

Pisces needs a loving supporter, a "soul brother or sister" who is able to tolerate its changing moods and its need for solitude or privacy. Emotions play a large part in the love life of Pisceans.

What has been said above for the Sun sign also applies to some extent to the rising sign, Moon sign, and, on occasion, the sign Mars occupies. The sign Venus is in tells more about the partner's basic nature than about one's own desires. It seems incorrect to associate Mars simply with men and Venus with women, although many astrologers continue to do so. In any horoscope Mars symbolizes one's own conscious sexual desires. The genital release is obtained through Pluto. Venus shows where, how, and with whom the union takes place.

Compatibility

If a person is seeking a face-to-face partner on the basis of broad intellectual growth and exchange of ideas he might do well to choose one whose sign is opposite his own Sun sign, as with Gemini for Sagittarius, or Pisces for Virgo. Such a relationship is something like a seesaw; the individuals at either end have to learn to give and take to the right degree and in the right manner in order for the relationship to be successful. In this type of arrangement one can establish a broad and effective sense of cooperation. On the other hand, the 180° relationship can become one of competition and strife if there are no favorable aspects to reinforce the Sun positions in the two charts. It is especially favorable to have the Moon and ascending signs between the charts either conjunct, sextile, or trine one another. The adjustment between yang signs is one of combining will with intellect: fire tends to be bold, aggressive, and speculative; air signs are self-expressive, more mentally reflective, particularly regarding social relationships. For the yin earth and water signs the opposition relationship shows how adjustments are made between practical needs and emotional needs, or between inner feelings and outward practical considerations.

Looking at it from one's own point of view, the most natural relationship of love would be with the sign which is 120° *after* one's Sun sign in the normal zodiacal sequence, as with Sagittarius for Leo, or Cancer for Pisces. Signs related in this way are always of the same zodiacal element, hence the similarity of interests and ideas about children, creative endeavors, recreation, and love in general. This is the relationship of "courtship," the most basic or heartfelt attraction one is likely to experience (ideally) through the zodiacal spectrum. Tradition has it that this is the most compatible of astrological attractions because the psychological makeup is similar. For example, the water signs Cancer and Pisces both have to do with feelings; Leo and Sagittarius express themselves through intuition; Gemini and Libra relate to the thinking mode; and Capricorn and Taurus would be inclined to share in what Jung calls the mode of sensation (empirical cognition).

The sign which is 120° *before* one's Sun sign is also related through likeness of zodiacal element. This is the most romantic, ideal, and expansive relationship. The individual is easily enthused by the other party. Aries is thus naturally stimulated by Sagittarius, and Sagittarius, in turn, is stimulated by Leo. To illustrate: Gemini is naturally attracted to the qualities inherent in Libra (the fifth sign after Gemini), but its highest ideals of communication, love, and freedom are found in Aquarius. All three are air signs. Libra has an immediate attraction to Aquarius; it holds to ideals of communication obtained through Gemini. Aquarius is fraternally attracted in the most heartfelt way to Gemini, while with Libra it finds ideas of harmony, justice, and equality in matters of love. Signs of the same element are naturally attracted to one another, but planets in other signs or the fact that different signs are rising may reduce the basic affinity. A Leo person (fire sign) with an earth sign rising and a large number of planets in earth signs may be less likely to choose a mate whose chart is predominately fire than one who has key planets in the earth and water signs. All that can be shown here is the ideal: it seldom happens that the sign appearing on the descendant (cusp of the seventh house), or the position of Venus, will correspond to what we most desire in a mate.

The sign which *follows* one's Sun sign by 60°, or a sextile aspect, is also considered to be a potentially compatible attraction because, through it, ideas and values can be shared and tested with some degree of ease. Examples of this would be Gemini for Aries, Capricorn for Scorpio, and Pisces for Capricorn. In this situation there is some degree of fraternity or a feeling of companionship. What counts most is adaptability and a kind of association that is rather informal and not overly demanding. Objectivity works to some advantage in effecting the best possible form of communication in this alliance.

Also inherently compatible through the sextile is the sign 60° *before* one's Sun sign in the zodiacal sequence, as with Aquarius for Aries, or Cancer for Virgo. In this combination one may realize the higher hopes of friendship which augment feelings of affection. In both of the sextilic relationships one is associating with either a yang or yin sign of the same gender as one's own Sun sign.

The sign *following* one's Sun sign by 90° shows those things to which one is subconsciously rooted. In this case, signs of the same zodiacal quality are involved, but they are of different functionality in terms of the elements. Examples are Cancer for Aries, Libra for Cancer, and Gemini for Pisces. The person who forms an alliance with the following sign squaring his own has to recognize the different motivational and psychological makeup of the other person. This combination can be constructive if the value of these differences can be understood, but often there is too much friction in this partnership to be conducive to feelings of warm mutuality. For the first sign in the sequence, one's own, this might be termed a dependent relationship wherein yang has to bend to yin, or vice versa. A maternal need may be present, and one's own sense of security is apt to be linked in some way to the conscious aims and purpose of the partner.

Another 90° relationship is formed by the sign square one's own, but *preceding* it in the sequence of the signs. This connection suggests a paternal effect in contrast to the square in the other direction. For Aries this would be Capricorn, for Cancer it would be Aries, and so on, for each of the signs. Rather than domestic matters being emphasized by the individual, there may be an orientation of personal values and aims toward the public in some way in which the partner plays an important role in helping the individual to achieve his objectives. But this is a basically frictional relationship requiring considerable effort and patience on the part of both parties. Where, in the previous case, one's subjective drives are tempered by private considerations and the feelings of the partner, in this instance they are subject to a more objective outward modification. A Leo person, for instance, is greatly affected at an emotional level by a Scorpio mate, especially in the area of sexual feelings; whereas a Taurus partner compels the Leo native to be oriented more to practical things important to his self-expression. With Leo, the Scorpio person is put in a situation where he has to learn to be less retiring and more self-expressive. The practical Taurus individual is made to give in to spending some of his talent or wealth by the Leo mate. A Scorpio person who marries an Aquarian may find in his partner the roots for a broader and more intellectual social relatedness. The Taurean may be able to obtain valuable associations from a marriage to an Aquarian that correspond to his highest conscious material aims; that is, in the form of altruism which has a practical goal. Through Taurus, Aquarius can find a materially sound foundation for its altruistic hopes and resources for its experiments. A Scorpio partner lends Aquarius will power and the necessary strength to perceive and regenerate weaknesses that may otherwise ruin the attempt to obtain an objective orientation. So it is with fixed signs.

This line of reasoning can be applied to the other signs which are related through the other two zodiacal qualities. In any case, the square, like the opposition, denotes a relationship which is essentially dynamic and perpetually adjustive. Friction can be either a constructive or a destructive force, depending upon how it is used or understood by the individuals concerned. Little can be taken for granted in 90° relationships. Those which are most successful are formed by people who strongly represent the positive qualities of their own Sun signs. There is less opportunity for success when either or both parties have brought to the relationship unresolved problems (broken building blocks) arising from the experiences of early childhood or through the parents. Moon and Saturn are important modifiers in quadrature alliances. One has to constantly meet the other person halfway, as a mature adult. Working for this kind of happiness is too trying for most people, but it has splendid possibilities if both people are at once realistic and sensitive to each other's needs.

When the individual forms an alliance with a person who has the Sun in the sign immediately *following* his own he may find that his basic aims are increased or benefited in some way by the partner. Examples of this 30°, or semisextilic, relationship are Taurus for Aries, Gemini for Taurus, and Cancer for Gemini. This tends to be the least sexual kind of alliance, there being a need to give priority to the satisfaction of some practical matter. The close proximity of Venus to the Sun—never more than 48° away—places some special emphasis on that planet in any semisextilic relationship. Also, Mercury's influence might be strongly felt because it is also close to the Sun.

The other 30° relationship involves the sign just *before* one's own. In this case, some sacrifice may be required of the individual. There might, in turn, be hidden rewards or support. What proves harmful is any degree of secrecy or ulterior motives through which one is taken advantage of in some way. The other sign could drain one's energy or cause a distortion of one's deeper sense of purpose. At the same time, one's worst shortcomings or fears might be amplified or personified by the other person. If the alliance is manifesting positively, however, it can be supportive of the individual's aims. All semisextilic situations involve signs of a different element, quality, and gender. They tend to be variable in their effect and are somewhat less stimulating than other alliances unless there are other contacts between the two horoscopes that enliven the relationship, particularly those involving aspects between the Moon, Mars, and Venus.

Partnerships between signs 150° apart, the distance of a quincunx aspect, are another type of basic zodiacal combination. Where they involve a sign *following* one's Sun sign in the zodiacal wheel they tend to emphasize some special purpose or reason for an alliance, often one that is practical in nature. Examples are Virgo for Aries, Aquarius for Virgo, and Scorpio for Gemini. In some way, this might be a "working" relationship where the individual is assisted by his partner. Overall, this is a variable and somewhat oblique alliance that depends on the other planets in the chart for stimulation in order for a favorable adjustment of aims and integration of needs. Again, Venus can play an important role because in a number of cases it will form a trine aspect to the Venus position in the partner's chart, which is a desirable contact between horoscopes.

The other 150° alliance occurs with the sign quincunx one's own, but *preceding* it in the zodiacal sequence, such as Aries for Virgo, Scorpio for Aries, and Leo for Capricorn. The partner in this type of relationship has a stimulating and regenerating effect on the individual, often in some indirect manner. There may be some modification in basic thoughts regarding sexual values; one person draws the other out, so to speak. This can be determined by noting the positions of the other planets, especially the Moon, Mars, and Venus. Scorpio has quite a different effect on Aries than Aries has on Scorpio, and the same is true for every quincunx relationship. The 150° distance between the two signs involved can hold many variables that affect the partnership.

One type of alliance remains to be discussed, and that is where the individual comes together with a person born under his own Sun sign. What could be more natural than to desire to be with someone who is like oneself? However, this arrangement can sometimes be the mark of an extreme narcissism, and there is also the danger that such a partner can reinforce and increase the worst faults in one's own character denoted by the Sun sign. In contrast, the relationship between two opposite signs suggests a much broader orientation, which, although frictional by nature, offers interesting challenges to both parties. The position of Mars in the one-sign relationship would be of vital importance in determining how broad the partnership actually is. The rising signs in the two charts would also say something about compatibility, as would the Moon.

It is a general observation that for the cardinal signs the secret of success in love lies in the ability to cooperate with others in meeting any crises that might arise. This demands energy, sensitivity to the feelings of others, a sense of justice, and loyalty. For the fixed signs a happy love life may depend upon their ability to overcome any values which are too rigid, while at the same time they should nurture a capacity to communicate their hopes and ideals to others, something which is usually easier for the mutable signs. The mutable signs might do well to spend more time defining, in advance, the nature of their commitment before giving their hearts to others.

Of course, everything that has been said so far about the compatibility of the Sun signs can also be applied to some degree to the rising sign, Moon sign, and the signs occupied by Mars and Venus. The houses that correspond to the signs are also very important in determining the nature of a person's love life, especially those containing the two luminaries, Mars and Venus and, to a lesser degree, the larger bodies. All of this has to be kept in mind when analyzing and comparing horoscopes. Superficial or impulsive judgments are much to be avoided in this very complex and sensitive phase of horoscopic interpretation. One can not be too thorough and conscientious, and one must also beware of letting his own feelings and ideas about love color the analysis of another's chart to an excessive degree.

Highlights in the Chart

There are no strict rules to follow in studying a person's love life as it is revealed in his horoscope. Nevertheless, there are some general things one can look for, such as noting which signs and houses Mars and Venus occupy and whether or not they are aspecting each other. The same can be done for the Sun and Moon because these form the main background upon which the Mars/Venus energies, modified by Saturn, Jupiter, and Mercury, are projected. The rising sign and the sign on the descendant (the house of partnerships) form an important axis, and planets in the first and seventh house are strongly modified by other bodies. Any planets in Leo or the fifth house will help to describe a person's ideas and deeper feelings about personal love and courtship and will show what he hopes to gain through any children he might have. Planets in Libra or in the seventh house affect the general atmosphere of exchange and adaption one undergoes in cooperative alliances. Scorpio and the eighth house reveal important things about the deeper (reproductive) currents of sexual feeling; they also have to do with the manner in which a person shares and combines his resources with those of the mate. In every case one has to consider such variables as geography, cultural traditions, current mores about love and sex, the prevailing world view, age, gender, and karma. Mars in Cancer trine Saturn in Scorpio means something quite different for an Eskimo hunter than it does for a married mortician in Los Angeles or a housewife in Iran.

Sexual contentment is not something separate from the other experiences of life. Wherever Mars is found in a chart, it will be most effective when it shows satisfaction in the overall concerns of that area. For example, a tenth house Mars is motivated to gain some degree of prominence or recognition, possibly through a career. To the degree that these desires are satisfied or frustrated they will affect the individual's vitality and success in sexual matters. It is also true that an unhappy love life would reflect upon the other matters of that position.

Comparing Horoscopes

In comparing two charts for compatibility, the first thing to note is the rising sign in each chart in order to see how much alike the basic attitudes and temperaments of the individuals are. It is often this outward personality factor to which another initially responds, rather than the deeper character described by the Sun sign. The next thing to observe is the position of Mars in each chart to see in what ways the outer drives are compatible. Then the Moon positions are compared to determine the differences in feelings and basic methods each person has for maintaining security. Affectional needs in each horoscope are defined by the positions of Venus. The house and sign positions of Mercury and Jupiter in the two charts might be compared in terms of the compatibility of intellectual and philosophical concerns. The positions of Uranus, Neptune, and Pluto are not usually as significant as the other planets in such comparisons, but they may act as important modifiers through their aspects to the other planets. Finally, the Sun positions are compared in order to determine the effect of combining the two wills. Close aspects between the Sun and Moon in one chart to the planets in the other chart are extremely important. One should also note any close aspects that Venus and Mars make between the two charts, either to each other, the two luminaries, or the rising sign. As a final observation note in which house the Sun of each falls in the chart of the other; then do the same for the Moon and Mars.

Several planets in one sign, when either of the luminaries or Mars is involved, usually means that one will have important contacts with people who have strong planets or rising sign in that zodiacal segment. If, in his own chart a person has Mars and Venus in frictional aspect with other planets, some complications and adjustments in the love life can be expected to arise; and even if his chart is "compatible" with another person's it does not guarantee that they will have a happy love life together. Astrology is not a science of wishful thinking. Time, it can be observed, provides each person with a unique character and a set of circumstances in which he can learn the lessons of life. He must evolve through his shortcomings and problems by using what free will he has to guide him. Certain people are helpful to him in this effort and others are not. It is not always easy to be sure that one has chosen the best companions. Astrology can help many to understand these choices; at the same time, it can make suggestions about what might be the most favorable relationships to pursue. Satisfying personal needs is important (Mars), but one has also to find emotional and practical security through the family (Moon) and through meaningful partnerships of cooperation with others (Venus). The part that should not be left out is the sense of responsibility and loyalty (Saturn) that helps a deeper relatedness endure. The mandala of human love includes four necessary qualities: opportunity for independent and spontaneous self-expression, the right means and degree of nourishment in both the physical and the emotional sense, a spirit of compromise and cooperation based on reason, and awareness of a greater whole to which one's relationships are attached.

In the two charts being compared, Mars and Venus might be in signs opposite, square (90° apart), or quincunx (150° apart) one another, and this can be either positive or negative in effect, depending upon the maturity and flexibility of the individuals concerned. Sex and love are always a combination of firmness and yieldingness, physically and psychically. The best arrangement is apt to be one where there is a mixture of close aspects between the two charts, involving the Sun and Moon, Venus, Mars, and Saturn. Jupiter can warm things up, but it may also cause an exaggeration of ardent feelings and ideals that weaken, rather than strengthen, a relationship. Uranus, Neptune, and Pluto may have some unusual effect in certain cases, but they are difficult to interpret when comparing charts.

Aspects Between Charts

In analyzing aspects between charts certain key phrases might be helpful. For conjunctions the astrologer can use something like "has an affinity with," "likeness to," "shares in a basic experience with," "identifies in purpose with," or "is of the same or a similar nature." For a sextile use "stimulates or accentuates," "favorably connects with the nature of," "communicates a sympathy for," "furthers the purpose or interest of," or "helps reveal a side of." For a square aspect use something like "is in conflict with," "is excited or activated by," "demands an adjustment between," "denotes potential problems between," or "greatly stimulates." For a trine use "blends well or harmonizes with," "favors one another," "supports," "favorably mirrors," "helps to fulfill," "facilitates the expression of," "is of a similar nature or persuasion," "shares in a common interest with," or "joins in the expression of." For the opposition use some phrase such as "requires an adjustment to," "counters," "complements," "antagonizes," "agitates," "collides with," "affects profoundly," "may be periodically out-of-phase with," "dramatically unites," or "insists upon a compromise between." For the semisextile use something like "is slightly favored by," "properly loses some of its power to," or "makes a minor adjustment necessary between." For the quincunx aspect use "is somewhat out-of-phase with," "seeks to work toward," "requires some regeneration between," "has to adjust to," or "brings the other out." These phrases are only suggestions. The reader is advised to find some of his own to use in comparing horoscopes.

Allowable orbs or distances between planets aspecting each other in the two charts may vary according to the practice of the particular astrologer doing the comparison. Strong aspects are those occurring within an orb of 5°. But the general picture should also be studied. A person who has the Sun at 3° Aries and one with the Sun at 28° Leo may not have the two positions in orb of a trine aspect, according to allowable orbs, but they are still in signs of the same element, and this is an important point in determining compatibility.

The Marriage Chart

A horoscope can be set up for the exact time and place of marriage. As a chart for a "beginning" it will reveal something about the direction that partnership is apt to go and the experiences which will be met along the way. The marriage chart cannot be interpreted exactly like a natal horoscope because it represents more than one person; nevertheless, an experienced astrologer should be able to glean something of interest from it, comparing its planets and angular house cusps with the natal positions of the husband and wife. The planets might be interpreted according to the following suggested procedure:

The Sun defines the main setting and purpose for the alliance. It has to do with mutual creative endeavors and children. To a large extent it describes the male or the yang partner.

Domestic matters, daily routines, and emotional ties are shown by the position of the Moon. It indicates the female or yin partner.

Mars has to do with the basis of the attraction and the level of energy in the relationship. It acts as a sort of barometer.

Venus describes the main basis for cooperation and exchange. It is the point where union between the two people is attempted. The details of the contract are also defined by Venus.

Saturn's position in the marriage chart has to do with duties, goals, and social responsibilities held in common. Through Saturn, the marriage touches the public realm. Traditional or paternal influences may be indicated by that planet. Certain obstacles might also be attributed to it.

The spirit of enthusiasm and (mutual) ideals is defined by Jupiter, which may also show in what way the individuals are tied together spiritually. In a general sense, Jupiter represents an area of expansion and potential opportunity for both parties. It may also have to do with mutual athletic interests or long journeys which are undertaken by the couple.

Uranus accounts for unexpected changes in the relationship, and it shows the effect of friends and other associations on the marriage. In a much higher sense, Uranus has to do with those mutual hopes and altruistic notions which the couple shares and which tie them to the broader issues of their fellowman.

Neptune's place is one of unsuspected changes, mutually necessary sacrifices, a sense of sorrow (if any), and deeper commitment that reaches beyond the narrower confines of marriage.

The position of Pluto may suggest unconscious ties, the manner in which resources are shared and combined, and possibly, the point where regeneration will be most needed in the partnership.

Minor planets, especially the three larger ones, Ceres, Pallas, and Vesta, might also be studied in the marriage chart in order to see whether or not their effect is felt in some small but important way.

The ruler of the rising sign, which is the ruler of the chart overall, should be studied, along with the ruler of the descending sign. Any planets in the first or seventh houses would seem to be emphasized in this type of chart.

Reflective Tendencies in Charts

It is a tradition to consider the seventh house of one's own natal chart as the first house of one's partner. Thus, in studying a chart, the individual's eighth house becomes the partner's second house, and so on, for each house. This approach is justified on the basis of the idea that every individual in some way reflects every other individual with whom he comes in contact. We are all of one species, sharing in the same changes and cosmic patterns. This is true biologically, astronomically, and spiritually. There are bonds between people, of varying valence of course, that go much deeper than may appear from the outside. Existence is a complex mosaic of these synchronous connections. The most reflective relationship or connection is that of Adam and Eve, that is, of a permanent and compelling union between the two sexes. Life itself springs from this union of yin and yang forces. The longer we stay with another person, the more our individuality becomes interwoven with his or hers (positively or negatively), and the more clearly his chart will reveal things about ourselves. Naturally, our own natal chart is our own master blueprint, but from our partner's chart we can see where we stand in the relationship from the viewpoint of their experience.

Similar charts can be set up for one's parents, children, and friends. Just as the individual's seventh house is the first house of his mate, the fourth house in his chart becomes, by analogy, his mother's first house, and his tenth house marks the first house of his father. His oldest or first child would be best described by his fifth house and the position of its ruler; that is, his fifth house would be the reflective first house of his child. The fifth house and any planets it contains would also reveal something about any subsequent children, but possibly with less strength. It might be that the fifth house represents one's first-born child; the sixth house, the second-born; the seventh, the third child; and so on; but this is a matter of speculation which should be approached carefully. Regarding special interest colleagues and friends, the individual's eleventh house becomes the first house of any broad association he may join.

There is another thing to look for in all kinds of relationships. In dealings with others one should notice how the same signs and degrees of the Zodiac continue to appear. For example, if one has Mars or Sun

Fig. 22.   Zodiacal design

at 25° Aries there will probably be stimulating contacts with people with planets or angular house cusps in that sign, near the degree, or in other signs where planets are near the 25th degree, such as 25° Capricorn or 25° Leo. There are many other things one can discover in comparing charts which will help in understanding relationships better. Just the same, the newcomer should avoid experimental or elaborate methods and untested concepts until he has mastered the fundamental principles of astrology. A simple and clear approach to the matter of compatibility will probably bring the most rewards. For instance, if in one chart a Mars position squares the Moon position in the other, one might begin with a simple statement that "the energy level and conscious drives of the one party are not in harmony with the feelings and instincts for security of the other." Then, the astrologer would note what houses and signs are involved and what other aspects or planetary relationships may reinforce or contradict this particular aspect. If comparing charts is not one of the astrologer's basic skills he should not attempt it. It is better to refer a client to a colleague who specializes in chart comparison and who has a good understanding of the reflective tendencies that exist between horoscopes.

Parents and Siblings

The main significators of the father in a horoscope are the Sun, Saturn, the tenth house, and the sign Capricorn. Older men and people in authority (men and women both) are also indicated by Saturn. The Moon, Cancer, and the fourth house relate more to the mother, women in general, and essentially yin or feminine matters. Brothers, sisters, playmates, and classmates are described by Mercury, Gemini, and the third house. The first house, Aries, and Mars are associated with the individual himself, while Venus, the seventh house, and Libra describe the partner, and generally, the individual relation with the opposite sex. It should be apparent that many of the relationships of adult life are to some degree reflections and variations of our childhood experiences with relatives and others close to us in the neighborhood of our home. To what extent we walk in our father's footsteps or cling to our mother's apron strings varies from individual to individual, but we are always linked to the past through our parents, even if only unconsciously. Our ambitions and inhibitions are also determined by our early environment and experiences. Mars, Mercury, and the Moon show the influence of this early environment as it relates to one's siblings and mother. Venus, Jupiter, and Saturn pull the individual away from this more insular orientation toward the realm of the father and the public as a whole. The first house and the rising sign are placed at the midpoint between the fourth and tenth houses: this means that the individual is placed between the two poles of parenthood. Everything that we need to augment or complement this subjective development is found in the seventh house and its cusp. The rising sign, especially if it corresponds to the first house, remains the most striking feature of our own personality; it is that point to which our parents and our mate most readily relate. The position of the ruler of the ascendant, along with the position and aspects of Mars, are significant modifiers of this outer temperament, and any aspects they might make to the Moon or Saturn will show additional involvements with the parents.

The rising sign is the most obvious part of our life available to all people we encounter; it is our point of self-awareness and identity.[2] The sign on the cusp of the fourth house and the position of its ruler has to do with the most private aspects of our life. On the seventh house cusp is the sign which represents the opposite qualities of our own outward personality. The tenth house cusp, the midheaven, has to do with the least private, or the most public phases of experience. Beginning with the first house and ending with the tenth house, one moves from what is most intimate or personal toward an increasingly objective orientation. The great modifications take place through the mother, the father, and one's spouse, with one's own children and siblings acting as somewhat less significant influences on one's development. Individual destiny is always linked to that of close relatives. After we leave the mother's breast (fourth house), form a union with our true love (seventh house), and profess our highest conscious goals (tenth house) we realize the true meaning of our own desires and aims (first house). The rising sign is the key to our main karma; the Sun sign shows how we go about fulfilling it. The cusps of the other three angular houses modify the rising sign most dramatically. The cusps of the intermediate houses have a less striking, although not unimportant, effect.

[2] It should be understood that the rising sign is not made to correspond exactly with the degree of the Zodiac appearing on the first house cusp in every system of astrology. Indeed, with the "hour of birth" system the angular house cusps seldom find an exact correspondence with the ascendant, descendant, midheaven, and nadir. For the most part, however, one can use the terms "first house" and "rising sign" synonymously if it is remembered that they are not quite identical.

Children

In discussing a person's relationship to his children, the same non-astrological variables which have already been mentioned have to be kept in mind, particularly those which are by nature cultural, geographical, and, in some cases, racial. The rearing of a farm boy in the Tibetan foothills will contrast remarkably with the childhood of a wealthy Jewish girl born under the same astrological patterns on the same day in New York City. They will experience similar responses to changes and events which occur in the course of their lives, but the environmental factors will differ, just as their karma does. Here is evidence that the place of birth is often as important as the time of birth.

A common significator for involvement with children is a strong emphasis in either Leo or the fifth house of the horoscope, although this does not always hold true for various reasons. Where there are no planets in either Leo or the fifth house and the majority of the planets are above the horizon, there may be less likelihood of having a (large) family; or at least that would not seem to be one's main goal or means of expression. The position of Saturn in the chart, and any planets in Capricorn or the tenth house may show how one is influenced by one's father in terms of values that have to do with rearing children. The Moon, Cancer, and the fourth house would similarly show something about the maternal side of one's role as a parent. This is true whether the individual is a man or a woman. The legacy of his own childhood has a powerful influence on the way in which he raises his own family. The Sun's position is a vital factor because it shows what deeper values and methods an individual will express through and with his own children. One might expect some trouble in raising children if the Sun, Moon, or Saturn are poorly placed. This is also true for Mars and Venus, which help to define the essential nature of a person's love life. Of course, this is true mostly for the nuclear family. It is quite a different matter when children are raised in a Uranian environment, such as that found in a commune.

It may be an irony of life that the individual's hopes (eleventh house) are opposed to his children's personal aims (fifth house). However, children can bring joy when the individual's highest philosophical and spiritual ideals (ninth house) correspond to the creative and expressive needs of his children. This idea is based on the fact that his fifth house of children is reckoned in his own horoscope as the children's first house, and that the fifth house following the individual's fifth house in his own ninth house of ideals. Where these high ideals are not present there might otherwise be happiness and rapport with children through play, sport, travel, or some mutually creative or adventurous endeavor.

That no person possesses the soul of his offspring is apparent because his own eighth house is that of death, and, as the fourth house following his own fifth house, it is where his children find their "roots" in the union of the sperm and ovum from which they are born. The parent merely provides the seed (and the mother, the womb) from which the child develops. The soul enters the body of the newborn individual at first breath. The cord is cut, and slowly he begins the long process of "individuation." A person is nonetheless linked to his ancestors: the fifth house following his tenth house (the father) is his own second house of resources (the second and eighth houses are opposed). And the second house is the tenth house following the house of children. We are linked to our forefathers through life (sperm) and material means, but not through death, as it is associated with the eighth house. The fourth house after the fifth house, the individual's own eighth house, represents the child's mother. This seems to represent a paradox. The eighth house has to do with the conception of the male and female gametes; it is the individual's own house of death; and, by analogy, it is the house of one's children's mother (which may not necessarily be a man's wife). Thus, at the very gateway of death, life begins in the mother's womb. The ejaculation of sperm is for the father a "little death." Is it not any wonder that man so compelled stands in awe of sex? He cannot avoid it while he lives, yet sometimes it frightens him as much as death itself.

The individual's eleventh house is the seventh following his fifth house, which, as already established, is the symbolic first house of his children. This indicates the importance of his associations and friends in helping his children determine what qualities they will later seek in a mate. The first faces which appear over the edge of the crib are very important to the infant and form part of his ideas about people in general later in life. The rule might be made that the quality, nature, and extent of the parent's objective relationships and friendships directly, though somewhat unconsciously, affect his child's choice of a partner later on. In essence, the parent's social graces (and sins) are visited upon the child. It is not simply the parents, the siblings, and other relatives that affect the early values of a growing child; it is also the friends and acquaintances of his parents.

The eleventh house following the individual's fifth house is his third house. Here, something is learned about his children's friends, hopes, and link to the future. Knowing all the things the third house represents, he might be able to determine the effect of his siblings and neighbors upon his children, and eventually, their own choice of friends and special interest associations. Thus, his brother or sister may in some way be more instrumental in helping his children realize their higher hopes than he is himself. The idea presented here is that our lives are interwoven in many ways with those of others, and that from our own charts we can see the development of our children.

Immediately following the fifth house is the individual's sixth house, which is studied in this manner as being the child's second house of personal possessions. What is possessed or acquired are the skills and practical values of the parent, who, in turn, had received them from his own family and parents. In a modern society this practical inheritance is less apparent because now children seldom follow in their parents' line of work or craft, or obtain the same practical instruction as their forebears. The individual's tenth house is the sixth house following his fifth house; therefore, it reflectively becomes the child's own house of employment and denotes those skills acquired while on the job. This correspondence accounts to some extent for the natural desire for parents to see their children "make it" by being recognized for their work or skills in some public way, but in a modern society parents are often disappointed because the criteria they (their generation) associate with success differ in many cases from the child's actual ability and interests. The parent's own second house is the tenth house from his fifth, and as such, shows how his resources and tools affect the potential career aspirations of his child. The practical orientation of the parent to his child is very different in these rapidly changing times from what it was in the past.

A person's twelfth house is the eighth house of his child, counting eight houses away from the fifth house. This could mean, as the early Greeks and others believed, that the "sins" and shortcomings are "visited" upon the child. The eighth house has to do with what we inherit; hence, in this instance, the parent's weakness and faults (neuroses perhaps) are acquired to some degree by the offspring. The twelfth house has to do with those things which are difficult to fathom or which are normally hidden from view. Counting from the fifth house, the parent's fourth house becomes the child's twelfth house. The fourth house relates to emotional attachments, sentiments, the individual's early environment, instincts for security, his mother, and tribal customs and taboos. Such traditions and subjective matters could hold a child back in his development, causing him to be too attached to his family (or nation) and the customs of his childhood. To what extent do one's own emotional makeup, habits, sense of security, and survival instincts give hidden support to his children, and to what extent do they become his children's "secret enemies," stifling their growth and their sense of security? It is probable that the unresolved childhood traumas and emotional problems of the parent reach out and undermine the security of his own children. It is equally as true that early love and affection have the reverse effect.

The seventh house of partnership in a person's chart becomes the third house of the child. This illustrates an important point: communication is the very essence of a happy family. The third house following the seventh house relates to the partner's own ability to communicate. This is the individual's own ninth house, and it is a point where all in the family—oneself, spouse, and children—can find agreement and spiritual rapport. The third house is also a compatible point of mutual interest for the entire family. The activities that hold a family together are found between these two complementary houses. Physical activities and travel are just two examples of how members of the family can find satisfaction as a group. Learning situations can also be stimulating for parents and children alike. Spiritual communion of some type is important in every family, even if it is only as simple an act as the joining of hands at the evening meal.

Raising children is the first art of life and one which requires the greatest attention and care. To want to ride on this carrousel with the idea that it brings only joy is to invite folly. Children do not belong to people, they *happen through* them; and they can also be a source of great sorrow, disappointment, and pain. The reasons for having children also vary. Most people follow psycho-biological urges and cultural imperatives in reproducing children. A few make conscious decisions to have children or not to have them, and many children are "accidentally" conceived.

The fifth house after the seventh house is the eleventh house, which is the partner's fifth house of children as viewed in one's own chart. It can provide insights about the aims of the partner regarding the rearing of children, these aims, of course, being a complement to one's own (as symbolized by the fifth house). In communal "marriages," the third house is the significator of children, since the third house is the fifth house following the eleventh.

To look at the parent in a child's chart, study the fourth house of the child's chart to gain insights about the mother, and do the same with the tenth house with respect to the father. The Moon will also tell something about the mother, and Saturn (and often the Sun) will be the best planet to study in order to determine the place of the father. One would also note any close aspects between the chart of a child and those of his parents.

Zodiacal Elements and Children

It should be clear that the fifth house in every horoscope provides information about the experiences and expectations that person has regarding children. Variations arise due to the fact that any of the twelve signs can be located at the fifth house within a twenty-four-hour period. Besides that, each of the four zodiacal elements is characterized by distinct values about raising children.

Fire signs naturally relate to the essence of youth. Those whose Sun signs are Aries, Leo, and Sagittarius take a personal pride in their children. The more they can inspire them in both play and ideals, the happier they will be as parents. A spirit of active involvement and guidance is required, but the fire sign parent has to be careful not to overpower the will of the child, particularly when that child has the Sun in either a water or earth sign. The parent himself needs a spontaneous attitude, a sense of humor and play, warm demonstrativeness, and a youthful viewpoint. The fire sign child and the fire sign parent generally find each other stimulating, but some degree of competition and an occasional clash of wills can be expected. The air sign child tends to be less intuitive and adventurous than the fire sign child, and he responds favorably to reason and a demonstrated sense of justice and fair play. The earth sign child might be pushed along too rapidly by a fire sign parent. He needs to learn the lessons of thoroughness and pragmatic intelligence more than to be taught how to "play his hunches," as the fire sign parent is inclined to do. The child with the Sun in a water sign is inclined to be more retiring, emotionally sensitive, and less bold than the fire sign parent.

The air sign parent emphasizes communication, education, sociability, and mutuality. Gemini and Libra may be somewhat better disposed for raising children than Aquarius, which finds its deeper needs satisfied more through objective communicative experiences with friends than through children (symbolized by the opposite sign, Leo). Gemini takes a lively interest in children, making a fairly good playmate and teacher. Libra lends the child a sense of justice, fair play, good manners, and grace. Reasonableness helps the air sign parent deal with the strong will of the fire sign child; it enables him to make the necessary materials available for the projects of the skillful earth sign child; it allows for the need for privacy of the water sign child; and it helps the air sign child to acquire an attitude of exchange and adaptability with others. But the air sign parent has to learn to be consistent, especially when it comes to discipline and establishing guiding rules for the child. Reason has to be tempered by a practical viewpoint, emotional sensitivity, and an intuitive awareness of the child's own aims. No child will respond favorably to a parent who is too rational (or rationalizing). What has been said here also applies to some extent to those with air signs rising or to those with the Moon in an air sign.

The earth sign type of parent does best to gently show his child the value of practical, down-to-earth things. Hobbies and other skillful activities can be encouraged, especially where the child is also an earth sign or has prominent planets therein. Being firm and consistent, but not too stiff or empirical, the devoted earth sign parent can teach his child the value of caring for their own possessions. A closeness to nature should be taught. Fire sign children can be made to realize that their schemes and desires for adventure always rest upon the quality of the materials and tools at their immediate disposal; they learn from the earth sign parent that ambitions and impulses must have substance. The air sign child learns how to intelligently bargain with others. The water sign child finds what it needs in order to protect itself and obtain maximum security. The earth sign parent finds satisfaction in seeing his child succeed in his chosen line of work. He can be proud if he has been able to impart a sense of thrift and thoroughness to that child, as well as a realistic approach to determining the quality and worth of things.

A parent who is strongly influenced by the water signs is motivated by a maternal instinct which is somewhat in contrast to the paternal tendency associated with the earth signs. The feelings of every child have to be nurtured and protected, and the proper shelter provided. In doing this the water sign parent has to guard against being too possessive or clinging, or the child's will power can be stifled. This is especially true if he is a fire or air sign. The fire sign child needs to learn to be sensitive to the feelings and desires of others; he cannot forever have the center of the stage or be the leader. For the earth sign child a loving tenderness and imaginative use of materials can be taught; he is shown the inner essence of the things he acquires. The air sign child learns from the water sign parent how to take into account the feelings and moods of others in the course of communication; he learns to be tactful. The water sign child is shown the value of receptivity and empathy and he is also taught how to guard his own feelings. A parent born under Cancer, Scorpio, or Pisces should try to make it clear to his children that there is always more than "meets the eye," that no job is ever quite done, that nothing is free from decay, that ambitions and love are both affected by present conditions, and that each person can only accomplish or contain so much in a given lifetime.

The interpretations which have been given above are general and they do not take into account the many variables which can occur in the charts of both parents and children. The main factors to study are the positions of the Sun, Moon, Saturn, and the sign rising. Also, the fifth sign following one's Sun sign holds clues about how one will raise children: for Aries that would be Leo, for Taurus the concepts of rearing children are found in Virgo, and so on. In the child's own chart the Sun and Saturn symbolize the father; the Moon's position (sometimes that of Saturn) shows the influence of the mother. The fourth house is related to the mother and the tenth to the father. Some astrologers reverse this, making the fourth house correspond to the father and the tenth to the mother. Marc Edmund Jones has referred in his many works to the fourth house as representing the "in depth" parent and the tenth the "outer link" parent. In this age of changing roles there may be good reason for viewing the two houses in this way.

In discussing love let us not pretend that it is contained in the hearts of Adam and Eve alone. True happiness depends just as much upon those conditions around us as upon our own desires, hopes, and intentions. In a chaotic world where human security (society) is threatened by overpopulation, war, pollution, depletion of natural resources, antiquated political and economic systems, and a proliferation of crime, there is hardly anyone living on the edge of technology who does not feel anxiety about the future—even if only subconsciously. Most people are reluctant to think about the welfare of their future descendants. They would rather hold to the Pollyanna idea that somehow things will get better. Those who are the freest and happiest together are probably those who face the problems of the future by living more intelligently in the present. At least, in such a family, the conscience is not subject to the nagging apprehensiveness that prevails in the modern "civilized" world. The happy family is the one which has a simple life style, effective means of communication among its members, mutual projects, and an affectionate respect for other life forms and the land upon which they live. The unhappy family is wasteful and the prevalent mood is "what's in it for me?" In discussing this complex subject it is difficult to end on a note of optimism. Certainly, the hope for man's future lies in his children and their children's children.

Friendship: Astrological Distinctions

Mercury represents siblings, neighbors, playmates, chance club members, peers, and acquaintances; in other words, all those relationships which are more or less informal, accidental, or lacking a definite aim or commitment that affects the world as a whole. Venus symbolizes a person's mate, partner, close comrade, competitor, or other face-to-face relationships involving two individuals who share a common (social) goal. Most people we associate with, outside of our immediate family, fall under the influence of these two planets. This includes many of those whom we call "friends."

True friendship, astrologically speaking, is an objective Uranian association willingly entered into in which the individual shares some broader goal or interest with the other person. A friend, in this manner of speaking, is a colleague. It is important, when analyzing charts, to distinguish among the effects of Mercury, Venus, and Uranus, much in the same way that one notes the differences (and similarities) of the three signs which those planets rule: Gemini, Libra, and Aquarius.

Also, the Sun sign and rising sign show fundamental characteristics to which we are attracted in others. We may marry according to what Venus indicates, hope for those friends described by Uranus, and long for the heartfelt relationships denoted by the Sun's position, but we may end up, for one reason or another, befriending those qualities indicated by the position of our Moon. The laws of attraction are very complex. Every planet in a horoscope has something to say about every relationship we form.

Other Relationships

There is not room here to go into detail about such relationships as grandparents, uncles and aunts, cousins, employers, and others. Certain houses of the horoscope, as shown below, are related to some of these relationships. Understanding how they are determined requires a familiarity with the basic meaning of the twelve houses and their corresponding signs. For example, one grandmother (mother's mother) is associated with the seventh house, and the other grandmother (father's mother) with the first house. The fourth house after the fourth house is the seventh, and the fourth house after the tenth house is the first. Learning these additional or secondary meanings expands one's understanding of the horoscope.

FIRST HOUSE: one's personal self, grandfather (mother's father), grandmother (father's mother), great-grandchildren, friends and colleagues of siblings, siblings of friends.

SECOND HOUSE: stepsiblings (mother's husband's children), friends of mother, mother of friend or colleague.

THIRD HOUSE: siblings, nonamorous peers and companions, acquaintances, neighbors, side-by-side relationships in general, children of friends, friends of children, playmates, classmates, early teachers, secretaries.

FOURTH HOUSE: mother, great-grandmother (mother's father's mother), great-grandmother (father's mother's mother), great-grandfather (mother's mother's father), great-grandfather (father's father's father), stepmother, female guardian, father-in-law, cousins (father's siblings' children), personal agents, landlord.

FIFTH HOUSE: children, great-great-grandchildren, fiancé, fiancée, lovers, friends of mate, partner or mate of friend.

SIXTH HOUSE: aunts and uncles (siblings of mother, spouses of father's siblings), co-workers, employees, assistants, servants, mentors, instructors (of practical skills).

SEVENTH HOUSE: mate or partner, comrade-competitors, face-to-face relationships in general, open enemies, playmates or peers of one's children, grandmother (mother's mother), grandfather (father's father), nephews and nieces (children of siblings), clients.

EIGHTH HOUSE: stepsiblings (father's wife's children), friends and colleagues of father, business partners.

NINTH HOUSE: siblings of mate or partner, grandchildren, siblings-in-law, mate or partner of siblings, teachers, teammates, fellow students, parishioners, travelers, foreigners in general.

TENTH HOUSE: father, great-grandmother (mother's mother's mother), great-grandmother (father's father's mother), great-grandfather (mother's father's father), great-grandfather (father's mother's father), stepfather, male guardian, mother-in-law, cousins (mother's siblings' children), superiors, personal managers, sponsors, employer.

ELEVENTH HOUSE: friends, colleagues, associations, club members, special interest affiliations, communal relationships, sons and daughters-in-law, stepchildren (spouse's children), political representatives, extraterrestrial humanoid beings(?).

TWELFTH HOUSE: uncles and aunts (siblings of father) (spouses of mother's siblings), hidden supporters, secret enemies, slaves, aliens, nonhumanoid extraterrestrial beings(?).

Astrological Meditation and Encounter

Without making specific suggestions about how it might be done, it seems to me that the symbols and principles of astrology could be applied to various types of interpersonal meditation. Each chart, after all, is a sort of mandala that uniquely expresses one's relationship with the solar system as a whole, and with other people in particular. Group meditation, as well as forms of group encounter, might be tried, where astrological concepts and individuals' charts could be used in some manner. Music, art, and astrology could probably be combined with other approaches to the human spirit, including those dating back to ancient traditions. Basic Sun signs, individual horoscopes, and knowledge of current planetary cycles would all be considered.

Astrology could prove to be an effective tool in group encounters. Sessions might be planned for signs of the same zodiacal element or quality, one particular sign, or on the basis of some other astrological factor held in common. For those who are more spiritually inclined, astrology can enrich a spirit of high communication and celebration which draws like-minded people closer to the cosmic forces from which they are born. Of course, this is a practice that is also subject to misunderstanding by those who have not tried the "cosmic sacrament." There is always the danger, here, as elsewhere, of the formation of narrow cults; on the other hand, there is a tendency to suppress or outlaw what is feared or not well understood. Astrology is a potentially useful tool for helping a person to focus on energies which might otherwise be ill-understood or which even can be psychologically destructive. Its universal quality makes it a powerful way to draw people together toward a spiritual center held in common. Just as all the planetary bodies revolve around the Sun with their own satellites, and as the spokes of the zodiacal wheel are tied to a common hub, there is a deeper sense of self in which all people with open hearts can share, regardless of their place in life. In the final analysis, astrology, which is a system of time-related archetypal categories, actually helps people to transcend those and other categories.

Appendix I

The Chronological Development of Astrology

c. 15,000 B.C.	Mesolithic man observes the lunar phases and the Sun's seasonal arrival at the equinoctical and solstitial points. Marks found on bones and antlers show the lunar phases.
6000 B.C.	Early observations of planets as "wanderers" in Babylon.
c. 2900 B.C.	Chinese philosopher/astrologer Fu Hsi invents the eight yin and yang trigrams of the *I Ching*.
2350 B.C.	Astrological predictions of Sargon I in Babylonia.
1700 B.C.	Further development of mundane astrology in Babylonia. Astrological-ceremonial solar megaliths constructed at Stonehenge, England.
c. 1500 B.C.	Aryan invasion of India introduces the first Mesopotamian ideas on astrology.
1375 B.C.	Sun worship in Egypt under Ikhnaton.
1150 B.C.	Further work done on the *I Ching* by King Wen and his son, the Duke of Chou.
1000 B.C.	Beginning of Indian mundane astrology. Octantal Zodiac in use.
747 B.C.	First records of eclipses in Mesopotamia.
6th century B.C.	Pythagoras develops the idea of the harmony of the spheres. Mesopotamian astrology continues to spread to India and Tibet where ideas intermin-

	gle. Persian invasions of Egypt introduce new astrological knowledge. Confucius adds commentaries to the *I Ching*.
5th century B.C.	Chaldean astrologers develop rules for erecting royal horoscopes.
409 B.C.	Date of the oldest known Babylonian horoscope for an individual: April 29, 409 B.C.
331 B.C.	Mesopotamian astrology introduced into Greece following Alexander's conquest of Babylon. Greek astrology takes on a more personal form, the Zodiac and planets being made to correspond to figures from their mythology; the Stoics are especially receptive to astrology. Greek astrology influences the metaphysical astrology of India.
280 B.C.	Berossus, the Chaldean historian/astrologer, relates events to star worship. The medical ideas of Hippocrates are apparently influenced by astrology. Rome begins to be strongly affected by Greek astrology.
150 B.C.	Esoteric writings in Egypt on astrology by Petosiris.
135 B.C.	Posidonius furthers astrology among Roman intellectuals.
99–45 B.C.	Nigidius Figulus of Rome makes predictions. Opposition from Cicero and the Epicureans to astrology.
70 B.C.	Greeks set up the first known personal horoscope based on the exact time of birth, thus deriving the ascendant.
30 B.C.	Emperor Augustus has his horoscope erected and interpreted by Thrasyllus, establishing a precedent followed by later Roman Emperors. The date of his birth was September 23, 63 B.C.
c. 4 B.C.	Magi/astrologers from Chaldea apparently predict the birth of Jesus Christ.
1st century A.D.	The first individual horoscope is used in China in addition to mundane predictions.
A.D. 10	The poet/astrologer Manilius publishes his *Astronomicon*, the first major Greek work on astrology. Certain Mediterranean mystery religions embrace astrology.

A.D. 140	Ptolemy of Alexandria publishes his *Tetrabiblos*, the first major textbook on astrology.
C. A.D. 300	Mayan priest/astronomers develop an accurate calendar. Greek thought continues to affect the development of astrology in India and elsewhere, where the twelve-sign Zodiac is adopted.
A.D. 354–430	St. Augustine leads an early Christian attack on astrology.
4th century A.D.	Under the reign of Constantine the Christian, Julius Firmicus Maternus supports astrology in his *Mathesis*.
A.D. 476	End of the Roman Empire; decline of astrology in the West.
6th century A.D.	In India, Vahara Mihira compiles astrological lore under the reign of King Vikramaditya.
A.D. 700–1200	Arabs continue divinatory astrology during the Dark Ages following the Fall of Rome. Astrology is reintroduced to medieval Europe via the universities of Spain during the Moorish invasions. Charlemagne (c. A.D. 800) helps further astrology in the West.
8th century A.D.	School of astrology established in Baghdad. Chinese astrology develops under Han Yü and Li Hsü-Chung.
9th century A.D.	Sabian star worship in Mesopotamia. Albumasar publishes his *Introduction to Astrology*. Jewish *Cabala* is created with the aid of Arabian astrologers.
11th century A.D.	Astrologer Alberuni records concepts of Hindu astrology during Islamic invasion of India. Arab and Greek concepts, in turn, continue to influence Hindu astrology.
A.D. 1000	Mayans observe solar/lunar data to predict such mundane events as weather, war, and natural disasters. Spanish and Portuguese invasions in the sixteenth century put an end to stellar science in the New World.
12th century A.D.	Adelard of Bath (England) helps reintroduce astrology in the Christian West after a journey to the Middle East.
13th century A.D.	St. Thomas Aquinas aids in the reconciliation of

	astrology with the Church. Universities in Spain and Italy establish chairs of astrology.
12th to 15th centuries A.D.	Astrology becomes more and more a decadent divinatory practice. Still, some serious scholars devote time to its study.
1400 to 1600 A.D.	Aztecs associate the planet Venus with the god Quetzaltcoatl. Wan Min-Ying of China publishes his *Compendium of Astral Sciences*.
15th to 16th centuries A.D.	The Renaissance favors development of astrology through the astrologer/physician Paracelsus and others. Astrology is associated with alchemy, magic, and other occult arts and practiced by Agrippa and others. A new system of house division is created by Regiomontanus.
A.D. 1543	The Copernican view of the universe is regarded by skeptical scientists as a refutation of geocentric astrology, thus bringing to a close the great humanitarian interest in astrology.
A.D. 1555	Nostradamus publishes his first sensational "prophecies." Catherine de Médicis passionately embraces astrology, as do several other rulers of this period.
A.D. 1571	Birth of Johannes Kepler, who sought to develop a new astrology. His teacher, Tycho Brahe, also practiced astrology.
A.D. 1666	Astrology is banished from the French Academy of Sciences.
17th century A.D.	Placidus de Titus, a Benedictine monk and teacher, publishes important astrological works. Morin de Villefranche, the court astrologer/physician of Louis XIV, publishes *Astrologica Gallica*.
A.D. 1675	William Lilly publishes the first major original work on astrology since Ptolemy and predicts the Great London Fire. However, astrology is still practiced mostly by quacks or those intellectually underground and it continues to decline during the "Age of Enlightenment."
A.D. 1781	William Herschel discovers Uranus.
A.D. 1824	Astrology is outlawed in England (*The Vagabond Act*).

A.D. 1828 — Raphael (Robert Gross Smith) publishes the *Manual of Astrology*, the first of an increasing number of popular works on astrology.

A.D. 1846 — The discovery of Neptune (and earlier Uranus) helps astrologers to begin to resolve some of the old ambiguities of their craft, although some critics erroneously see this as a further refutation of astrology.

late 19th century A.D. — Theosophists, Rosicrucians, and occultists in England and the United States show a deeper interest in astrology. Some use pseudonyms such as Leo, Zadkiel, and Raphael. The revival of astrology spreads to the Continent, especially to Germany and France.

A.D. 1908 — Llewellyn George establishes an astrological school in Los Angeles, California.

C. A.D. 1920 — Evangeline Adams succeeds in getting the practice of astrology legalized in New York. The forerunner of the American Federation of Astrologers is founded by George.

A.D. 1930 — Pluto's discovery is celebrated by stellar science. Astrology becomes more popular through the newspapers in England and elsewhere. Astrology begins to be strongly influenced by depth psychology.

C. A.D. 1940 — Popular predictive astrology continues to flourish. At the same time, serious-minded astrologers continue their observations.

A.D. 1966 — The psychedelic revolution helps to create a deep and sweeping interest in astrology at many levels. The writings of serious astrologers gain wide appeal, especially among the younger generation. This seems to be a great turning point for astrology.

C. A.D. 1970 — Important new works by a new generation of astrologers are published. At the same time, popular astrology continues to personalize the Zodiac through the arts and elsewhere. Scientific interest in the subject increases.

Appendix II

Zodiacal Keywords

As has been pointed out throughout this book, pure zodiacal manifestations are rare. Nevertheless, certain keywords seem to fit one sign better than others. Following is a list of keywords, some of which could certainly be applied to other signs in the same zodiacal element. For instance, Aries "inspires," but so do Leo and Sagittarius.

Aries

action	beginner	combativeness	debut
adamant	blaze	command	decision
alert	brave	congenital	declaration
ammunition	brazen	conquest	defiance
announce	bright	conspicuous	demeanor
anterior	brute	contumacy	discovery
armor		conviction	
arousal	caprice	countenance	ebullience
arrowhead	catapult	courage	ejaculate
ascendancy	centurion	crest	elementary
assail	challenge	criterion	emanation
awakening	champion	curiosity	embolden
	coagency	cutthroat	emergence
baton	cocksure		energy
bayonet	coercion	dauntless	engender

entrance
envisage
essence
essentiality
eureka
excitation
exigency
expediency
exploit
exploration

fanfare
fervor
fetching
fighter
firemaker
first
flash
flicker
focus
force
forefront
foresight
forthright
fortitude
fresh
furnace

generate
genesis
germinate
glance
glaring

hale
hammer
harbinger
head
headlong
headstrong
heady
hegemony

helm
herald
heroic
highlight
horn
hurl
hurtle

identification
identity
ignition
illuminate
immature
immediacy
impact
impassioned
impatience
impel
imperative
impervious
impetuousness
impetus
impression
impudence
incandescent
incendiary
incense
incentive
inception
inchoate
incinerate
incise
incitement
individuality
inflame
infuriate
ingress
inimitability
initial
initiation
innocence
inspire

intimidation
intransigence
intrepid
intrinsic
introduce
intrusion
invade
invigorate
invincibility
irascible
irradiate
irrepressibility
irritation
irruption
issue

jack-in-the-box

keynote
kindle
knife
knock

lance
launch
leading
leaning
liberate
lever
liberty
lively
lucid

maestro
mainspring
mark
marshal
martial
melody
microcosm
might
militant

model
motif

naïveté
narcissism
narrow
nascent
neophyte
newcomer
newfangled
nick
notion

obvious
offensive
opening
openmindedness
original
originate
ostensible
outburst
overt
overture

pacemaker
paradigm
particularization
penchant
perception
personalization
pioneer
poignant
point
point-blank
pointer
pose
potent
power
preamble
precedent
precipitant
precocity

precursor
predilection
preface
prelude
premature
premeditate
premiere
presumptuous
primary
primer
principal
priority
pristine
proboscis
proceed
proclaim
proclivity
prodigy
projector
prologue
promotion
propensity
propulsion

prospect
protégé
prototype
proud
provocation
punch

quickening

radiance
rambunctious
rapid
rash
razor
refulgent
restlessness
robust
rush

scan
scepter
self-command
self-propelled

self-reliance
sharp
slash
soliloquy
source
spark
spartan
spring
sprout
stamp
stimulate
straightforward
strike

temerity
temper
thesis
torch
trenchant
trigger
twinkle

unequivocal

uniqueness
urge
usher

vainglory
vanguard
vernal
verve
view
vigilant
vigor
visage
visualization
vital
vivacious
vivid
volition
volley

wake
weapon
whim
will

Taurus

abundance
accumulation
acquisition
adequacy
affluence
amount
annuity
appraisal
aptitude
assessment
attachment
avarice
awkwardness

bank

bluntness
bountiful
business
buy

calmness
capability
commence
commercial
commonsense
competence
composition
concern
concrete
configuration

conservatism
consistency
constancy
construction
contentment
continuity
cornerstone
criterion
cupidity

deal
deposit
determination
diligence
domestication

dullness
durable

earn
earthen
efficaciousness
endowment
engineer
enrich
estimate
evaluation
expend
expense

figure

finance
firmness
fitness
fortification
fortune
foundation

gain
gift
greed
grindstone

hidebound
hone

impatience
impenetrability
inflexibility
installation
instrument
investment

label
ledger
lucrative
lucre

manufacture
market
material

materialism
materialization
means
merchandise
monetary

necessity

obdurate
obtain

paraphernalia
patience
pay
persevere
pertinacity
philistine
pocket
ponderous
possess
possession
pouch
practical
pre-emption
price
production
profit
property
purchase
purse

reckon
recompense
remuneration
resolute
resource
resourcefulness
restraint
reward
rudiment
rumination

safe
salary
sale
sample
satisfactory
sculpture
smooth
solid
spend
stability
stamina
stanch
steady
stinginess
stipulate
stout
strong
stubbornness
substance

substantiation
sustainment

tabulate
talent
tally
tangible
tenure
thoroughness
till
tool
touchstone
trade
trademark

unbending
utilization

valuation
value
Vishnu

wampum
ware
wealth
well-off
worth

Gemini

abstraction
acquaintance
adaptability
adeptness
advertisement
ambivalence
anagram
anecdote

antenna
aphorism
author

bilateral
bilingual
binary
bipolarity

brief
briefing
brochure
brother

caprice
chameleon
changeableness

charm
chum
cleverness
colloquial
colloquy
comment
communication
concomitant

congeniality
contact
conundrum
convey
correlation
correspondence
courier
cursory

definition
deftness
description
dexterity
diagram
dialogue
dialectic
dichotomy
diction
dilettante
discursive
discussion
disjunction
disquietude
documentary
double

education
eloquence
embrace
enigma
enquire
en route
epigram
episode
errand
essay
explanation
extemporize

fast
fickleness
finesse

flair
fleet
flexibility
fluency
flutter
fraternize
freethinker

garrulity
gazette
geniality
gesticulation
gesture
glossary
gossip
grammar
graphic
greeting

handy
hearsay
hurry
hypothesis

ideation
illustration
impart
imprint
impromptu
improvise
inconsistency
information
ingenuity
inscription
interesting
interpretation
intimation
itinerant

jabber
jaunty
juxtaposition

ken
kinetic

language
lateral
learning
letter
lexicography
limber
lithe
locution
logical
loquacious
lyrical

malleability
manuscript
memorandum
mental
mercurial
message
mobile
motorist
motto
mutable

narration
nearby
neighbor
news
nimble
notebook

offer
offhand
oratorical
oscillate

page
parable
paradox
parallel

paraphrase
paper
parchment
parlance
passageway
passerby
path
pendulum
persiflage
peruse
plagiarize
platitude
playmate
pliable
postal
prate
prestidigitation
propinquity
pupil

read
recount
referee
remark
repartee
resilient
restive
restless
riddle
road
route
rumor

quaver
quick-witted
quotation

salutation
saunter
saying
scintillate
shallow

shift
sibling
side-by-side
sidekick
sidestep
signal
stereotype
straw vote
study
subscription
superficial

supple
swift
syllogism

tale
telegraph
telephone
transcript
transient
translation
tentative

topic
touch
trip

vagabond
verbal
verbosity
vernacular
versatile
vibrate
vicinity

visit
vocabulary
voice
volatile

windmill
word
write

Cancer

absorption
accommodation
accustom
akin
ancestry
anchor
anticlimax
antique
apron
aqueduct
assurance
auction
auld lang syne
awning

bag
bargain
barricade
bassinet
bath
boarding house
bottom
bowl
bulwark
bushel
buttress
buxom

cache
capacity
care
chamber
chauvinism
clan
clannishness
clinging
collection
commodity
common
community
compartment
compatriot
consensus
consume
cosanguinity
crabbed
crabby
cranky
crib
cubbyhole
custom
customary
customer

dairy

dawdle
defense
defensiveness
denizen
devour
diaphragm
domain
dome

eat
emotionally
empathy
enclosure
encompass
endemic
environment

familiarity
fancier
favorite
fealty
feast
fecundity
feelings
fertile
festival
feud

flood
flow
fluid
flume
flush
flux
fodder
folk
fondness
foodstuff
forage
forbear
foster
founder
fount
fountain
foyer
freehold
fretful
fructify
fulcrum
full
fumble
fundamental
furnish
furnishings
furniture

fuss

galley
garden
garner
gather
gauche
gear
genetic
genre
glue
gluttony
goblet
gourd
gourmand
gourmet
granary
grapple
grasp
greenhouse
grocery
gross
grub
grubstake
grudge
grumble
guardian
gush
gusto

habiliment
habit
habitat
habitation
haggard
halter
hatchery
headquarters
headwaters
heirloom
henpeck
heredity

heritage
hesitant
hoard
hodgepodge
hold
holding
home
homeland
homemade
homespun
homestead
hospitality
host
hostel
hostess
house
household
housewife
hovel
huddle
hug
hush
hut
hutch

idiom
imbue
implant
impressionability
inclination
incubator
indigenous
indomitability
inert
ingest
inhabit
inhabitant
innkeeper
inside
insular
insulation
irrigation

keepsake
kin
kindred
kinsfolk
kinship
kitchen

lady
landlord
latency
levee
lineage
livable
local
locality
location
lodge
loyal
lubricant

majordomo
material
matriarchy
matrix
matron
meander
mediocre
medium
mellifluous
mellow
memento
memory
menu
milieu
milkmaid
milkman
mnemonic
moist
mood
moodiness
mother
motherland

municipal

nadir
nap
nest
nestle
niche
nipple
nourishment
nursemaid
nurture
nutrient

occupancy
occupy
orientation

pabulum
pacification
pack
package
pamper
pantry
patriot
paunch
peevishness
phlegmatic
picnic
pinch
pincushion
plain
plebeian
plenitude
pot
pour
precinct
prolific
prosaic
protection
provide
provision

quaint
receptacle
reception
receptivity
recess
recipe
remembrance
reminiscent
repast
replete
reservoir
residence
retrospect
room and board
root
rotunda
rustic

salve
sanction
scoop
sectarian
security

sedentary
sediment
sensitivity
sensitization
sentiment
sentimental
settlement
shed
shelter
shield
shop
shutter
siesta
sieve
site
sloppy
sloth
slouch
slovenly
sludge
sluice
slump
smock
snivel

snooze
snug
snuggle
sojourn
solace
solicitude
soothe
soup
souvenir
spa
spread
stall
staple
station
stew
storage
store
stow
supply
support
sustain

tenacity
tenet

tent
throwback
topsy-turvy
torrent
totem
town
town bell
townspeople
tribe
tub

unfoldment
upbringing

village
vise

warehouse
welcome
wholesome
wickerwork
wigwam
wishy-washy

Leo

adoration
afferent
aggrandizement
allegory
amateur
amativeness
amazement
amusement
animation
ardor
aroma
august
auspiciousness

autocracy
avocation

backbone
benevolence

caper
celebration
celebrity
character
childishness
children
colorful

colossal
connoisseur
convivial
core
creativity
cruelty
cynosure

dally
dazzlement
delight
demonstration
despotism

direction
display
distraction
diversion
dominance
dominion
dramatization

earnestness
edification
effulgence
elation
enjoyment

enrapture
enterprise
entrepreneur
epicure
exhilaration
exuberance
exultant

fable
fad
fashion
fiancé
fiancée
fiat
flamboyance
flaunt
flirtation
flourish
folklore
frivolity
frolic
fun
funny

gaiety
gala
gallivant
gambol
game
garish
gaudiness
gild
gladness
glee
glisten
glorification
glow
golden
grandstand
gumption

happiness

heartfelt
heart-to-heart
hearty
hedonism
Herculean
hilarity
hobby
holiday
humor

impresario
inamorata
indolence
insatiability
iridescence

jocose
jocular
jocund
joke
joy
jubilation

laugh
lavish
leisure
lethargy
levity
lionize
loud
love
lover
luminary
luminous
luster
lusty
luxuriant
luxury

magnanimous
magnificence
majesty

matinee
merriment
merry-go-round
mirth
monarchy
morale
munificence

offspring
opulence
ornament
ornate
orotund
ostentation
outing
ovation
overbearing
overjoy

pageant
palace
palette
palpitate
panoply
parable
paramour
pastime
peacock
performance
persuasion
pet
philander
play
playboy
playground
pleasure
plethora
pomp
pompous
portrayal
pride
primogeniture

procreation
prodigal
promise
proposal
protagonist
pulsate

quintessence

rapture
recreation
regal
regale
regalia
reign
relish
repertoire
resplendent
reverie
ribald
rich
roar
roister
romance
royal

sanguine
satiate
scene
self-expression
serenade
shine
show
silly
spectacular
splendid
splendor
spree
squander
stage
strength
sundial

swagger

tale
theater
throne
toy

tyrannical

vacation
vivify
vogue
voluptuary

warmth
wholehearted
willful

zany
zest

Virgo

abridgment
acclimation
accuracy
acumen
adjustment
agenda
aid
allowance
amenability
amendment
analysis
ancillary
annotate
antidote
antiseptic
application
appraisal
apprenticeship
aseptic
assignation
assignment
assimilation
assist
assistant
assortment
audit
authentication

betrothal
broom
brush
budget

busy

calculation
calibrate
catalogue
categorization
certification
clean
clinical
competency
compile
compliance
concession
confirmation
conscientiousness
conscription
conservation
consignment
contraception
correction
co-worker
craft
craftsmanship
cringe
criticism
crop
cultivation
curative
custodian

dependability
detail

develop
diagnosis
diet
digest
digestion
discernment
discretion
discrimination
dispensary
dispensation
dispense
dissemination
distillation
dossier
dowry
dungarees

effectiveness
efficiency
embellishment
emend
employment
engage
enlistment
entourage
entrust
enumerate
equanimity
equipment
exactitude
examination
excellence

expound

facilitate
factory
fastidiousness
faultfinding
fawning
feasible
format
formula
fraction
frugal
fussiness

garrison
gauge
glean
governess
grange
groom
guild

handiwork
hardware
harvest
health
heed
helot
help
helpful
henchman
humbleness

husbandry
hygiene
hypochondria

immaculate
impeccable
indenture
indoctrination
industry
infirmity
insignia
inspection
instruction
instrument
inventory
itemize

job

labor
lackey
laconic
livelihood

maiden
maintenance
manual
mechanic
mechanism
medical
mend
menial
mentor
mercantile
merchant
method
meticulousness
mild
mill
miller
minimize
minion

modesty
mollification
monotony
muster

nomenclature
notary

obsequious
observant
observation
occupation
ordering
outfit
outline
output
overhaul

painstaking
paltry
parcel
pasture
pattern
peddle
pensive
penurious
peon
perfect
perfunctory
perspicacity
pertinence
petty
pinpoint
placate
placement
pleasant
ply
polish
porter
portion
postscript
practice

pragmatism
precision
preen
preparation
prescribe
prim
probity
problem-solving
procure
proletarian
proofread
prophylactic
prudence
punctilious
purity
purvey

qualification
qualify
querulous

ramification
ration
rectify
refine
regent
regimen
regiment
relevant
reliable
remedial
repair
reparable
replenish
report
respite
restoration
restorative
review
rig
ripe
rote

routine

salubrious
sanitary
schedule
scheme
scrupulous
scrutinize
servant
serve
service
serviceman
servile
shepherd
shoptalk
simplicity
skepticism
skill
sober
sort
specialize
specify
squeamish
stable
statistics
stipend
strict
submission
subordinate
subservient
subsistence
succinct
summarize
supplicate
systematic

tailor
technical
technique
tedium
therapeutic
thresh

thrift
tidy
toil
training
transaction
treatment
tried
trifle

trim
trivial
true-blue

umpire
utensil
utility
utilize

validate
variety
vassal
vend
verify
vestal
virtuosity
vocation

voluntary
vouch

waiter
work
workmanship

Libra

accentuation
accomplice
accord
address
aesthetics
affair
affinity
agreement
allegiance
allurement
aloofness
also
ambassador
amiability
amicability
and
another
antagonism
antithesis
appeal
apportionment
approbation
approval
arbitration
arrangement
attraction
attunement
audition
augment

balance
beautification
bipartisan
buoyancy

choice
classical
cohabit
coincident
coitus
combination
commensurate
companion
comparative
comparison
compatibility
compeer
compensate
competition
complaisance
compliance
compliment
compromise
concede
conciliation
concurrent
congruity
conjugate
connection

connubial
consent
consonance
consort
consultation
contention
contest
contract
contradiction
contrapuntal
contrariwise
contrast
contravene
controversy
cooperation
cooperator
coordination
cope
counselor
counteract
counterpart
counterpoise
couple
courtesy
covenant

debate
decorous
deference

detachment
détente
diplomat
disputation
dissension
divergence
division
duel
duet

emancipation
endorsement
engagement
enhancement
equable
equality
equalization
espouse
etiquette
exchange

face-to-face
faithfulness
fidelity
foil
forensic
forum

glide

go-between
golden rule
grace
gracefulness
gracious

harmony
helpmate
husband
hymeneal

insipidity
intercede
interdependence
intermediary
interpose

justice

lawsuit
levelheaded
liberal
literary
litigate

maneuver
marriage
match
mate
matrimony

measurement
median
mediation
middle
monogamy
mutual

negotiate
nuptial

objectification
objective
obligation
opponent
oration

pair
parity
parley
parry
partition
partnership
peace
peer
penmanship
Ping-Pong
plaudit
pleasant
pledge
poise

polarize
polemic
protocol
public
publicity

quorum

rapport
ratiocination
rationality
rationalization
rearrange
reason
reciprocal
recital
recommend
reconciliation
reflection
relatedness
responsive
retaliate
retort
revue
rival
rostrum

seesaw
sociable
social

spouse
stalemate
subpoena
summon
symmetry

tact
tantamount
teeter-totter
testify
tête-à-tête
tit for tat
toastmaster
truce
tune

ultimatum
unification
union

vacillation
versus
vow

war
waver
wedding
weigh
wife

Scorpio

adhesion
alarm
anesthesia
annexation
aphrodisiac
appeasement
ashes
assassinate

astonishment
avalanche

balefulness
baptism
barb
benefit
bequest

bewitch
bleakness
booty

cataclysm
catastrophe
catharsis
caustic

clarification
clearance
coalesce
compost
compress
compulsion
concentration
conception

condense
confiscation
congealment
constriction
consummation
convert
copulation
corrosion
coup de grâce
coup d'état
cremation
curtail

damage
deaden
death
deflation
demise
demolition
demotion
denature
denude
denunciation
deposition
depreciation
destruction
deter
detergent
devastation
discipline
disconnect
dislodge
dismantlement
dismember
dispel
dispossess
disruption
dissection
dissolution
divorcement
drain
drastic

dunghill

ecstasy
ejection
elimination
engrossment
enrichment
enticement
eradicate
erasure
erosion
erotic
excavate
excise
excrete
execution
expenditure
expose
expropriation
expulsion
expunge
exterminate
extinguish
extraction
extrasensory
        perception
extricate

fascination
fertilizer
fixation
forfeiture
fulminate
fumigate
fury
fuse

gallows
guarantee

havoc
heir

hostility

immersion
implosion
impregnation
indebtedness
indemnity
inheritance
inject
insemination
insurance
intensification
introspection
investigation

jealousy
jettison

kill

laxative
legacy
lessen
liquidate
loan
loss

macabre
maelstrom
magnetism
malignant
maraud
matador
mire
moat
moderation
molt

no man's land
nullification

obituary

obliterate
obsession
offering
onerous
opacity
orgasm
outhouse
overcome
owe

penetration
peril
perish
pernicious
persistent
phallus
pharmacy
philter
pierce
pillage
poison
portend
possession
potion
predatory
premium
preservation
prevention
prey
prize
proscribe
prosecute
puncture
pungent
purgative

quicksand

raffle
rampage
rapine
ravage

ravish
raze
rebate
reclaim
recompense
reconstruct
redeem
redress
reduce
refit
refund
regeneration
reimburse
reject
rejuvenation
release
remodel
remove
renascence
rend
renew
renovate
reorganize
reorientation
repeal
repel
repossess
reprisal
reproduce
rescind
research

resolution
restitution
retain
revamp
revenge
revenue
revise
revoke
riddance
rift
rip
risk
rupture

sacrilege
sadism
salvage
sanguinary
satanic
scare
schism
scorn
scour
scourge
secede
secretiveness
seize
sensuous
septic
sepulchral
setback

sever
sexual release
Shiva
siege
slaughter
slaughterhouse
snare
solution
solvent
spank
spawn
spoil
squelch
stabilization
sterilize
sting
stockade
stockpile
suppurate
surgery

tantalize
tax
tempt
terrify
therapy
thwart
tithe
toll
torment
tornado

torture
toxic
trance
transfigure
transform
transmutation
transplant
treasure
trial
turbulent

unction
undermine
upheaval

venereal
vengeance
venom
victim
virulence
vortex

weave
web
whip
whirlpool
will
withhold
wrath
wrench

Sagittarius

academic
acquittal
adventure
advocacy
agility
alien

alumnus
amelioration
aspiration
athlete
audacity
avidity

avowal

belief
bigotry
brave

candidness
carriage
catechism
cavalier
cheer
chivalry

college
cordiality
credo
crescendo
crusade

daring
dart
dauntlessness
declamation
demagoguery
disclosure
discourse
dissertation
doctrine
dogma

education
elucidation
emblazon
emblem
emigration
emissary
emulation
encouragement
enlightenment
enunciation
envoy
epic
equestrian
equine
eruption
exaggeration
exhilaration
exoneration
expansion
expatiate
expedition
expert
evangelism

fanaticism

faraway
flag
forecast
foreign
forthrightness
frankness
frontier

gallantry
gallop
gamble
gavel
generosity
genuine
glorious
gospel
graduate
grandiloquence
gregarious
guidance
gullibility

hike
homiletics
horseplay
hunch

ideal
idealization
ideology
imperial
improvement
ingenuousness
international
intrepidity
invocation

jest
journey
joust
joviality
judgment

judicious
jurisprudence
jury
juvenile

knight-errant

lampoon
lecture
legal
legend
legion
literary
luck

magnification
maneuver
matriculate
metaphysics
mobility
mobilization

opportunity
optimism
orison

paean
panegyric
parade
parson
passenger
pastor
pedagogy
pedantry
pennant
pep
philosophy
polyglot
popinjay
postulate
prance
prayer

preach
prescience
probation
procession
projection
promoter
promulgate
prophecy
proselytize
publish
pulpit

quest
quixotism

rally
realization
recklessness
religion
reveal
revelation
revere
rhapsody
rhetoric
ride
ridicule
roam
rogue
romantic

sacred
safari
saga
sapient
savant
scholar
school
scope
score
scout
scripture
search

sententious
sermon
sincerity
slogan
solicit
soothsaying
sophism
speculation
sport
sportsmanship
stadium
stag
stealth
student

tackle
teach

text
thanksgiving
theology
thrill
tour
tournament
traffic
transfer
translate
transmit
transport
travelogue
trek
tribunal
tribune
triumph
troop

truck
truism
truth
tutor

understanding
university

valise
valor
vanquish
varsity
vaunt
vehicle
venture
veracity
verdict

victory
visionary
voluble

wager
wagon
wander
wanderlust
widespread
wisdom
wiseacre
worship
wrangle

zeal
zealot

Capricorn

acclamation
accomplished
accomplishment
achievement
acknowledge
administration
affirmation
aloofness
ambition
aplomb
apotheosis
assiduous
astuteness
authentic
authority
authorization

blessings
boss
bureaucracy

cairn
capital
capitalism
capitalization
career
caution
chief
circumspection
citadel
commemoration
commend
composure
concern
condescension
confirmation
congruous
contrivance
control
conventionality
crucial

cube
cynicism

decree
dedication
deification
deliverance
demagoguery
designation
dictum
dignity
disdain
dispassion
distinctiveness
dry

éclat
elaboration
elevation
embodiment

eminence
emporium
emulation
epitome
equilateral
establishment
exaltation
example
executive
exemplary
extol

father
forbid

gentility
gentleman
gentry
goal
grouchy

grumpy

hallmark
haughtiness
high-handed
homage
honor

illustrious
immortalization
impassivity
imperturbability
insensitivity
institute
integrity

ladder
largesse
laudable
limelight
lofty
long-standing

management
manipulation
martyrdom
masterpiece
mature
maximum
merit
milestone
misanthropy
monopolize
monumental

noble
notable

obedience
office holder
official
officiate
officiousness
opus
order
ordinance
organization
organize
outstanding
ovation
overlord

panorama
paragon
paramount
parsimony
paternal
patriarch
patron
peak
pedigree
penthouse
pinnacle
policy
politic
praise
praiseworthy
pre-eminent
preside
president
prestige
pretension
priggish
prissy
prominent

promotion
proper
providence

recognition
rectitude
regulate
relic
renown
reputation
reserve
resolve
respect
respectable
responsibility
result
reticence

sagacious
salience
salute
satire
seal
sedate
shrewd
snob
socialite
solemn
sourpuss
sponsor
staid
stalwart
standard
statuesque
stature
stern
stiff

stodgy
stolid
sullen
supercilious
superintendent
superior
superiors
supervise
supremacy

taciturn
time-honored
timely
top
tradition
tribute
trophy

uppermost
upright
urban
urbane
urn

venerable
vertical
viceroy

watchtower
well-done
well-known
well-made
well-thought-of
wit

zenith

Aquarius

acquiescence
aerial

affiliation
aggregation

alienation
altogether

altruism
amalgamation

among
anarchy
angel
anthropology
assemblance
association
assonance
automation
avant-garde

bizarreness

camaraderie
carelessness
census
choir
circulation
coexist
cohere
cohesion
colleague
commingle
committee
communal
commune
communion
communism
company
compound
confederation
conference
confrere
conglomerate
congregation
congress
conjoin
conspiracy
convergence
conviviality
convocation
cooperative
corporate

cosmopolitan
coterie
council
crew
crony
cult

delegation
diffusion
disorder
dispersion
disrespect
divergence
diversification
diversity

eccentricity
efferent
effervescence
effusion
elasticity
electrification
emancipation
enfranchise
enfranchisement
erratic
estrangement
expectation
experimentation
explosion

federation
forgive
fraternity
freedom
free love
free trade
friendship
future

galvanic

heterodox

heterogeneous
high-minded
hope
hopefulness
humanitarian

insurgence
integrate
intellectual
intelligentsia
interaction
intercommunicate
intermarry
intermingle
interplay
interpolation
interracial
intersperse
interweave
invention
involvement

join
junction

kaleidoscope
knowledge

league
legislate
legislature

majority
malcontent
meeting
membership
merge
mingle
miscegenation
modern

open-minded

orchestra
organization
overthrow

panel
panelist
parliamentary
participate
partisan
party
patchwork
patent
pavilion
permutation
philharmonic
planetarium
plebiscite
plenary
poll
polytechnic
popular
postgraduate
potpourri
powwow
privilege
progress
prolixity

radical
rampant
reassurance
rebel
referendum
reform
remonstrate
rendezvous
representation
resurrect
reunion
revival
revolt
riot

robot

scatter
share
shareholder
shatter
shock
solidarity
sophisticate
sorority
spacious

spectator
sundry
surplus
swarm
symphony
symposium
syndication
synthesis

team
together

transcend
trust
trustee
turnout

unanimous

variation
varicolored
variegated
ventilate

vicissitude
vote

wayward
wing
worldly-wise
worldwide

zigzag

Pisces

abstruseness
addict
afterthought
allegory
alleviation
allurement
ambiguity
ambrosia
ambulance
anomaly
anonymity
anthology
apostasy
argot
asceticism
assuagement
atonement
atrophy
atypical

basement
bazaar
bedlam
beggar
beguilement
bewilderment
blight

blind
burglary

cabal
calumny
camera
cant
capitulate
capsize
captive
caravan
caudal
cessation
charity
charlatan
chicanery
circumnavigate
circumvention
clairvoyance
clandestine
cloister
closing
cocoon
comatose
commiserate
compassion
comprehensive

conclusion
confession
confluence
confound
confusion
conjuror
connivance
conscience
consequence
consolation
constraint
contagion
contaminate
contemplation
continence
contraband
convalescence
convict
cool
corruption
counterfeit
cowardice
creep
crestfallen
crime
cripple
cryptic

culpable
cunning

debasement
debilitation
debility
decadence
deception
decompose
dedication
defamation
defection
defilement
deformity
degeneration
degradation
dejection
demobilize
departure
depletion
depot
depravity
depression
dereliction
desecration
desertion
desolation

despoilment
despondence
destitution
deterioration
deviation
deviousness
devotion
diffidence
dilapidation
dilation
discharge
discomfort
disentangle
disguise
disintegration
dismal
dismay
disqualification
dissipation
dissociation
distortion
disunited
dole
dolefulness
donation
dope
dormant
dormitory
double-cross
doubt
downheartedness
dream
drone
drowsy
drug
drunk
dubious
dumb
dungeon
dupe

eclectic

eeriness
elastic
eleemosynary
elegiac
elixir
embargo
embarrassment
embezzlement
enchantment
encircle
endmost
enemy
enshrine
enslave
enthrallment
envelop
epidemic
escape
esoteric
espionage
evacuation
evasion
eventuate
exclusion
excommunication
exile
exit
exodus
exotic
expulsion
extraordinary

faith
fakir
falsity
farewell
far-reaching
fermentation
fetter
foot
footstool
forgery

fraud
frustration
fuel
fugitive
furtive
futility

gamut
gang
gangster
ghostly
global
gloom
goblin
grief
grotesqueness
guile

hallowed
hallucination
handicap
haunt
haven
hermitage
hibernate
hidden
hinder
hindsight
hood
horde
humiliation

imagination
immeasurability
immure
impairment
impediment
implicit
incapacitation
incarcerate
incorporeality
index

inertness
infirmity
inmate
intangibility
internment
intoxicate
intrigue
inundation
invalid
inward
irony
isolation

jinx
junk

labyrinth
laggard
lame
lament
languish
last
latent
libation
lonesome
lost
lugubriousness

machination
mask
masquerade
melancholy
meliorate
menagerie
mendacity
mendicant
mercy
metaphor
miracle
mirage
miscellaneous
misery

mislead
mission
mitigate
mob
muddle
multifarious
mummy
muse
mystery
mystical

narcotic
navigation
neglect
net
nunnery
nurse

obfuscate
oblique
obscure
occlude
odd
oddity
odyssey
ostracize
outcast
outlandish
outlaw

panacea
pandemonium
pantheon
paralyze
pardon
pariah
parole
password
pathetic
pathos
penalty
penitence

penitentiary
pent
permeate
perplexity
persecution
phantasm
phantasmagoria
phantom
philanthropy
phobia
piety
pilgrimage
pillow
piracy
plastic
poach
pollute
poor
poorhouse
powerless
predicament
premonition
presentiment
pretend
prevarication
priceless
priory
privacy
privation
prison
prostrate
puzzle

quandary
quiescent

radar
recant
recluse
recover
recuperation
refrain

refuge
rehabilitate
relaxation
relief
relinquish
remand
remorse
remote
repent
repose
reproach
resign
rest
restful
restrain
restrict
retirement
retribution
retrospect
rob
rummage
runaway

sabotage
sad
saint
salon
saloon
salvation
sanctuary
sanctum
sandman
sanitarium
saturate
save
scandal
screen
seance
seclusion
secrecy
sedative
seduction

self-pity
self-sacrifice
self-undoing
sequester
serenity
shrine
shun
sick
silent
silhouette
siren
slave
slum
slumber
sneak
sob
solitary
solitude
soporific
sorrow
sot
spelunker
stifle
still
strange
submerge
subterranean
subtlety
succor
suffer
suffusion
superstition
surrender
surreptitious
surround
symbolization
sympathy

taboo
telepathy
temple

terminus
thralldom
torpid
tragedy
tramp
trance
tranquilize
transition

trap
turbid

ubiquitous
ulterior
underprivileged

veil

veneration
vicarious
voodoo
voyage

wastebasket
weird
welfare

witch
wither
wizard
woe
worn-out
wretch

zymurgy

Bibliography

The works selected for this bibliography are but a few of those available on the subject of natal astrology. Being a general sampling, it does not include books that cover special areas of concern.

BACHER, ELMAN. *Studies in Astrology* (4 Vols.). Oceanside, California: The Rosicrucian Fellowship, 1964.

CARTER, CHARLES E. O. *Principles of Astrology* (5th ed.). Wheaton, Illinois: Theosophical Publishing House, 1963.

DAVISON, RONALD C. *Astrology*. New York: Arc Books, Inc., 1967.

DE VORE, NICHOLAS. *Encyclopedia of Astrology*. New York: Philosophical Library, 1947.

EVANS, COLIN. *The New Waite's Compendium of Natal Astrology* (rev. ed.). Revised by BRIAN E. F. GARDENER. London: Routledge and Kegan Paul Limited, 1967.

GEORGE, LLEWELLYN. *A to Z Horoscope Maker and Delineator* (16th ed.). St. Paul, Minnesota: Llewellyn Publications, 1967.

GOODMAN, LINDA. *Sun Signs*. New York: Taplinger Publishing Co., Inc., 1968.

HONE, MARGARET. *Modern Textbook of Astrology* (rev. ed.). New York: Samuel Weiser, Inc., 1972.

JONES, MARC EDMUND. *Astrology: How and Why It Works*. Baltimore: Penguin Books, Inc., 1969.

LEO, ALAN. *The Art of Synthesis* (rev. ed.). New York: Samuel Weiser, Inc., 1971.

LEWI, GRANT. *Heaven Knows What* (rev. ed.). St. Paul, Minnesota: Llewellyn Publications, 1971.

LYNDOE, EDWARD. *Astrology for Everyone*. New York: E. P. Dutton and Co., Inc., 1970.

MACNEICE, LOUIS. *Astrology*. Garden City, New York: Doubleday and Co., Inc., 1964.

McCAFFERY, ELLEN. *Graphic Astrology*. Richmond, Virginia: Macoy Publishing, 1952.

MOORE, MARCIA, and DOUGLAS, MARK. *Astrology the Divine Science*. York Harbor, Maine: Arcane Publications, 1971.

PARKER, DEREK and JULIA. *The Compleat Astrologer*. New York: McGraw-Hill Book Company, 1971.

RUDHYAR, DANE. *The Practice of Astrology*. Baltimore: Penguin Books, Inc., 1971.

SAKOIAN, FRANCES, and ACKER, LOUIS S. *The Astrologer's Handbook*. New York: Harper and Row, Publishers, 1973.

TYL, NOEL. *The Principles and Practice of Astrology*. St. Paul, Minnesota: Llewellyn Publications, 1973.

VAUGHAN, RICHARD B. *Astrology in Modern Language: How to Read Your Character and Destiny through the Stars*. New York: G. P. Putnam's Sons, 1972.

Index